SCORE RELIABILITY

SCORE RELIABILITY

CONTEMPORARY THINKING ON RELIABILITY ISSUES

Editor

BRUCE THOMPSON

Texas A&M University

SAGE Publications
International Educational and Professional Publisher
Thousand Oaks ▪ London ▪ New Delhi

For information:

Sage Publications, Inc.
2455 Teller Road
Thousand Oaks, California 91320
E-mail: order@sagepub.com

Sage Publications Ltd.
6 Bonhill Street
London EC2A 4PU
United Kingdom

Sage Publications India Pvt. Ltd.
M-32 Market
Greater Kailash I
New Delhi 110 048 India

Printed in the United States of America

Library of Congress Cataloging-in-Publication Data

Thompson, Bruce, 1951-
  Score reliability: Contemporary thinking on reliability issues / by
Bruce Thompson.
      p. cm.
Includes bibliographical references and index.
  ISBN 0-7619-2626-7 (pbk.)
  1. Psychological tests--Design and construction. 2. Educational tests
and measurements--Design and construction. I. Title.
  BF176 .T45 2002
  150´.28´7--dc21

                          2002006881

05   06   07   08   09   7   6   5   4   3   2

Acquiring Editor:	C. Deborah Laughton
Editorial Assistant:	Veronica Novak
Production Editor:	Diana E. Axelsen
Copy Editor:	Kris Bergstad
Typesetter:	C&M Digitals (P) Ltd., Chennai, India
Cover Designer:	Janet E. Foulger

Contents

Preface

We engage in measurement every day. We may weigh ourselves each morning. We look at attractive people and estimate how tall they are in relation to us. Or we look at an appealing dessert and estimate how many inches eating the big splurge will add to some cherished portion of our anatomies.

Some of us are consistently accurate in estimating calories (or their consequence: inches) from visual inspection of desserts. Some of us are accurate some of the time and wildly inaccurate at other times, with no discernable pattern. Such are the questions of reliability (and unreliability).

When the consequences of somewhat unreliable measurement are relatively minor, imperfect measurement may be of little concern. But when we make "high stakes" decisions (e.g., whether to turn off the respirator because the measure of brain wave activity indicates the patient has died, or whether a high school diploma should be awarded), we had better be careful that the scores upon which we base our decisions are sufficiently reliable that our resulting decisions are reasonable.

Estimating the reliability of scores can present challenges. And as Cunningham (1986) noted, "Despite its being relatively easy to compute, there are few subjects in the field of measurement more difficult to understand than reliability" (p. 101). This reader is designed to explain basic concepts of score reliability in an accessible manner.

Specifically, the reader presents basic concepts of (a) score reliability, (b) reliability induction (i.e., inferring that scores are reliable by invoking reliability coefficients from a prior study, such as a test manual), and (c) reliability generalization (RG). RG is a meta-analytic technique in which different studies (not different people) provide the basis for exploring score reliability.

Many of the chapters in this reader first appeared in *Educational and Psychological Measurement*, a leading journal in measurement and statistics that was founded more than 60 years ago by a very influential psychologist named Frederic Kuder. The citations for chapters originally appearing as articles are indicated in footnotes at the start of these chapters.

The chapters originally appearing as articles have been only lightly edited. For example, citations originally appearing as "in press" have been updated. Page numbers in the original publication are indicated within narrative in bold square brackets (e.g., [157]).

To minimize excessive redundancy, some content from reprinted articles has been eliminated. These excisions are indicated with ellipses in bold square brackets (e.g., [. . .]). However, some redundancy has been maintained across chapters, so students who are reading only selected chapters may do so without omitting important concepts.

The reader has been written with the premise that you already know some basic concepts in statistics (e.g., the variance, the SD, and their symbols) and some analyses (e.g., the basic elements of an analysis of variance), although you are not expected to be an expert in these topics.

The reader covers basic concepts in "classical" (or "true score") test theory (e.g., Chapter 1). The reader also covers the basic elements of "modern" test theory (e.g., "generalizability" theory). But the reader does not cover all aspects of measurement, such as "item response theory" (or "latent trait measurement"). These IRT topics are important, but are covered elsewhere in more technical and comprehensive books (e.g., Crocker & Algina, 1986), chapters (cf. Cantrell, 1999; Hennard, 2000), or articles (Fan, 1998; MacDonald & Paunonen, in press).

The reader is not intended as a primary textbook for measurement classes. Instead, it is designed as a supplementary resource that fleshes out the key reliability concepts in an accessible manner.

The Exercises in the reader were developed to promote just such reflection. They focus on understanding coefficient alpha, and on the construction of confidence intervals for reliability coefficients. They also seek to promote personal impressions regarding the quality (or lack thereof) of the treatments of measurement issues within the published literature, and some skills for conducting "reliability generalization" (RG) studies.

Hopefully the reader will help you to think about these various issues. Thinking is what in no small part helps make for good research, and for better measurement as well!

Bruce Thompson

The thoughtful comments of the following reviewers are gratefully acknowledged:

Richard Gorsuch, Fuller Theological Seminary
Steven Katsikas, Carlos Albizu University
Ralph O. Meuller, The George Washington University
Bruce G. Rogers, University of Northern Iowa
Claudia R. Wright, California State University, Long Beach

References

Cantrell, C. E. (1999). Item response theory: Understanding the one-parameter Rasch model. In B. Thompson (Ed.), *Advances in social science methodology* (Vol. 5, pp. 171-192). Stamford, CT: JAI Press.

Crocker, L., & Algina, J. (1986). *Introduction to classical and modern test theory.* New York: Holt, Rinehart and Winston.

Cunningham, G. K. (1986). *Educational and psychological measurement.* New York: Macmillan.

Fan, X. (1998). Item response theory and classical test theory: An empirical comparison of their item/person statistics. *Educational and Psychological Measurement, 58,* 357-381.

Hennard, D. H. (2000). Item response theory. In L. Grimm & P. Yarnold (Eds.), *Reading and understanding more multivariate statistics* (pp. 67-97). Washington, DC: American Psychological Association.

MacDonald, P., & Paunonen, S. V. (in press). A Monte Carlo comparison of item and person statistics based on item response theory versus classical test theory. *Educational and Psychological Measurement.*

PART I

Basic Concepts in Score Reliability

1

Understanding Reliability and Coefficient alpha, Really

Bruce Thompson
Texas A&M University
and
Baylor College of Medicine

Abstract

Because tests are not reliable, it is important to explore score reliability in virtually all studies. The present chapter explains the most
frequently used reliability estimate, coefficient alpha, so that the
coefficient's conceptual underpinnings will be understood. Too few
researchers understand (a) what data features impact alpha or
(b) the characteristics and possible range of alpha.

As lamented in other chapters in this reader, it is unfortunately all too
common to find authors of education and psychology journal articles
describing the "reliability of the test" or stating that "the test is reliable."
This "sloppy speaking" (Thompson, 1992, p. 436) at face value asserts an
obvious untruth, because reliability is a property that applies to scores, and
not immutably across all conceivable uses everywhere of a given measure
(Thompson, 1994b). The same measure, administered 100 times, may yield
100 different reliability coefficients (Vacha-Haase, 1998).

As Wilkinson and the APA Task Force on Statistical Inference (1999) recently emphasized:

> It is important to remember that a test is not reliable or unreliable. . . . Thus, authors should provide reliability coefficients of the scores for the data being analyzed even when the focus of their research is not psychometric. (p. 596)

The purpose of the present chapter is to explain the basic idea of score reliability, and in particular to focus on the properties of the most commonly reported reliability estimate: Cronbach's alpha.

Nature of Score Reliability

Each of us engages in measurement every day. For example, many of us begin our day by stepping on a scale to measure our weight. Some days when you step on your bathroom scale you may not be happy with the resulting score. On some of these occasions, you may decide to step off the scale and immediately step back on to obtain another estimate. If the second score is half a pound lighter, you may irrationally feel somewhat happier, or if the second score is slightly higher than the first, you may feel somewhat less happy.

But if your second weight measurement yields a score 25 pounds lighter than the initial measurement, rather than feeling happy, you may instead feel puzzled or perplexed. If you then measure your weight a third time, and the resulting score is 40 pounds heavier, you probably will question the integrity of *all* the scores produced by your scale. It has begun to appear that your scale is exclusively producing randomly fluctuating scores.

In essence, your scale measures "nothing." That is, measurement protocols measure "nothing" when the scores they produce are completely unrelated to any and all systematic or nonrandom dynamics, such as your weight, or how much new information you learned in a course, or your attitudes or beliefs.

When measurements yield scores measuring "nothing," the scores are said to be "unreliable." At the other extreme, if the measurement yielded scores with no elements whatsoever of random fluctuation, the scores would be described as perfectly reliable. The idea of evaluating the psychometric integrity of scores as regards these influences is not new. Spearman (1904, 1910) articulated the original conceptualizations of "reliability" and ways to evaluate score reliability that have come to be called "classical test theory," primarily only because these ideas were formulated a long time ago.

Since Spearman's time, modern theories of measurement have conceptualized alternative ways of thinking about and evaluating score reliability. Prominent among these "modern" theories are "generalizability theory" (Cronbach, Gleser, Nanda, & Rajaratnum, 1972) and "item response theory" or "latent trait theory" (cf. Rasch, 1960, but also see Fan, 1998). For accessible treatments of these two modern test theories, see Shavelson and Webb (1991) and Henard (2000), respectively.

In practice, score reliability is a matter of degree, because all scores include some random fluctuations and are not perfectly reliable. There are *no* perfect scores. Even the U.S. official atomic clock maintained by the National Bureau of Standards loses a second or so each century.

Implications for Research Practice

It is important to evaluate score reliability in *all* studies, because it is the reliability of the data in hand in a given study that will drive study results, and not the reliability of the scores described in the test manual (cf. Vacha-Haase, Kogan, Tani, & Woodall, 2001; Vacha-Haase, Tani, Kogan, Woodall, & Thompson, 2001). There are two ways in which score unreliability may compromise study results.

First, poor score reliability may compromise the ability of the scores to measure intended constructs (e.g., academic achievement, self-concept, attitudes toward school). In other words, poor score reliability may compromise what is called score "validity."

Second, poor score reliability may compromise the ability of a study to yield noteworthy effects. This includes the ability of the study to yield "statistically" significant, "practically" significant, or "clinically" significant results (Thompson, 2002). As Wilkinson and the APA Task Force on Statistical Inference (1999) emphasized, in each study, "Interpreting the size of observed effects *requires* [italics added] an assessment of the reliability of the scores" (p. 596).

Reliability and Validity

Score validity deals with the degree to which scores from a measurement measure the intended construct. A more specific and elegant definition is provided by the Joint Committee on Standards for Educational Evaluation (1994), which produced the first standards for professional conduct ever certified as *the* American national standards by the American National Standards Institute (ANSI). The Joint Committee noted that:

> Validity concerns the soundness or trustworthiness of the inferences that are made from the results of the information gathering process. . . . Validation is the process of compiling evidence that supports the interpretations and uses of data and information collected. (p. 145)

The example of the bathroom scale can again be invoked to explain the concept of validity. Let's presume that upon repeated uses on a given morning your bathroom scale (to your possible disappointment) repeatedly yields the same estimate of your weight: 200 pounds. This evidence suggests that the scores may be reliable. However, if you inferred from your score(s), "Gosh, I must be brilliant, because an IQ of 200 is quite high," questions of score validity might arise!

Score reliability clearly is a *necessary but not sufficient* condition for score validity. That is, perfectly unreliable scores measure nothing. If the scores purport to measure something/anything (e.g., intelligence, self-concept), and the scores measure nothing, the scores (and inferences from them) cannot be valid. Scores can't both measure nothing and measure something. The only time that perfectly unreliable scores could conceivably be valid is if someone was designing a test intended consistently to measure nothing. But people do not ever design tests to measure nothing, because measurements of random fluctuations are already widely available in the form of dice and coin flips and other mechanisms.

Indeed, some "modern" measurement theories, such as generalizability theory, blur the distinction between score reliability and score validity (cf. Brennan, 2001). This is because some measurement theories focus simply and directly on whether score integrity is adequate or inadequate, across any and all forms these inadequacies may take.

Questions of validity are important in research studies, because our inferences regarding study outcomes will be compromised if our scores are invalid. For example, we might conduct an experiment to determine whether eating a dozen donuts at breakfast every day will raise intelligence. We might randomly assign 50 people, half to a regimen of eating 12 donuts each morning for 6 months, and half to eating their regular diet for 6 months.

At the end if the study, if we measured post-intervention IQ by weighing each person on a bathroom scale, and the donut group had a mean score 30 units higher than the control group, we might erroneously conclude that eating donuts can cause higher IQ. Of course, the integrity of our inferences in any study turns on the critical premise that the scores in the study are reliable and valid.

By the way, the use of the bathroom scale in these examples has the appeal that most of us can relate to the example, especially as regards score reliability. The disadvantage of the example is that obviously no researcher would ever measure IQ with a bathroom scale.

But score validity questions and answers are in practice never this clear (Moss, 1992, 1995; Shepard, 1993). This is because the constructs many of us measure are often abstract, and the constructs themselves are sometimes defined incompletely, because our theories are often incomplete or vague. Furthermore, the process of establishing validity is not simple. And we must establish that the scores measure intended constructs and support intended inferences, but also that the scores do *not* measure what they are not supposed to measure.

Nevertheless, if we want to conduct inquiries that yield meaningful results, we simply cannot escape the responsibility of establishing the integrity of the data we are actually analyzing. Unfortunately, some people have difficulty addressing these essential psychometric issues, because their training has ill equipped them for this particular adventure (Aiken, West, Sechrest, & Reno, with Roediger, Scarr, Kazdin, & Sherman, 1990). As Pedhazur and Schmelkin (1991) observed, "[a]lthough most programs in sociobehavioral sciences, especially doctoral programs, require a modicum of exposure to statistics and research design, few seem to require the same where measurement is concerned" (p. 2).

Reliability and Significance

When researchers conduct studies, they interpret their results by invoking some combination of one or more of three types of significance: "statistical" significance, "practical" significance, and "clinical" significance (Thompson, 2002).

Statistical significance evaluates the probability or likelihood of the *sample* results, given the sample size, and assuming that the sample came from a population in which the null hypothesis is exactly true (Cohen, 1994; Thompson, 1996). Since its inception (cf. Boring, 1919), but especially in recent years, the use of statistical significance to interpret results has been harshly criticized by some scholars (Schmidt, 1996). For example, Schmidt and Hunter (1997) suggested that statistical significance tests should be banned, arguing that, "Statistical significance testing retards the growth of scientific knowledge; it never makes a positive contribution" (p. 37). On the other hand, scholars such as Abelson (1997) have argued equally forcefully that if these tests did not exist, they would have to be invented.

Practical significance quantifies the extent to which sample results diverge from the null hypothesis (Kirk, 1996). There are several dozen "effect size" statistics (e.g., Cohen's d, η^2, ω^2, R^2, adjusted R^2) that can be used for this purpose (Elmore & Rotou, 2001). Available choices are described by Snyder and Lawson (1993), Olejnik and Algina (2000), and Thompson (2002).

The recent fifth edition of the APA (2001) *Publication Manual* now emphasizes that,

> For the reader to fully understand the importance of your findings, it is *almost always necessary* to include some index of effect size or strength of relationship in your Results section. . . . The general principle to be followed . . . is to provide the reader not only with information about statistical significance but also with enough information to assess the magnitude of the observed effect or relationship. (pp. 25-26, emphasis added)

At least 20 journals (e.g., *Educational and Psychological Measurement*) have published editorial policies explicitly requiring effect size reporting (cf. Snyder, 2000). Included in this list are the flagship journals of the American Counseling Association and the Council of Exceptional Children, distributed to the 55,000+ members of both of these organizations.

Clinical significance addresses the question, "Are treated individuals as a group indistinguishable from normals with respect to the primary complaints following treatment?" (Kendall, 1999, p. 283). Although practical and clinical significance are related concepts, they are not identical effects. For example, in two interventions to treat depression, in both studies the depressed intervention groups might have postintervention depression scores lower by 10 points, but "in the first study all participants might nevertheless still require hospitalization following the intervention, while in the second study with the same effect size many or even all of the participants might no longer require hospitalization" (Thompson, 2002, p. 66). Clinical significance focuses on how many study participants have moved across the boundaries for diagnostic categories, such as depression or reading disability.

Poor score reliability compromises the capacity to obtain all three types of significance. At the extreme, perfectly unreliable scores are perfectly random and cannot yield statistically, or practically, or clinically significant results. Thus, establishing that the data being investigated in a given study are reliable is a prerequisite for even subsequently analyzing any of the three types of significance.

Current Score Reliability Reporting Practices

Because "reliability is a characteristic of data" (Eason, 1991, p. 84), researchers must attend to the influence that the participants themselves have on score quality in every study. As Thompson (1994b) explained, because total score variance is an important aspect of reliability, the participants involved in the study will themselves affect score reliability: "the same measure, when administered to more heterogenous or more homogenous sets of subjects, will yield scores with differing reliability" (p. 839).

Given the diversity of participants across studies, simple logic would dictate that authors of *every* study should provide reliability coefficients on the scores for the data being analyzed, even in nonmeasurement substantive inquiries. As Pedhazur and Schmelkin (1991, p. 86, emphasis in original) argued,

> Researchers who bother at all to report reliability estimates for the instruments they use (many do not) frequently report only reliability estimates contained in the manuals of the instruments or estimates reported by other researchers. Such information may be useful for comparative purposes, but it is imperative to recognize that the *relevant reliability estimate is the one obtained for the sample used in the [present] study under consideration.*

However, reporting reliability coefficients for one's own data is the exception, rather than the norm, as several chapters in this reader make abundantly clear. Too few reliability estimates for analyzed data are provided in both journals (Meier & Davis, 1990) and doctoral dissertations (Thompson, 1994a).

For example, Meier and Davis (1990) reported, "[T]he majority (95%, 85%, and 60%) of the scales described in the [three *Journal of Counseling Psychology*] JCP volumes [1967, 1977, and 1987] were not accompanied by reports of psychometric properties" (p. 115). In an examination of the *American Educational Research Journal (AERJ)*, Willson (1980) reported that only 37% of *AERJ* articles explicitly provided reliability coefficients for the data analyzed in the studies. He concluded "that reliability . . . is unreported in . . . [so much published research] is . . . inexcusable at this late date" (p. 9). Fortunately, some journals have better records as regards these analytic and reporting practices (cf. Thompson & Snyder, 1998).

Pedhazur and Schmelkin (1991) commented on the cause of these practice oxymorons, and pointed a finger at doctoral programs that do not require the rigorous study of measurement. These authors concluded, "It is, therefore, not surprising that little or no attention is given to properties of measures used in many research studies" (p. 3).

A Primer on Coefficient α

Even within only classical test theory there are numerous ways to estimate the reliability of scores (e.g., internal consistency, test-retest, form equivalence). However, by far the most commonly used estimate (Hogan, Benjamin, & Brezinksi, 2000) is Cronbach's (1951) coefficient alpha (α), which is an internal consistency estimate. Internal consistency estimates have the practical appeal that they require only that a single measure is given only one time. Stability (or test-retest) coefficients require that the measure must be administered at least twice, such that scores from the two measurements can be correlated to obtain a reliability coefficient. Equivalence estimates require that two forms of a measurement must be administered, so that scores from the two forms can be correlated to obtain a reliability coefficient.

Classical Formulation

Dawson (1999) has noted that any analog of r^2, including the reliability coefficient, can be conceptualized as the ratio of some subcomponent of the total score variance to the total score variance. He noted that,

One alternative formula with which to compute the r^2 effect size is:

$$r^2 = SOS_{EXPLAINED} / SOS_{TOTAL}.$$

... Formula (1) is a *general* formula for effect for all parametric univariate methods. For example, this formula is correct for r^2, for R^2 (a regression effect size), and eta^2 (an ANOVA and t-test effect size). Conceptually, this formula asks, "what portion (or percentage) of the total information can an extraneous variable explain or predict?" Thus, any variance-accounted-for r^2 effect size is a ratio of variances; the formula could also be written as:

$$r^2 = V_{EXPLAINED} / V_{TOTAL}$$
$$= [SOS_{EXPLAINED} / (n-1)] / SOS_{TOTAL} / (n-1).$$

Because formula (2) contains $n-1$ in both the numerator and the denominator, and these terms cancel, formula (1) is the more usual and convenient expression of this very general formula. (Dawson, 1999, pp. 105-106)

Algebraically, variance and sums-of-squares are squared (i.e., area-world) statistics, and ratios of these statistics yield results in the same squared metric (e.g., r^2, eta^2, α).

Estimation via KR-20. The seminal formula for an estimate of internal consistency can be traced to the famous algorithm presented as the 20th formula within the article by Kuder and Richardson (1937). In addition to articulating the KR-20 formula, Kuder also was the founding editor of *Educational and Psychological Measurement.* The KR-20 estimate is computed as:

$$\text{KR-20} = K/(K-1) \, [1 - (\textstyle\sum p_k q_k / \sigma_{\text{TOTAL}}^2)],$$

where K is the number of items, p_k is the proportion of people with a score of 1 on the kth item, q_k is the proportion of people with a score of 0 on the kth item, and σ_{TOTAL}^2 is the variance of the scores on the total test.

KR-20 works with any tests for which items are dichotomously-scored, such as cognitive tests for which answers have been scored right-wrong. However, the formula may also be used with attitude items that have been dichotomously-scored (e.g., "yes"–"no", "agree"–"disagree").

The KR-20 formula works only for measures composed of dichotomously-scored items, because for such items the variance of the scores on the kth item (i.e., σ_k^2) equals $p(q)$. For example, consider item $k = 1$ on which three examinees scored "0" (e.g., wrong, or "agree," or "false") and five examinees scored "1" (e.g., right, or "disagree," or "true"). Here the variance of the item scores could be computed using the conventional formula for variance, as follows:

Person	X_1	$-M_1$	$=x_1$	x_1^2
1.	0	$-.625$	$=-.625$	.3906
2.	0	$-.625$	$=-.625$	.3906
3.	0	$-.625$	$=-.625$	.3906
4.	1	$-.625$	$=.375$	.1406
5.	1	$-.625$	$=.375$	.1406
6.	1	$-.625$	$=.375$	.1406
7.	1	$-.625$	$=.375$	.1406
8.	1	$-.625$	$=.375$	.1406
Sum	5			
Mean	.625			
SOS				1.8750
$\sigma^2 = \text{SOS}/n$				.2343

When items are scored "0" or "1," the mean of the item scores equals the proportion (p) of the people who scored "1" (i.e., here, $p = .625$). Because $q = 1 - p$, here q is $1 - .625 = .375$. For these values of p and q, $p(q) = .625(.375) = .2343$. Of course, this also equals the variance (σ^2) of the item scores for the kth item. Obviously, this alternative formula has the appeal that the alternative variance formula is easier to compute than is the conventional variance formula. [One implication of this formula for variance is that variance for item scores for dichotomously-scored items can never exceed $\sigma_k^2 = .25$; see Reinhardt (1996) and Henson (2001) for an excellent discussion.]

Estimation via Cronbach's α. Because formula KR-20 may be applied *only* with measures incorporating exclusively dichotomously-scored ability or attitude items, Cronbach (1951) subsequently proposed a more general estimate of internal consistency that may be applied with measures involving items of *any* form, including items that are dichotomously scored:

$$\alpha = K/(K-1)\,[1 - (\textstyle\sum \alpha_k^2 / \alpha_{\text{TOTAL}}{}^2)],$$

where K is the number of items, $\sum \sigma_k^2$ is the sum of the k item score variances, and $\sigma_{\text{TOTAL}}{}^2$ is the variance of the scores on the total test. Of course, for measures consisting exclusively of dichotomously-scored items, α = KR-20, because the only differences in the two formulas involves the use of $\sum p_k q_k$ as against $\sum \sigma_k^2$, and for dichotomously-scored items each kth $p_k q_k$ equals each kth σ_k^2, and across all k items $\sum p_k q_k = \sum \sigma_k^2$.

The General Linear Model (GLM) in Measurement. Dawson (1999) emphatically makes the point that the same general linear model (GLM) permeates all substantive and measurement contexts:

> The presence of the general linear model (GLM) across both substantive and measurement analyses can also be seen in the computation of coefficient alpha (Cronbach, 1951) as the ratio of two variances. (p. 109)

It was previously noted that substantive effect sizes (e.g., r^2, R^2, eta^2) are computed as the same ratios.

However, the Table 1.1 data can be used to create a paradox that can only be resolved via a deeper understanding of coefficient α (and analogously coefficient KR-20). For the Table 1.1 data, involving scores of 10 people on a $K = 7$ item test, α may be computed using formula KR-20 as

$$
\begin{aligned}
\text{KR-20} &= K/(K-1)\,[1 - (\textstyle\sum p_k q_k / \sigma_{\text{TOTAL}}{}^2)] \\
&= 7/(7-1)\,[1 - (\{.25 + .25 + .25 + .25 + .25 + .25 + .25\} / .25)] \\
&= 7/6\,[1 - (\{.25 + .25 + .25 + .25 + .25 + .25 + .25\} / .25)] \\
&= 1.166667\,[1 - (\{.25 + .25 + .25 + .25 + .25 + .25 + .25\} / .25)] \\
&= 1.166667\,[1 - (1.75 / .25)] \\
&= 1.166667\,[1 - 7]
\end{aligned}
$$

Table 1.1   Illustrative Calculation of Coefficient α

				Item				
n_i/Statistic	1	2	3	4	5	6	7	TOTAL
1.	1	0	1	0	1	0	1	4
2.	0	1	0	1	0	1	0	3
3.	1	0	1	0	1	0	1	4
4.	0	1	0	1	0	1	0	3
5.	1	0	1	0	1	0	1	4
6.	0	1	0	1	0	1	0	3
7.	1	0	1	0	1	0	1	4
8.	0	1	0	1	0	1	0	3
9.	1	0	1	0	1	0	1	4
10.	0	1	0	1	0	1	0	3
p	.5	.5	.5	.5	.5	.5	.5	
q	.5	.5	.5	.5	.5	.5	.5	
σ^2	.25	.25	.25	.25	.25	.25	.25	.25

NOTE: This illustration is adapted from Reinhardt (1996).

$$= 1.166667 \, [-6]$$
$$= -7.0.$$

This result is anomalous, because it has been argued that α is a variance-accounted-for statistic expressed in a squared metric. How then can we achieve $\alpha = -7.0$ as a correctly computed result? This paradox suggests that psychometrically alpha involves more than only variances and their ratios to each other. Exploring the nature of these dynamics is important to understanding alpha.

While from a learning perspective it is important to understand how and why alpha can be negative, and indeed less than -1.0, in practice such a result may mean either that the scores are quite unacceptable, or alternatively that the wrong measurement model has been used to estimate reliability (Komaroff, 1997; Krus & Helmstadter, 1993). Feldt and Brennan (1989, pp. 110-111) and Lord and Novick (1968, pp. 47-50) describe various measurement models and their assumptions. The fit of these alternative measurement models can be evaluated using structural equation modeling (SEM) (Jöreskog & Sörbom, 1989, pp. 76-96), although these methods are considerably beyond the scope of the present treatment. In any case, the "take home" message is that (a) mathematically α can be negative (and even < -1.0) and (b) when this happens, something is really wrong as regards the evaluation of the integrity of the scores (i.e., either the wrong measurement model is being used to estimate reliability, or the scores are incredibly bad).

Coefficient α as an Index of Internal Consistency

Logically, a statistic that evaluates internal consistency should yield higher values for test data from items for which item scores are highly correlated. The previous paradox is resolved when we understand that the variance of the composite or total scores (σ_{TOTAL}^2) is not only a function of the item variances (σ_k^2), *but also of the covariances (COV_{XY}) of the item scores with each other*. Thus, α (and KR-20) do evaluate in part how correlated the item scores are with each other. [Recall that $r_{XY} = COV_{XY} / \{SD_X (SD_Y)\}$, so therefore $COV_{XY} = r_{XY} \{SD_X (SD_Y)\}$.]

Case 1: Item Score Correlations (and Covariances) Are All 0

As Sax (1974, p. 182) noted, "only when the covariances among [all] items are 0 will SD^2 [the variance of the total scores] equal $\sum pq$." Table 1.2 presents a data set with exactly these characteristics.

The previously declared formulas for alpha make obvious the need for three pieces of information to calculate an estimate: (a) the number of items on the measure, (b) the sum of the item score variances, and (c) the variance of the composite (total) scores on the measure. Here the number of items is five. As indicated in the Table 1.2 note, the sum of the five variances presented within the table is 1.10.

Given the item variances and covariances, the variance of the composite scores computed by totaling the item scores can be found using formula 5.15 from Crocker and Algina (1986, p. 95):

$$\sigma_{TOTAL}^2 = \sum \sigma_k^2 + [\sum COV_{ij} \text{ (for } i < j) * 2].$$

As reported in Table 1.3, for the Table 1.2 data for which the covariances for all pairs of item scores are 0, the variance for the composite (or total) scores therefore can be computed as:

$$\sigma_{TOTAL}^2 = 1.10 + [0 * 2]$$
$$= 1.10 + 0 = 1.10.$$

For these data, solving for α yields:

$$\alpha = K/(K-1) [1 - (\sum \sigma_k^2 / \sigma_{TOTAL}^2)]$$
$$= 5/(5-1) [1 - (1.10/1.10)]$$
$$= 5/(4) [1 - (1.10/1.10)]$$
$$= 1.25 [1 - (1.10/1.10)]$$

Table 1.2   Covariance and Correlation Matrices for Case #1
            (All Item Correlations Are 0)

Var.	Variance/Covariance					Correlation				
	1	2	3	4	5	1	2	3	4	5
1.	**.25**					1.00				
2.	.00	**.24**				.00	1.00			
3.	.00	.00	**.24**			.00	.00	1.00		
4.	.00	.00	.00	**.16**		.00	.00	.00	1.00	
5.	.00	.00	.00	.00	**.21**	.00	.00	.00	.00	1.00

NOTE: The sum of the item score variances $= .25 + .24 + .24 + .16 + .21 = 1.10$. Variances reported in the variance/covariance matrix are presented in **bold**.

Table 1.3   Variance of the Composite (Total) Scores Computed as a Function of Item Variances and Covariances

Pair		COV and SD²			r and SD			
I	J	COV_{ij}	VAR_i	VAR_j	COR_{ij}	SD_i	SD_j	Product
1	2	.00	.25	.24	.00	.50	.49	.00
1	3	.00	.25	.24	.00	.50	.49	.00
1	4	.00	.25	.16	.00	.50	.40	.00
1	5	.00	.25	.21	.00	.50	.46	.00
2	3	.00	.24	.24	.00	.49	.49	.00
2	4	.00	.24	.16	.00	.49	.40	.00
2	5	.00	.24	.21	.00	.49	.46	.00
3	4	.00	.24	.16	.00	.49	.40	.00
3	5	.00	.24	.21	.00	.49	.46	.00
4	5	.00	.16	.21	.00	.40	.46	.00
Sum		.00						.00
Sum*2		.00						

NOTE: The "Product" or r times SD_i times SD_j equals the covariance for a given kth pair of items (e.g., $COV_{1,2} = r_{1,2} \times SD_1 \times SD_2 = .00 \times .50 \times .49 = .00$).

$$= 1.25 [1 - 1]$$
$$= 1.25 [0] = 0.$$

The result is logical. If α measures how internally consistent test scores are based on the degree to which the item scores measure the same constructs, when the item scores are all perfectly uncorrelated, the score reliability indeed should be zero!

Table 1.4   Covariance and Correlation Matrices for Case #2
(*All Item Correlations Are +1*)

Var.	Variance/Covariance					Correlation				
	1	2	3	4	5	1	2	3	4	5
1.	.25					1.00				
2.	.24	.24				1.00	1.00			
3.	.24	.24	.24			1.00	1.00	1.00		
4.	.20	.20	.20	.16		1.00	1.00	1.00	1.00	
5.	.23	.22	.22	.18	.21	1.00	1.00	1.00	1.00	1.00

NOTE: For all three data sets (cases #1, #2, and #3) the sum of the item score variances = 1.10. Variances reported in the variance/covariance matrix are presented in **bold**.

Table 1.5   Variance of the Composite (Total) Scores Computed as a Function of Item Variances and Covariances

Pair		COV and SD²			r and SD			
I	J	COV_{ij}	VAR_i	VAR_j	COR_{ij}	SD_i	SD_j	Product
1	2	.24	.25	.24	1.00	.50	.49	.24
1	3	.24	.25	.24	1.00	.50	.49	.24
1	4	.20	.25	.16	1.00	.50	.40	.20
1	5	.23	.25	.21	1.00	.50	.46	.23
2	3	.24	.24	.24	1.00	.49	.49	.24
2	4	.20	.24	.16	1.00	.49	.40	.20
2	5	.22	.24	.21	1.00	.49	.46	.22
3	4	.20	.24	.16	1.00	.49	.40	.20
3	5	.22	.24	.21	1.00	.49	.46	.22
4	5	.18	.16	.21	1.00	.40	.46	.18
Sum		2.183					2.183	
Sum*2		4.366						

Case 2: Item Score Correlations Are All +1

Logically, if α measures the internally consistency of scores, when item scores are perfectly correlated, then α should equal 1. Table 1.4 presents statistics for data with this characteristic. For these data the variance for the composite (or total) scores, using the Table 1.5 results, therefore is

$$\sigma_{TOTAL}^2 = 1.10 + [2.183 * 2]$$
$$= 1.10 + [4.366] = 5.466.$$

Solving for α yields:

$$\alpha = K/(K-1) [1 - (\sum \sigma_k^2 / \sigma_{TOTAL}^2)]$$
$$= 5/(5-1) [1 - (1.10/5.466)]$$
$$= 5/(4) [1 - (1.10/5.466)]$$

Table 1.6   Covariance and Correlation Matrices for Case #3
                 (*Item Correlations Have Mixed Signs*)

Var.	Variance/Covariance					Correlation				
	1	2	3	4	5	1	2	3	4	5
1.	.25					1.00				
2.	.24	.24				1.00	1.00			
3.	.24	.24	.24			1.00	1.00	1.00		
4.	−.20	−.20	−.20	.16		−1.00	−1.00	−1.00	1.00	
5.	−.23	−.22	−.22	.18	.21	−1.00	−1.00	−1.00	1.00	1.00

Table 1.7   Variance of the Composite (Total) Scores Computed as a Function
                 of Item Variances and Covariances

Pair		COV and SD2			r and SD			
I	*J*	COV_{ij}	VAR_i	VAR_j	COR_{ij}	SD_i	SD_j	Product
1	2	.24	.25	.24	1.00	.50	.49	.24
1	3	.24	.25	.24	1.00	.50	.49	.24
1	4	−.20	.25	.16	−1.00	.50	.40	−.20
1	5	−.23	.25	.21	−1.00	.50	.46	−.23
2	3	.24	.24	.24	1.00	.49	.49	.24
2	4	−.20	.24	.16	−1.00	.49	.40	−.20
2	5	−.22	.24	.21	−1.00	.49	.46	−.22
3	4	−.20	.24	.16	−1.00	.49	.40	−.20
3	5	−.22	.24	.21	−1.00	.49	.46	−.22
4	5	.18	.16	.21	1.00	.40	.46	.18
Sum		−.35						−.35
Sum*2		−.71						

$$= 1.25 \, [1 - (1.10/5.466)]$$
$$= 1.25 \, [1 - .201]$$
$$= 1.25 \, [.798] = .998.$$

Case 3: Item Score Correlations Have Mixed Signs

Table 1.6 presents a data set for which some pairs of item scores have +1 correlation coefficients, and other pairs have −1 correlation coefficients. For these data the variance for the composite (or total) scores, using the Table 1.7 results, therefore is

$$\sigma_{TOTAL}^{2} = 1.10 + [-.35 * 2]$$
$$= 1.10 + [-.71] = .386.$$

Solving for α yields

$$\begin{aligned}
\alpha &= K/(K-1) \, [1-(\textstyle\sum \sigma_k^2 / \sigma_{TOTAL}{}^2)] \\
&= 5/(5-1) \, [1-(1.10/.386)] \\
&= 5/(4) \, [1-(1.10/.386)] \\
&= 1.25 \, [1-(1.10/.386)] \\
&= 1.25 \, [1-2.847] \\
&= 1.25 \, [-1.84] = -2.30.
\end{aligned}$$

Thus, the paradox of a negative statistic ostensibly in a squared metric has arisen once again. The paradox can be resolved if the formula for coefficient α is presented (Sax, 1974, p. 181) as:

$$\begin{aligned}
\text{KR-20} &= [K/(K-1)] \, [(\sigma_{TOTAL}{}^2 - \textstyle\sum \sigma_k^2) / \sigma_{TOTAL}{}^2)] \\
&= [5/(5-1)] \, [(.386-1.10)/.386)] \\
&= [5/(4)] \, [(.386-1.10)/.386)] \\
&= 1.25 \, [(.386-1.10)/.386)] \\
&= 1.25 \, [-.71/.386)] \\
&= 1.25 \, [-1.84] = -2.30.
\end{aligned}$$

Now what is the psychometric meaning of the result $-.71$ in the numerator of the above expression?

Perusal of Table 1.7 reveals that $-.71$ is 2 times the sum of the unique item covariances (i.e., the sum of the off-diagonal covariances for *both* redundant off-diagonal triangles within the item score variance/covariance matrix). Thus, psychometrically α (and KR-20) involves the ratio of the sum of all the item score covariances (a squared-metric statistic) to the variance (a squared-metric statistic) of the composite (or total) scores.

Is the ratio of the sum of item score covariances to the total score variance a ratio of apples to oranges (i.e., of two unlike entities to each other)? No, because, in addition to both being in a squared metric, like the numerator sum of item covariances, the denominator variance in the previous formulation is itself in part a function of covariances, as suggested by the formula for the composite (total) score variance from Crocker and Algina (1986, p. 95) that was previously presented:

$$\sigma_{TOTAL}{}^2 = \textstyle\sum \sigma_k^2 + [\textstyle\sum \text{COV}_{ij} \, (\text{for } i < j) * 2].$$

Reflection on the previous alternative formula indicates that coefficient α will tend to be bigger when the item score covariances (and correlations) are both large and in the same direction (e.g., all positive). This is only logical, given the psychometric view of α as a measure of the internal consistency of the items!

Summary

Regrettably, due to poor curricula in most doctoral programs (Aiken et al., 1990), many doctoral students and university faculty do not understand score reliability or what factors most affect score reliability (see Reinhardt, 1996, for one excellent review). Both published articles (Dawis, 1987; Willson, 1980) and dissertations (Thompson, 1994a) are accordingly more embarrassing.

An especially pernicious practice has been the tendency to test the statistical significance of score reliability coefficients (r_{XX}) using "nil" null hypotheses (i.e., H_0: r_{XX} = 0.0; see Cohen, 1994). Thus, Abelson (1997) commented on statistical tests of measurement study results using nil null hypotheses:

> And when a reliability coefficient is declared to be nonzero, that is the ultimate in stupefyingly vacuous information. What we really want to know is whether an estimated reliability is .50'ish or .80'ish. (Abelson, 1997, p. 121)

Fortunately, the author guidelines of some journals have become more enlightened as regards such practices:

> Statistical tests of such coefficients in a measurement context make little sense. Either statistical significance tests using the [nil] null hypothesis of zero magnitude should be by-passed, or meaningful null hypotheses should be employed. (Thompson, 1994b, p. 844)

The present chapter has reviewed the psychometric underpinnings of internal consistency coefficients with a view toward facilitating a deeper true understanding of what these estimates evaluate. For further insight, the reader is referred to Henson (2001) or Reinhardt (1996).

Nevertheless, we can conclude by showing that essentially both KR-20 and coefficient α are particularly sensitive to how related item scores are to each other, as measured by the covariances of the item scores. Recall that one formula for internal consistency (Sax, 1974, p. 181) is:

$$KR\text{-}20 = [K/(K-1)]\ [(\sigma_{TOTAL}{}^2 - \textstyle\sum \sigma_k^2)/\sigma_{TOTAL}{}^2)].$$

In the previous discussion it was also noted that the variance of the total (or composite) scores can be computed with statistics from the item scores, as follows (Crocker & Algina, 1986, p. 95):

$$\sigma_{TOTAL}{}^2 = \sum \sigma_k^2 + [\sum COV_{ij} \text{ (for } i < j) * 2].$$

Combining these two formulas, we see that the rightmost portion of the KR-20 and α formulas could be expressed as:

$$(\sum \sigma_k^2 + [\sum COV_{ij} \text{ (for } i < j) * 2] - \sum \sigma_k^2) / (\sum \sigma_k^2 + [\sum COV_{ij} \text{ (for } i < j) * 2]).$$

This reformulation makes it abundantly clear that the item score covariances play an important role in both the numerator and the denominator of the estimate. Or, in the words of Guilford and Fruchter (1978), "It is only by virtue of their entering into the covariance terms that the item variances contribute to internal consistency. The intercorrelations of the items are the essential sources of this kind of reliability" (p. 424).

It has been noted that Cronbach's α is a "lower-bound" estimate of score reliability (cf. Crocker & Algina, 1986). That is, the actual reliability will not be smaller than the α estimate, and may be larger. On the other hand, Brennan (2001) noted that "if data are collected on a single occasion, an estimate of reliability based on such data will almost certainly overestimate reliability when interest is in generalizing *over* occasions" (p. 8, emphasis in original). And as Thompson (1991) emphasized, that is often exactly what we wish to be able to do.

In other words, when we estimate a score reliability we invoke a given measurement model. We obtain our most accurate estimate of score reliability when our (a) measurement model and (b) our model for using the scores both match. Several of the following chapters elaborate on this important idea.

References

Abelson, R. P. (1997). A retrospective on the significance test ban of 1999 (If there were no significance tests, they would be invented). In L. L. Harlow, S. A. Mulaik, & J. H. Steiger (Eds.), *What if there were no significance tests?* (pp. 117-141). Mahwah, NJ: Lawrence Erlbaum.

Aiken, L. S., West, S. G., Sechrest, L., & Reno, R. R., with Roediger, H. L., Scarr, S., Kazdin, A. E., & Sherman, S. J. (1990). The training in statistics, methodology, and measurement in psychology. *American Psychologist, 45,* 721-734.

American Psychological Association. (2001). *Publication manual of the American Psychological Association* (5th ed.). Washington, DC: Author.

Boring, E. G. (1919). Mathematical vs. scientific importance. *Psychological Bulletin, 16,* 335-338.

Brennan, R. L. (2001). Some problems, pitfalls, and paradoxes in educational measurement. *Educational Measurement: Issues and Practices, 20*(4), 6-18.

Cohen, J. (1994). The earth is round ($p < .05$). *American Psychologist, 49,* 997-1003.

Crocker, L., & Algina, J. (1986). *Introduction to classical and modern test theory.* New York: Holt, Rinehart and Winston.

Cronbach, L. J. (1951). Coefficient alpha and the internal structure of tests. *Psychometrika, 16,* 197-334.

Cronbach, L. J., Gleser, G. C., Nanda, H., & Rajaratnum, N. (1972). *The dependability of behavioral measures: Theory of generalizability for scores and profiles.* New York: John Wiley.

Dawis, R. V. (1987). Scale construction. *Journal of Counseling Psychology, 34,* 481-489.

Dawson, T. E. (1999). Relating variance partitioning in measurement analyses to the exact same process in substantive analyses. In B. Thompson (Ed.), *Advances in social science methodology* (Vol. 5, pp. 101-110). Stamford, CT: JAI Press.

Eason, S. (1991). Why generalizability theory yields better results than classical test theory: A primer with concrete examples. In B. Thompson (Ed.), *Advances in educational research: Substantive findings, methodological developments* (Vol. 1, pp. 83-98). Greenwich, CT: JAI Press.

Elmore, P., & Rotou, O. (2001, April). *A primer on basic effect size concepts.* Paper presented at the annual meeting of the American Educational Research Association, Seattle, WA. (ERIC Document Reproduction Service No. ED 453 260)

Fan, X. (1998). Item response theory and classical test theory: An empirical comparison of their item/person statistics. *Educational and Psychological Measurement, 58,* 357-381.

Feldt, L. S., & Brennan, R. L. (1989). Reliability. In R. L. Linn (Ed.), *Educational measurement* (3rd ed., pp. 105-146). Phoenix, AZ: Ornyx.

Guilford, J. P., & Fruchter, B. (1978). *Fundamental statistics in psychology and education* (6th ed.). New York: McGraw-Hill.

Henard, D. H. (2000). Item response theory. In L. Grimm & P. Yarnold (Eds.), *Reading and understanding more multivariate statistics* (pp. 67-97). Washington, DC: American Psychological Association.

Henson, R. K. (2001). Understanding internal consistency reliability estimates: A conceptual primer on coefficient alpha. *Measurement and Evaluation in Counseling and Development, 34,* 177-189.

Hogan, T. P., Benjamin, A., & Brezinksi, K. L. (2000). Reliability methods: A note on the frequency of use of various types. *Educational and Psychological Measurement, 60,* 523-531.

Joint Committee for Standards on Educational Evaluation. (1994). *The program evaluation standards: How to assess evaluations of educational programs.* Newbury Park, CA: Sage.

Jöreskog, K. G., & Sörbom, D. (1989). *LISREL 7: A guide to the program and applications* (2nd ed.). Chicago: SPSS.

Kendall, P. C. (1999). Clinical significance. *Journal of Consulting and Clinical Psychology, 67,* 283-284.

Kirk, R. (1996). Practical significance: A concept whose time has come. *Educational and Psychological Measurement, 56,* 746-759.

Komaroff, E. (1997). Effect of simultaneous violations of essential tau-equivalence and uncorrelated error on coefficient alpha. *Applied Psychological Measurement, 21,* 337-348.

Krus, D. J., & Helmstadter, G. C. (1993). The problem of negative reliabilities. *Educational and Psychological Measurement, 53,* 643-650.

Kuder, G. F., & Richardson, M. W. (1937). The theory of the estimation of test reliability. *Psychometrika, 2,* 151-160.

Lord, F. M., & Novick, M. R. (1968). *Statistical theories of mental test scores.* Reading, MA: Addison-Wesley.

Meier, S. T., & Davis, S. R. (1990). Trends in reporting psychometric properties of scales used in counseling psychology research. *Journal of Counseling Psychology, 37,* 113-115.

Moss, P. A. (1992). Shifting conceptions of validity in educational measurement: Implications for performance assessment. *Review of Educational Research, 62,* 229-258.

Moss, P. A. (1995). Themes and variations in validity theory. *Educational Measurement: Issues and Practice, 14*(2), 5-12.

Olejnik, S., & Algina, J. (2000). Measures of effect size for comparative studies: Applications, interpretations, and limitations. *Contemporary Educational Psychology, 25,* 241-286.

Pedhazur, E. J., & Schmelkin, L. P. (1991). *Measurement, design, and analysis: An integrated approach.* Hillsdale, NJ: Lawrence Erlbaum.

Rasch, G. (1960). *Probabilistic models for some intelligence and attainment tests.* Copenhagen: Danmarks Paedagogiske Institut.

Reinhardt, B. (1996). Factors affecting coefficient alpha: A mini Monte Carlo study. In B. Thompson (Ed.), *Advances in social science methodology* (Vol. 4, pp. 3-20). Greenwich, CT: JAI Press.

Sax, G. (1974). *Principles of educational measurement and evaluation.* Belmont, CA: Wadsworth.

Schmidt, F. L. (1996). Statistical significance testing and cumulative knowledge in psychology: Implications for the training of researchers. *Psychological Methods, 1,* 115-129.

Schmidt, F. L., & Hunter, J. E. (1997). Eight common but false objections to the discontinuation of significance testing in the analysis of research data. In L. L. Harlow, S. A. Mulaik, & J. H. Steiger (Eds.), *What if there were no significance tests?* (pp. 37-64). Mahwah, NJ: Lawrence Erlbaum.

Shavelson, R., & Webb, N. (1991). *Generalizability theory: A primer.* Newbury Park, CA: Sage.

Shepard, L. A. (1993). Evaluating test validity. In L. Darling-Hammond (Ed.), *Review of research in education* (Vol. 19, pp. 405-450). Washington, DC: American Educational Research Association.

Snyder, P. (2000). Guidelines for reporting results of group quantitative investigations. *Journal of Early Intervention, 23,* 145-150.

Snyder, P., & Lawson, S. (1993). Evaluating results using corrected and uncorrected effect size estimates. *Journal of Experimental Education, 61,* 334-349.

Spearman, C. E. (1904). The proof and measurement of association between two things. *American Journal of Psychology, 15,* 72-101.

Spearman, C. E. (1910). Correlation calculated from faulty data. *British Journal of Psychology, 3,* 271-295.

Thompson, B. (1991). Review of *Generalizability Theory: A Primer* by R. J. Shavelson & N. W. Webb. *Educational and Psychological Measurement, 51*(3) 1069-1075.

Thompson, B. (1992). Two and one-half decades of leadership in measurement and evaluation. *Journal of Counseling and Development, 70,* 434-438.

Thompson, B. (1994a, April). *Common methodology mistakes in dissertations, revisited.* Paper presented at the annual meeting of the American Educational Research Association, New Orleans. (ERIC Document Reproduction Service No. ED 368 771)

Thompson, B. (1994b). Guidelines for authors. *Educational and Psychological Measurement, 54,* 837-847.

Thompson, B. (1996). AERA editorial policies regarding statistical significance testing: Three suggested reforms. *Educational Researcher, 25*(2), 26-30.

Thompson, B. (2002). "Statistical," "practical," and "clinical": How many kinds of significance do counselors need to consider? *Journal of Counseling and Development, 80,* 64-71.

Thompson, B., & Snyder, P. A. (1998). Statistical significance and reliability analyses in recent *JCD* research articles. *Journal of Counseling and Development, 76,* 436-441.

Vacha-Haase, T. (1998). Reliability generalization: Exploring variance in measurement error affecting score reliability across studies. *Educational and Psychological Measurement, 58,* 6-20.

Vacha-Haase, T., Kogan, L., Tani, C. R., & Woodall, R. A. (2001). Reliability generalization: Exploring reliability coefficients of MMPI clinical scales scores. *Educational and Psychological Measurement, 61,* 45-59.

Vacha-Haase, T., Tani, C. R., Kogan, L. R., Woodall, R. A., & Thompson, B. (2001). Reliability generalization: Exploring reliability variations on MMPI validity scale scores. *Assessment, 8,* 391-401.

Willson, V. L. (1980). Research techniques in *AERJ* articles: 1969 to 1978. *Educational Researcher, 9*(6), 5-10.

Wilkinson, L., & APA Task Force on Statistical Inference. (1999). Statistical methods in psychology journals: Guidelines and explanations. *American Psychologist, 54,* 594-604. [reprint available through the APA Home Page: http://www.apa.org/journals/amp/amp548594.html]

EXERCISE SET 1

There is no better way to understand coefficient α than to compute alpha values for different data sets, and to explore what features of data most dramatically affect estimated score reliability. One way to do this is to create data within an SPSS data window, and then execute the RELIABILITY procedure. Once the data file has been created, the data can be edited within the data window to determine how different changes impact estimates of score reliability. This can be done by inputting item data as numbers into the data window (e.g., "0" = item wrong, "1" = item right; or "1" = "strongly agree," "2" = "agree," "3" = "disagree," "4" = "strongly disagree"). In fact, SPSS can be used to score cognitive tests, and then analyze score integrity, as illustrated in the syntax presented in Appendix EX1.A.

However, a spreadsheet program (e.g., Excel, Lotus) is an even more flexible tool, because all the analyses can be run in a single screen, and all the computations are done automatically as data are created or altered. Appendix EX1.B presents a spreadsheet program that can be executed in Excel to analyze data for 10 people on any 7-item measure. Thus, this program can be used to analyze the data in Table 1.1 in Chapter 1.

To create this program on your computer, double click on the Excel icon on your computer desktop, or (a) click on the START icon, (b) click on the PROGRAMS choice in the menu, and then (c) click on the Excel choice in the next menu. Excel will then be open.

Spreadsheets are matrices with letters (e.g.,"A", "B", "C") defining columns, and numbers (e.g., "1", "2", "3") defining rows. Together, letters and numbers define cells. For example, the "A1" cell is the upper-left-most cell, "B1" is the top cell in the second column, and "A2" is the cell in the second row of the first column.

In a given cell you can enter (a) numbers (e.g., "1", "2" [typed *without* the quotation marks]), (b) letters (e.g., "p", "Var" [typed *without* the quotation marks]), or (c) formulas (e.g., "=1+2", "=1−B13", "=SUM(B3:B12))/ $A12" [typed *without* the quotation marks, and *not* case sensitive]). Create the spreadsheet presented in Appendix B.

Leave blank cells that have nothing typed in them in Appendix B. These are the cells ("B3" through "H12") where you will type your data. As you later enter your data, the computer will automatically solve each of the formulas. Thus, after all your data have been input, cell "F26" will *not* show "=C25*F25", but will instead give the coefficient α for the data you have entered.

After you have created the spreadsheet program, enter the Chapter 1 Table 1.1 data to make sure that your results match Table 1.1 and thus everything has been entered properly. Then the following activities may help you to better understand (a) item variance, (b) total score variance, (c) and alpha and the KR-20 coefficients.

Variances of Item Scores

Cells "B3" through "B12" contain the scores of the 10 people on item number 1. Enter different item scores (use only numbers) in these 10 cells.

1. Enter all zeros in these 10 cells. What is "*pq*" (output in cell "B15") and what is the variance of the item scores (output in cell "B16") computed using the conventional formula for variance ($\sigma^2 = SOS/n$)?

2. Enter all ones in these 10 cells. What is "*pq*" (output in cell "B15") and what is the variance of the item scores computed using the conventional formula for variance ($\sigma^2 = SOS/n$) output in cell "B16"?

3. Enter a mixture of zeroes and ones in these 10 cells. What is "*pq*" (output in cell "B15") and what is the variance of the item scores computed using the conventional formula for variance ($\sigma^2 = SOS/n$) output in cell "B16"?

4. Enter a mixture of ones and twos in these 10 cells. What is "*pq*" (output in cell "B15") and what is the variance of the item scores computed using the conventional formula for variance ($\sigma^2 = SOS/n$) output in cell "B16"? Will the "*pq*" formula work for *any* items on which responses are dichotomously-scored?

5. Enter a mixture of ones, twos, threes, and fours in these 10 cells. What is "*pq*" (output in cell "B15") and what is the variance of the item scores computed using the conventional formula for variance ($\sigma^2 = SOS/n$) output in cell "B16"? Does the "*pq*" formula for item score variance work for nondichotomous item scores?

6. For any possible mixture of ones, and/or twos, and/or threes, and/or fours, what 10 scores yield the largest possible variance? For 10 scores

restricted to be ones, and/or twos, and/or threes, and/or fours, does the item score variance under these constraints have a mathematical maximum limit?

7. For any possible mixture of ones and/or twos only, what 10 scores yield the largest possible variance? For 10 scores restricted to be ones and/or twos, does the item score variance under these constraints have a mathematical maximum limit?

Variances of Total Scores

The "total" score for each person is computed by summing the responses of a given person to the seven items. These scores are computed automatically as the responses of all 10 people to the seven items are entered in cells "B3" through "H12".

8. Limit the data for item scores to values of only zeros or ones. For this situation, what combination of total scores yields the largest variance of the total scores? For this situation (i.e., 10 scores restricted to be zeroes, ones, twos, threes, fours, fives, sixes, or sevens), does the item score variance under these constraints have a mathematical maximum limit?

Reliability Estimates

9. Limit the 70 (10 × 7) data points to be zeroes or ones. Flip a coin to decide what number to enter in each cell. Enter a "0" if you flip a heads; enter a "1" if you flip a tails. What is α? Why?

10. Modify the data so the item score variances are all small while at the same time trying to make the variance of the total scores big. As you are more successful in doing so, what happens to α?

Reliability "Prophecy" Applications

When score reliability is estimated to be unsatisfactory, or alternatively in some cases unnecessarily large given the decision context, the question arises regarding what can be done to modify the measurement to more closely achieve desired score reliability. Test length is one factor that might be expected to impact score reliability.

If a test is scored right-wrong (or disagree-agree), and there are 10 items, the total scores can range only from "0" to "10". If 5 additional items are added, then the total scores may range from "0" to "15". Of course, if 5 items are added, and all of the new items are missed (or answered "0" = "disagree"), the scores on the 15 items will still range from "0" to "10". Or, if 5 new items are added, and everyone correctly answers the new items (or answers "1" = "agree"), then the range of the scores will again be unaltered as regards variability (although the scores will now range from "5" to "15").

Predicting New Reliability

The Spearman-Brown "prophecy" formula can be used to guide judgment regarding these decisions. Where r_{xx}^* is the estimated reliability of a lengthened (or shortened) measure, and k is how many times longer (e.g., 2, 2.5, 4) or shorter (e.g., 0.7, 0.5) the measure is made, and r_{xx} is some estimate of score reliability for the original measure, the new reliability can be estimated as:

$$r_{xx}^* = (k * r_{xx}) / (1 + (k - 1) * r_{xx}).$$

Note that if the test length is doubled, because $(k - 1)$ equals 1, the formula simplifies to:

$$r_{xx}^* = (k * r_{xx}) / (1 + r_{xx}).$$

For example, if the original score reliability is .4, and the measure is doubled in length, the estimated new score reliability would be:

$$(2 * 0.4) / (1 + (2 - 1) * 0.4)$$
$$(0.8) / (1 + (1) * 0.4)$$
$$(0.8) / (1 + 0.4)$$
$$(0.8) / (1.4)$$
$$0.571.$$

Of course, the reasonableness of this estimate turns on the absolutely *critical* assumptions that (a) the new items are similar in quality to the original items and (b) the people measured with the new test form are similar to the people in the initial sample. (To emphasize this point, note what Vacha-Haase says in Chapter 13 about the short and long forms of the Bem Sex Role Inventory.)

11. If the original reliability estimate is .4, and the measure is tripled in length, what would estimated score reliability be? If the measure was shortened by half (i.e., $k = .5$), what would estimated score reliability be?

12. Given an initial estimate of $r_{XX} = .4$, solve for $r_{XX}*$ for k values of 1 (if $k = 1$, shouldn't $r_{XX}* = r_{XX}$?), 2, 3, 4, 5, 6, and 7. For each increment in test length, does $r_{XX}*$ increase by a constant amount?

Solving for k

It is also possible to use the prophecy formula to solve for k using as input a desired reliability ($r_{XX}*$):

$$k = ((r_{XX}*) * (1 - r_{XX})) / ((r_{XX}) * (1 - r_{XX}*)).$$

For example, if initial score reliability is .34, and desired reliability is .507, k is:

$$((0.507) * (1 - 0.34)) / ((0.34) * (1 - 0.507))$$
$$((0.507) * (0.66)) / ((0.34) * (0.493))$$
$$0.334 \quad / \quad 0.167$$
$$1.996.$$

Again, the estimate presumes the new items are similar in quality to the original items. If the new items are worse than the original items, the score reliability for the new measure will not be as high as desired. Alternatively, if the new items are better than the original items, reliability for the new scores will be even higher than desired.

13. If the original reliability estimate is .8, and the desired reliability is .93, how much longer does the measure need to be? If the original reliability estimate is .8, and the desired reliability is .7, by what factor (k) will the measure be shortened?

Appendix EX1.A.   SPSS Syntax to Score and Analyze Test Data

In this example, person ID# is typed in columns 1-9 in the data file typed and saved in ASCII "*.txt" format as a file named in this example "SCORTEST.TXT". Each person's name is typed in columns 11-20. Answers from the 5-item multiple choice are typed as capital letters (i.e., "A", "B", "C", "D", "E", or a space if the item is omitted); the reading of the data is case sensitive. These answers are typed in columns 22-26.

```
SET printback=listing .
DATA LIST
  FILE='a:scortest.txt' FIXED RECORDS=1 TABLE
  /1 id 1-9 name 11-20 (A) v1 to v5 (1X,5A1) .
EXECUTE .
TITLE 'scortest.sps  ***************************************' .
list variables=name v1 to v5/cases=9999/format=numbered .

COMMENT .
COMMENT  The input item response data IS _case sensitive_ !!! .
subtitle '0.  Score items for correct answer !!!!!!!!!!!!I!!!' .
execute .
recode v1 ('A'=0) ('B'=0) ('C'=0) ('D'=1) (' '=0) INTO rwrong1 .
recode v2 ('A'=1) ('B'=0) ('C'=0) ('D'=0) (' '=0) INTO rwrong2 .
recode v3 ('A'=0) ('B'=1) ('C'=0) ('D'=0) (' '=0) INTO rwrong3 .
recode v4 ('A'=0) ('B'=0) ('C'=1) ('D'=0) (' '=0) INTO rwrong4 .
recode v5 ('A'=1) ('B'=0) ('C'=0) ('D'=0) (' '=0) INTO rwrong5 .
compute total=sum(rwrong1 to rwrong5) .
print formats rwrong1 to rwrong5 (F1) total (F2) .
descriptives variables=total/save .
list variables=name rwrong1 to rwrong5 total ztotal/
  cases=999/format=numbered .
variable labels
  rwrong1 'scored right^wrong'
  rwrong2 'scored right^wrong'
  rwrong3 'scored right^wrong'
  rwrong4 'scored right^wrong'
  rwrong5 'scored right^wrong'
  total 'total number of right answers' .
frequencies variables=total .
subtitle '1.  Get basic reliability statistics ############' .
execute .
COMMENT .
COMMENT  Note. Mean of 0,1 is item _p_ value  !!!!!!!!!!!!!!! .
reliability variables=rwrong1 to rwrong5/
  scale(total)=rwrong1 to rwrong5/
  model=alpha/statistics=all/summary=total .
```

Appendix EX1.B.   Spreadsheet Commands to Compute α

	A	B	C	D	E	F	G	H	I
1					Item				Total
2	Person	1	2	3	4	5	6	7	Score
3	1								=SUM(B3:H3)
4	2								=SUM(B4:H4)
5	3								=SUM(B5:H5)
6	4								=SUM(B6:H6)
7	5								=SUM(B7:H7)
8	6								=SUM(B8:H8)
9	7								=SUM(B9:H9)
10	8								=SUM(B10:H10)
11	9								=SUM(B11:H11)
12	10								=SUM(B12:H12)
13	p	=SUM(B3:B12)/$A12	=SUM(C3:C12))/$A12	=SUM(D3:D12))/$A12	=SUM(E3:E12))/$A12	=SUM(F3:F12)/$A12	=SUM(G3:G12))/$A12	=SUM(H3:H12))/$A12	
14	q	=1-B13	=1-C13	=1-D13	=1-E13	=1-F13	=1-G13	=1-H13	
15	pq	=B13*B14	=C13*C14	=D13*D14	=E13*E14	=F13*F14	=G13*G14	=H13*H14	
16	Var	=VARP(B3:B12)	=VARP(C3:C12)	=VARP(D3:D12)	=VARP(E3:E12)	=VARP(F3:F12)	=VARP(G3:G12)	=VARP(H3:H12)	
17	SD								=I16^.5
18									
19	n of					Sum of		Total	
20	items					Item V		Var	
21	=H$2	=B21			1	=SUM(B16:H16)		=I16	
22	=B21	=C21-1			1	=F21		=H21	
23		=B22/C22			1	=F21		=H21	
24					1	1-G24	=F23/H23		
25		=C23				=C25*F25	= ALPHA		
26									
27									

2

Correcting Effect Sizes for Score Reliability

A Reminder That Measurement and Substantive Issues Are Linked Inextricably

Frank Baugh
Texas A&M University

[254]

Abstract

The present chapter emphasizes that measurement issues must be explicitly considered even in studies that focus on substantive questions. First, dynamics associated with insufficient attention being paid to score reliabilities in substantive studies are discussed. Next, reasons to adjust affect size indices for score unreliability are presented. Finally, some procedures for adjusting effect sizes for score reliability are briefly reviewed.

Baugh, F. (2002). Correcting effect sizes for score reliability: A reminder that measurement and substantive issues are linked inextricably. *Educational and Psychological Measurement, 62*, 254-263.

Most social science researchers are aware of the roughly 80 year old controversy (cf. Boring, 1919) regarding statistical significance testing (Pedhazur & Schmelkin, 1991). Although there are thoughtful supporters of null-hypothesis testing (e.g., Abelson, 1997; Cortina & Dunlap, 1997; Frick, 1996; Robinson & Wainer, in press), researchers increasingly recognize the limitations of the statistical method Rozeboom (1997) described as "the most bone-headed misguided procedure ever institutionalized in the rote training of science students" (p. 335). This awakening is attributable to the efforts of various scholars (e.g., Cohen, 1990, 1994; Harris, 1991; Kupersmid, 1988; Rosnow & Rosenthal, 1989; Thompson, 1993, 1996) who have repeatedly noted the inability of p values to inform judgments regarding result importance (Thompson, 1993), measure the size of an effect (Thompson, 1999), or establish result replicability (Cohen, 1994).

Today more and more journal editors recognize the weakness of the American Psychological Association publication manual's (APA, 1994) "encouragement" (p. 18) to authors to provide effect size information and [255] have hence promulgated journal-specific policies requiring that effect sizes are reported (cf. Baugh & Thompson, 2001). For example, the editorial policies of the APA *Journal of Applied Psychology* declared, "So far, I have not heard a good argument against presenting effect sizes. Therefore, unless there is a real impediment to doing so, you should routinely include effect size information in the papers you submit" (Murphy, 1997, p. 4). Similarly, the APA Task Force on Statistical Inference suggested that researchers "*always* provide some effect-size estimate when reporting a p-value" (Wilkinson & APA Task Force on Statistical Inference, 1999, p. 599). Moreover, the new fifth edition of the APA *Publication Manual* (2001) emphasized:

> For the reader to fully understand the importance of your findings, it is *almost always necessary* to include some index of effect size or strength of relationship in your Results section. You can estimate the magnitude of effect or the strength of the relationship with a number of common effect size estimates. . . . The general principle to be followed . . . is to provide the reader not only with information about statistical significance but also with enough information to assess the magnitude of the observed effect or relationship. (pp. 25-26, emphasis added)

Effect size reporting is increasingly recognized as a necessary and responsible practice (Henson & Smith, 2000). However, even with the new APA (2001) publication standards and multiple scholarly works explicating the effect size concept (e.g., Kirk, 1996, in press; Snyder & Lawson, 1993; Thompson, 2002), many researchers do not fully understand the important factors that bear on these estimates. Score reliability, a central concept under the measurement domain, is one such factor that can exact a potentially pernicious influence on effect size interpretations (Henson, 2001). As Thompson (1994) noted,

> The failure to consider score reliability in substantive research may exact a toll on the interpretations within research studies. For example, we may conduct studies that could not possibly yield noteworthy effect sizes given that score reliability inherently attenuates effect sizes. Or we may not accurately interpret the effect sizes in our studies if we do not consider the reliability of the scores we are actually analyzing. (p. 840)

As effect size reporting becomes the norm for empirical investigations, an awareness of the potentially detrimental impact of score reliability on these estimates is paramount. Yet, multiple investigations of the educational and psychological literature have suggested that some researchers remain naïve about score reliability and its potential influence on effect size estimates (Meier & Davis, 1990; Thompson & Snyder, 1998; Vacha-Haase, Ness, Nilsson, & Reetz, 1999; Willson, 1980). [256]

The present chapter emphasizes that measurement issues must be explicitly considered even in studies that focus on substantive questions. The chapter first reviews dynamics associated with insufficient attention being paid to score reliabilities in substantive studies. Next, reasons to adjust affect size indices for score unreliability are discussed. Finally, some procedures for adjusting effect sizes for score reliability are briefly reviewed.

Insufficient Attention to Score Reliability

Measurement quality continues to be a critically important consideration even in nonmeasurement, substantively-oriented studies. Nunnally (1982) aptly characterized its role:

> Science is concerned with repeatable experiments. If data obtained from experiments are influenced by random errors of measurement, the results are not exactly repeatable. Thus, science is limited by the reliability of measuring instruments and by the reliability with which scientist use them. (p. 1589)

Likewise, Thompson (1990) emphasized, "measurement integrity is critical to the derivation of sound research conclusions" (p. 585). Eason (1991) concurred, noting "Behavioral measurements that yield reliable results are of paramount importance for social scientists . . . [because] measurement integrity is crucial to sound scientific inquiry" (p. 83).

Unfortunately, disregard for the central role of measurement in empirical investigations has been and remains widespread in the social sciences. For example, Kuder (1941), in his introductory editorial of the well-known APA journal *Educational and Psychological Measurement*, noted that "Improved methods in measurement are being developed and significant research is being done in many fields. In spite of this rising interest, measurement is still a stepchild" (p. 3). Some five decades later Thompson (1994) highlighted various advances in measurement dynamics but concluded, "in at least some respects, measurement does remain something of a stepchild" (p. 837). Indeed, Aiken et al. (1990) have empirically documented the decreased allocation of curricular space to measurement training within doctoral programs.

It is therefore not surprising that studies of the literature as regards the evaluation of reliability have documented poor practice (Meier & Davis, 1990; Thompson & Snyder, 1998; Vacha-Haase et al., 1999; Willson, 1980). For example, Willson (1980) lamented, "That reliability . . . is unreported in almost half the published research is . . . inexcusable at this late date" (pp. 8-9).

Why have measurement issues been largely ignored? Pedhazur and Schmelkin (1991) offered one possible explanation: [257]

> Measurement is the Achilles' heel of sociobehavioral research. Although most programs in sociobehavioral sciences, especially doctoral programs, require a modicum of exposure to statistics and research design, few seem to require the same where measurement is concerned. . . . It is, therefore, not surprising that little or no attention is given to properties of measures used in many research studies. (pp. 2-3)

Consequently, as Thompson and Vacha-Haase (2000) noted, today "students with terminal degrees in education and psychology first enter their training based upon scores from a computer-adaptive GRE testing that upon their graduation they could not intelligently explain or evaluate" (p. 180).

Others have suggested that "telegraphic ways of speaking" (Thompson & Snyder, 1998, p. 438) about reliability has led to misunderstandings about the nature of reliability. Some researchers routinely make statements suggesting that a given "test is reliable" (Meier & Davis, 1990; Thompson, 1994; Thompson & Snyder, 1998; Vacha-Haase, 1998; Vacha-Haase et al., 1999). Thus, some graduate students and researchers, alike, come to believe that an "instrument's reliability" can be proven once and for all. As a result, those students and researchers may ignore measurement issues, erroneously believing that scores from a given measure will eternally be as reliable as were the test manual data gathered with the same instrument, regardless of to what diverse groups these prior reliabilities are generalized via "reliability induction" (cf. Vacha-Haase, Kogan, & Thompson, 2000; Whittington, 1998).

Why Adjust Effect Sizes for Score Reliability?

Social scientists make contributions to the field through empirical investigations that demonstrate a replicable effect size. However, the accuracy and replicability of reported effects is largely dependent on the reliability of the scores being analyzed (Vacha-Haase et al., 1999). Because all analyses in the General Linear Model are correlational, various effect size estimates analogous to r^2 can always be computed, even in ANOVA or t-test analyses.

Johnson (1944) long ago noted that errors of measurement tend to attenuate obtained effects below the true values and also cause observed effects to fluctuate across studies. Therefore, an argument can be made that score reliability should be accounted for when estimating and interpreting effect sizes. Spearman was the father of the concept of reliability, and he long ago (1910) emphasized:

> For an estimate of the correlation between two things is generally of little scientific value, if it does not depend unequivocally on the nature of the things, but just as much on the mere efficiency with which they happen to have been measured. (p. 271) [258]

Likewise, Thompson and Snyder (1998) commented,

> The concern for score reliability in substantive inquiry is not just some vague statistician's nit-picking. Score reliability directly (a) affects our ability to achieve statistical significance and (b) attenuates the effect sizes for the studies we conduct.... In other words, because measurement error variance is generally considered random, measurement error inherently attenuates effect sizes. It certainly may be important to consider these dynamics as part of result interpretation, once the study has been conducted. (p. 438)

Ignoring the presence of measurement error variance and its influence on effect size can seriously limit the business of science.

In a similar vein, Hunter and Schmidt (1994) described measurement error as one of the many potential imperfections in a given study. The ultimate goal of researchers is to design and implement a perfect study. Unfortunately, no study is free of imperfections or "artifacts" (Hunter & Schmidt, 1994). As a result, even scores with reasonably acceptable reliability do not provide perfectly accurate effect size parameter estimates.

Interpretation of effects without correcting for score unreliability is equivalent to assuming the scores are perfectly reliable even when evidence to the contrary is recognized. Therefore, correcting effect estimates for the unreliability of scores "is essential to the development of cumulative knowledge" (Hunter & Schmidt, 1994, p. 324).

Adjusting Effect Sizes for Score Reliability

There are literally dozens of effect sizes (cf. Kirk, 1996), and the appropriate correction for reliability may be expressed differently for different effect indices. But some general concepts regarding the corrections will be reviewed here.

Hunter and Schmidt (1994) and Hunter, Schmidt, and Jackson (1982) have been among the theorists highlighting the common sources of noise that often lower obtained effect sizes. In addition, these authors like others proposed methods of correcting effect sizes for score unreliability (i.e., noise). The procedure yields an estimate of the effect size that one might expect to find in a perfect study (Rosenthal, 1984, 1994).

The correction technique is based on the notion that study artifacts can be systematic or unsystematic. However, information about the size and extent of the artifact is required for the application of a useful correction formula. For example, correcting for the influence of random measurement error for a dependent variable's measurement necessitates knowledge about the reliability of scores on that variable (Hunter & Schmidt, 1994).

Researchers should also keep in mind that artifact information must be of the appropriate type. In the context of corrections for measurement error, an [259] estimate of the proper reliability coefficient must be utilized. Failure to do so is likely to result in an inaccurate correction (Hunter & Schmidt, 1990).

Hunter and Schmidt (1994) indicated that the majority of systematic artifacts attenuate the population correlation ρ. Specific artifacts attenuate ρ differentially and knowledge of the artifact allows for the quantification of influence on the effect estimate. For example, reliability coefficients for scores on dependent variables provide an estimation of the amount of random measurement error present in the dependent variable scores. In this context, a reliability coefficient is the artifact parameter determining the extent of influence measurement error had on the effect size.

As mentioned earlier, score unreliability attenuation usually results in the obtained correlation (effect) being lower than the population effect parameter (Hunter & Schmidt, 1994). Because the attenuation can be expressed simply as a product of the actual correlation value and an "artifact multiplier" (Hunter & Schmidt, 1994, p. 325), the following formula can be applied in cross-sectional correlation studies to estimate the amount of reduction for the population effect realized in the sample effect size:

$$\rho_O = a_i \, \rho,$$

where ρ_O is the attenuated observed effect parameter, ai represents the artifact multiplier in a given case, and ρ is the unattenuated population correlation. In other words, "Because we cannot do the study perfectly (e.g., without measurement error), this study imperfection produces an artifact that systematically reduces the actual correlation parameter" (Hunter & Schmidt, 1994, p. 325). Hence, greater measurement error leads to smaller values of a_i and thus larger reductions in the observed effect.

The artifact for measurement error in the dependent variable scores can be computed as

$$a_i = r_{YY}^{.5},$$

with r_{YY} equal to the reliability coefficient for the dependent variable scores, so that an $r_{YY} = .81$ is analogous to an $a_i = .9$. Plugging this value into the estimation equation identifies a 10% reduction of the population effect parameter in the form of the observed sample effect:

$$\rho_O = .9 \, \rho.$$

The same equation applies for measurement error present in independent variable scores in a cross-sectional correlation study. Experimental studies require a different yet similar equation. Hunter and Schmidt (1990, 1994) [260] provide a detailed explication of the analogous equation for experimental studies.

This type of correction can also be applied to "standardized difference" effect sizes (Kirk, 1996). For example, a Cohen's d can be converted into an r using Cohen's (1988, p. 23) formula #2.2.6:

$$r = d \, / \, [(d^2 + 4)^{.5}],$$

or an analogous formula. Then a correction for unreliability can be invoked, and the corrected r can be converted back into a corrected d using Friedman's (1968, p. 246) formula #6:

$$d = [2 \ (r)] \ / \ [(1 - r^2)^{.5}].$$

Conclusion

Correction of effect sizes for unreliability of scores has obvious benefits and yet requires considerable caution—the correction itself can yield an adjusted effect size correlation greater than 1.00 (Guilford, 1954; Johnson, 1944; Rosenthal, 1991; Spearman, 1910). Rosenthal (1984) recommended that researchers taking advantage of the correction procedure report *both* the adjusted and unadjusted effect estimates. Attenuation adjustments to effect sizes are not the norm, therefore, presentation of both adjusted and unadjusted estimates allows ready comparisons of effect sizes across studies. As Henson (2001) recently noted, "because so few researchers report reliability [for their own data], and even fewer interpret effects in light of reliability, the practical impact of this affect attenuation is largely unknown" (p. 186).

Comparisons of the effects in a given study with those in all related prior studies is exactly the suggested use of effect sizes (Wilkinson & APA Task Force on Statistical Inference, 1999). Too many researchers inappropriately use cutoffs for "low," "medium," and "large" effects to interpret the results in a given study. This is *not* the best use of effect indices. As Thompson (2001) recently noted, "if people interpreted effect sizes [using fixed bench-marks] with the same rigidity that $\alpha = .05$ has been used in statistical testing, we would merely be being stupid in another metric" (pp. 82-83).

In addition, reporting both reliability-corrected and uncorrected effect sizes acknowledges the presence of measurement error in all analyses and calls attention to its impact. Routine exposure to such reports will invariably have a positive impact on thinking within the field.

The limitations of statistical significance tests led a multitude of social scientists to call for improved practice as regards effect sizes. The wise counsel of these scholars (cf. Hyde, 2001; Kirk, 2001; Vacha-Haase, 2001) has culminated in the new APA Publication Manual's (APA, 2001) emphasis on reporting these useful estimates. This was most definitely good news. Unfortunately, [261] the battle for appropriate attention to measurement issues, and specifically score reliability, in some respects seems to have just begun. As the winds of change continue to shape responsible research practice, it is hoped that researchers will give more thoughtful consideration to the influence that measurement error variance exerts on effect sizes.

References

Abelson, R. P. (1997). A retrospective on the significance test ban of 1999 (If there were no significance tests, they would be invented). In L. L. Harlow, S. A. Mulaik, & J. H. Steiger (Eds.), *What if there were no significance tests?* (pp. 117-141). Mahwah, NJ: Erlbaum.

Aiken, L. S., West, S. G., Sechrest, L., & Reno, R. R., with Roediger, H. L., Scarr, S., Kazdin, A. E., & Sherman, S. J. (1990). The training in statistics, methodology, and measurement in psychology. *American Psychologist, 45,* 721-734.

American Psychological Association. (1994). *Publication manual of the American Psychological Association* (4th ed.). Washington, DC: Author.

American Psychological Association. (2001). *Publication manual of the American Psychological Association* (5th ed.). Washington, DC: Author.

Baugh, F., & Thompson, B. (2001). Using effect sizes in social science research: New APA and journal mandates for improved methodology practices. *Journal of Research in Education, 11*(1), 120-129.

Boring, E. G. (1919). Mathematical vs. scientific importance. *Psychological Bulletin, 16,* 335-338.

Cohen, J. (1988). *Statistical power analysis for the behavioral sciences* (2nd ed.). Hillsdale, NJ: Erlbaum.

Cohen, J. (1990). Things I have learned (so far). *American Psychologist, 45,* 1304-1312.

Cohen, J. (1994). The earth is round ($p < .05$). *American Psychologist, 49,* 997-1003.

Cortina, J. M., & Dunlap, W. P. (1997). Logic and purpose of significance testing. *Psychological Methods, 2,* 161-172.

Eason, S. (1991). Why generalizability theory yields better results than classical test theory: A primer with concrete examples. In B. Thompson (Ed.), *Advances in educational research: Substantive findings, methodological developments* (Vol. 1, pp. 83-98). Greenwich, CT: JAI Press.

Frick, R. W. (1996). The appropriate use of null hypothesis testing. *Psychological Methods, 1,* 379-390.

Friedman, H. (1968). Magnitude of experimental effect and a table for its rapid estimation. *Psychological Bulletin, 70,* 245-251.

Guilford, J. P. (1954). *Psychometric methods* (2nd ed.). New York: McGraw-Hill.

Harris, M. J. (1991). Significance tests are not enough: The role of effect-size estimation in theory corroboration. *Theory & Psychology, 1,* 375-382.

Henson, R. K. (2001). Understanding internal consistency reliability estimates: A conceptual primer on coefficient alpha. *Measurement and Evaluation in Counseling and Development, 34,* 177-189.

Henson, R. K., & Smith, A. D. (2000). State of the art in statistical significance and effect size reporting: A review of the APA Task Force report and current trends. *Journal of Research and Development in Education, 33,* 285-296.

Hunter, J. E., & Schmidt, F. L. (1990). *Methods of meta-analysis: Correcting error and bias in research findings.* Newbury Park, CA: Sage.

Hunter, J. E., & Schmidt, F. L. (1994). Correcting for sources of artificial variation across studies. In H. Cooper and L. V. Hedge (Eds.), *The handbook of research synthesis* (pp. 323-336). New York: Russell Sage Foundation.

Hunter, J. E., Schmidt, F. L., & Jackson, G. B. (1982). *Meta-analysis: Cumulating research findings across studies.* Beverly Hills, CA: Sage. [262]

Hyde, J. E. (2001). Reporting effect sizes: The roles of editors, textbook authors, and publication manuals. *Educational and Psychological Measurement, 61,* 225-228.

Johnson, H. G. (1944). An empirical study of the influence of errors of measurement upon correlation. *American Journal of Psychology, 57,* 521-536.

Kirk, R. E. (1996). Practical significance: A concept whose time has come. *Educational and Psychological Measurement, 56,* 746-759.

Kirk, R. E. (2001). Promoting good statistical practices: Some suggestions. *Educational and Psychological Measurement, 61,* 213-218.

Kirk, R. E. (in press). The importance of effect magnitude. In S. F. Davis (Ed.), *Handbook of research methods in experimental psychology.* Oxford, UK: Blackwell.

Kuder, G. F. (1941). Presenting a new journal. *Educational and Psychological Measurement, 1,* 3-4.

Kupersmid, J. (1988). Improving what is published: A model in search of an editor. *American Psychologist, 43,* 635-642.

Meier, S. T., & Davis, S. R. (1990). Trends in reporting psychometric properties of scales used in counseling psychology research. *Journal of Counseling Psychology, 37,* 113-115.

Murphy, K. R. (1997). Editorial. *Journal of Applied Psychology, 82,* 3-5.

Nunnally, J. C. (1982). Reliability of measurement. In H. E. Mitzel (Ed.), *Encyclopedia of educational research* (pp. 1589-1601). New York: Free Press.

Pedhazur, E. J., & Schmelkin, L. P. (1991). *Measurement, design, and analysis: An integrated approach.* Hillsdale, NJ: Erlbaum.

Robinson, D. H., & Wainer, H. (in press). On the past and future of null hypothesis significance testing. *Journal of Wildlife Management.*

Rosnow, R. L., & Rosenthal, R. (1989). Statistical procedures and the justification of knowledge in psychological science. *American Psychologist, 44,* 1276-1284.

Rozeboom, W. W. (1997). Good science is abductive, not hypothetico-deductive. In L. L. Harlow, S. A. Mulaik, & J. H. Steiger (Eds.), *What if there were no significance tests?* (pp. 335-392). Mahwah, NJ: Erlbaum.

Rosenthal, R. (1984). *Meta-analytic procedures for social research.* Beverly Hills, CA: Sage.

Rosenthal, R. (1991). *Meta-analytic procedures for social research* (rev. ed.). Newbury Park, CA: Sage.

Rosenthal, R. (1994). Parametric measures of effect size. In H. Cooper & L. V. Hedges (Eds.), *The handbook of research synthesis* (pp. 231-244). New York: Russell Sage Foundation.

Snyder, P., & Lawson, S. (1993). Evaluating results using corrected and uncorrected effect size estimates. *Journal of Experimental Education, 61,* 334-349.

Spearman, C. (1910). Correlation calculated from faulty data. *British Journal Of Psychology, 3,* 271-295.

Thompson, B. (1990). ALPHAMAX: A program that maximizes coefficient alpha by selective item deletion. *Educational and Psychological Measurement, 50,* 585-589.

Thompson, B. (1993). The use of statistical significance tests in research: Bootstrap and other alternatives. *Journal of Experimental Education, 61,* 361-377.

Thompson, B. (1994). Guidelines for authors. *Educational and Psychological Measurement, 54,* 837-847.

Thompson, B. (1996). AERA editorial policies regarding statistical significance testing: Three suggested reforms. *Educational Researcher, 25*(2), 26-30.

Thompson, B. (1999). If statistical significance tests are broken/misused, what practices should supplement or replace them? *Theory & Psychology, 9,* 165-181.

Thompson, B. (2001). Significance, effect sizes, stepwise methods, and other issues: Strong arguments move the field. *Journal of Experimental Education, 70,* 80-93.

Thompson, B. (2002). "Statistical," "practical," and "clinical": How many kinds of significance do counselors need to consider? *Journal of Counseling and Development, 80,* 64-71. [263]

Thompson, B., & Snyder, P. A. (1998). Statistical significance and reliability analyses in recent JCD research articles. *Journal of Counseling and Development, 76,* 436-431.

Thompson, B., & Vacha-Haase, T. (2000). Psychometrics is datametrics: The test is not reliable. *Educational and Psychological Measurement, 60,* 174-195.

Vacha-Haase, T. (1998). Reliability generalization: Exploring variance in measurement error affecting score reliability across studies. *Educational and Psychological Measurement, 58,* 6-20.

Vacha-Haase, T. (2001). Statistical significance should not be considered one of life's guarantees: Effect sizes are needed. *Educational and Psychological Measurement, 61,* 219-224.

Vacha-Haase, T., Kogan, L. R., & Thompson, B. (2000). Sample compositions and variabilities in published studies versus those in test manuals: Validity of score reliability inductions. *Educational and Psychological Measurement, 60*, 509-522.

Vacha-Haase, T., Ness, C., Nilsson, J., & Reetz, D. (1999). Practices regarding reporting of reliability coefficients: A review of three journals. *Journal of Experimental Education, 67*, 335-341.

Whittington, D. (1998). How well do researchers report their measures? An evaluation of measurement in published educational research. *Educational and Psychological Measurement, 58*, 21-37.

Willson, V. L. (1980). Research techniques in AERJ articles: 1969 to 1978. *Educational Researcher, 9*(6), 5-10.

Wilkinson, L., & APA Task Force on Statistical Inference. (1999). Statistical methods in psychology journals: Guidelines and explanations. *American Psychologist, 54*, 594-604.

3

A Brief Introduction
to Generalizability Theory

Bruce Thompson
Texas A&M University
and
Baylor College of Medicine

Abstract

Generalizability theory is an important "modern" measurement theory. "G" theory has important advantages over classical test theory, including the ability to (a) consider *simultaneously* multiple sources of measurement error, (b) consider measurement error interaction effects, and (c) estimate reliability coefficients for both "relative" and "absolute" decisions. But most noteworthy of all, generalizability theory is an important "way of thinking" about score reliability.

Generalizability or "G" theory (Cronbach, Gleser, Nanda, & Rajaratnum, 1972) is a modern measurement theory, as opposed to older classical or true-score measurement theory (Spearman, 1904, 1910). As noted in Chapter 1, classical test theory decomposes "observed" scores (and their corresponding score variances: $\sigma^2_{OBSERVED} = \sigma^2_{TRUE} + \sigma^2_{ERROR}$) into two components: "true" scores and measurement "error" scores. The ratio of systematic variance to observed variance is the score reliability coefficient ($r_{XX} = \sigma^2_{TRUE} / \sigma^2_{OBSERVED}$). True scores and true score variances can be estimated in various ways (e.g., test-retest, internal consistency). These classical theory reliability estimates remain the most frequently reported estimates (Hogan, Benjamin, & Brezinksi, 2000).

As noted in Chapter 1, the same general linear model is employed throughout both statistics and measurement (Dawson, 1999) to partition variance into component parts, and to create ratios of subcomponents of variance to observed variance (e.g., r^2, R^2 in multiple regression, η^2 in ANOVA, and reliability coefficients in measurement). The fact that ANOVA partitions score variance into component parts suggests that ANOVA methods might be applied in a measurement context to estimate variance components and then use these components to estimate score reliability.

The "G" theory articulated by Cronbach et al. (1972) builds on historical applications of ANOVA in estimating reliability coefficients (Hoyt, 1941; Lindquist, 1953; Medley & Mitzel, 1962). Like classical theory, "G" theory also can be used to partition observed score variance into only two parts: true and measurement error variance.

But unlike true score theory, which *always* invokes only two partitions of observed score variance, "G" theory can be used to partition observed variance into numerous subcomponents (Eason, 1991). Specifically, "G" theory can be used to subdivide measurement error variance further into its own variance subcomponents. As Jaeger (1991) explained,

> Cronbach and his associates . . . effectively demonstrated that it was no longer necessary to restrict decompensation of variation in individual's observed test scores to two components—variation attributed to true differences among individuals, and variation attributed to a conglomeration of systematic and random sources. . . . Indeed, this latter component of variation could be dissected further to gain an understanding of the systematic sources of variation that contributed to what we heretofore considered an undifferentiable mass, simply "error." (p. ix)

There are at least three very important advantages to invoking more than two partitions of observed score variance ($\sigma^2_{OBSERVED}$).

Advantages of Generalizability Theory

Simultaneous Estimation of Different Measurement Error Variances (σ^2_{ERROR})

The classical measurement theorist might administer a test twice, and compute the ratio of systematic to observed or total score variance as an estimate of score reliability (r_{XX}). This researcher might be pleased if 90% of the observed score variance was deemed reliable $(r_{XX} = .90)$, and only 10% was deemed unreliable.

The same researcher, erring on the side of caution, might go farther to explore score reliability and also administer two equivalent forms of the measure: form X and form Y. Again, the researcher might be delighted to find that 90% of the observed score variance was once again considered reliable, and only 10% was estimated to be unreliable.

However, these two procedures are *not* estimating that the same measurement error variance is 10%. Instead, these two procedures are estimating different error variances (AERA/APA/NCME, 1999). If the researcher really desires to generalize over both repeated measurement and equivalent forms, then these two 10%s are actually *separate* and *cumulative*. For these data a better reliability estimate might be .80!

Measure Error Interaction Effects

In ANOVA language, measurement error variance (σ^2_{ERROR}) can originate in several different *main effect* sources. For example, the items may be imperfect. Or test takers may not respond in a stable manner over time. Or raters may not uniformly employ the set of rating criteria.

Of course, researchers who have used ANOVA in substantive (i.e., non-measurement) studies know that in a multiway (or multifactor) design main effects may all have zero sum-of-squares and η^2 values, but still have noteworthy or even huge *interaction effects*. Interaction effects are separate effects of the ways on the outcome variable that are independent of each other and of the main effect influences on the outcome variable. Indeed, if the study involves an equal number of people in each design cell (i.e., a "balanced" design), then all the main and interaction effects are literally perfectly uncorrelated with each other (cf. Hester, 2000; Thompson, 1985).

This is one of the most counterintuitive dynamics in analyses in both statistics and measurement, and perhaps for this reason interaction effects are not understood by even some seasoned researchers (Rosnow & Rosenthal, 1989a). Indeed, Rosnow and Rosenthal (1989b) noted that interaction effects are "probably the universally most misinterpreted empirical results in psychology" (p. 1282). How can an interaction effect have nothing (zero, nada) to do with the main effects that together are involved in defining a given interaction effect?

The best explanation may be to invoke the metaphor of a drug interaction. One drug (no antihistamine vs. one regular dose of antihistamine) may have little or no main effect on the average ability of people to drive a car. A second drug (no wine vs. one glass of cabernet sauvignon) may have little main effect on the average ability of people to drive a car. However, taking an antihistamine and drinking wine together may have an effect over and above the sum of the two main effects taken separately.

ANOVA interaction effects for decades have been recognized as critically important in substantive research. For example, in his APA presidential address, Lee Cronbach (1957) noted that interventions (e.g., teaching methods, therapy techniques) may not be equally effective for all types of people (e.g., very bright people, people seeking remedial instruction). On this basis he strongly recommended the routine search for "aptitude-treatment interaction (ATI) effects" that focus on identifying what interventions will work best for different people, as opposed to the quixotic main-effects search for interventions that work best for absolutely everybody.

Interaction effects can also be very important in a measurement context. In other words, not only are main effect sources of measurement error variance separate and cumulative, they may also interact to create still more separate effects in the form of interactions expressed as yet more measurement error variance!

In analysis of variance the sum-of-squares and the η^2 for a main effect will both be zero if the means being evaluated are all equal. The sum-of-squares and the η^2 will become larger as the means differ to a greater degree.

Table 3.1 presents a two-way measurement design for a study involving two raters judging the skating performance of three skaters on each of two trials. Here the mean scores across the two raters (Colleen and Fred) ignoring trials (i.e., the rater main effect) are exactly equal: $\overline{X}_{Colleen} = 4.0 = \overline{X}_{Fred} = 4.0$. Consequently, the rater main effect sum-of-squares is zero. If all we knew was that two judges yielded the same mean ratings for three skaters each skating twice, we might at first glance be encouraged to think that the scores had some integrity.

The mean scores across the two trials (Trial #1 and Trial #2) ignoring raters (i.e., the trials main effect) are also exactly equal: $\overline{X}_{Trial \#1} = 4.0 = \overline{X}_{Trial \#2} = 4.0$. Again, the trials main effect sum-of-squares is zero. Again, if that was all we knew about the scores, we might be encouraged to believe that the scores were reliable.

However, the raters-by-trials two-way interaction effect for these data is quite dramatic. For example, on Trial 1 Colleen rates skater Kelly a "1," but judge Fred rates the same performance a "5." Indeed, when the trials and the raters are considered *simultaneously*, the ratings are never identical ("1" vs. "5"; "2" vs. "6" . . ., "7" vs. "3")!

Clearly the skaters would not be sanguine regarding the integrity of these scores. From a perspective simultaneously considering the combined

Table 3.1   Heuristic Example of Measurement Interaction Effects

| Skater | Judge #1 | | Judge #2 | |
	Time #1	Time #2	Time #1	Time #2
Kelly	1	5	5	1
Deborah	2	6	6	2
Wendy	3	7	7	3

effects of raters and trials on scores (i.e., the interaction effect) the scores seem unduly variable. Indeed, they may be deemed so variable due to inter-action effects that the credibility of all the scores would probably be called into question.

Non-zero measurement error main effects occur, for example, if some raters are more severe than other raters by a constant amount across the pool of judgments. Or a non-zero main effect for occasion might occur if all test takers did better (or worse) by a constant amount on a second test administration.

A non-zero item × occasion measurement error interaction effect, on the other hand, would occur if some test items were interpreted differently upon different administrations of a test. A non-zero rater × occasion measurement error interaction would occur if only some raters varied the severity of their judgments across rating occasions. A non-zero ratee × rater measurement error interaction effect would occur if some judges were inconsistent in evaluating a subsample of the ratees. These kinds of interaction effects can reasonably be anticipated in many measurement situations.

In fact, it may appear unreasonable to assume that such interactions never occur or are always irrelevant. Yet that is exactly what classical test theory assumes, because classical test theory (a) creates only a single esti-mate of measurement error variance at a time and (b) never estimates mea-surement error interaction effects. Only generalizability theory evaluates the interaction effects that create their own additional sources of measure-ment error variance.

"Absolute" Versus "Relative" Decisions

There are two ways that test scores may be used in making decisions. First, for a given set of scores the only focus may be upon score order. For example, a university might award a lucrative scholarship to the three Ph.D. applicants each year with the highest GRE scores regardless of what the scores are. This is called a "relative" decision.

Second, scores might be interpreted by invoking a standard or cutoff. For example, all persons who answer at least 70% of all test items correctly might be awarded a high school diploma regardless of how many students this is or of what proportion of high school seniors would pass under these conditions. This is called an "absolute" decision.

Classical test theory can compute score reliability estimates only for "relative" decisions. Let's say a 10-item state licensure test was created to determine which medical school graduates would be licensed as physicians. Two forms of the test were developed and then administered to four M.D.s in a counterbalanced order (i.e., two receive Form X first, two receive Form Y first) to evaluate test equivalence.

Here is the hypothetical number of right answers on the tests:

	Form X	Form Y
Douglas	6	1
Jan	7	2
Jane	8	3
Ronald	9	4

On the theory that 70% is a commonly used benchmark for passing tests, the state medical board has decided that seven or more right answers will be passing scores meriting licensure.

In classical test theory no special reliability coefficients can be estimated for "absolute" decisions. Classical test theory reliability estimates presume "relative" decisions. The equivalence reliability for this situation is computed as the bivariate correlation between scores on test forms. For these data this coefficient is 1.0.

The data make clear that invoking measurement models that do not honor the dynamics of a given decision context can lead to inappropriate conclusions. Clearly, based on the preliminary measurement study, in this example licensure candidates who have just spent years in grueling study in medical school would care a great deal which of the two perfectly equivalent test forms they were assigned to take.

"G" theory has real advantages in that reliability estimates are computed in different ways for different types of decisions. The reliability coefficient for the two applications conceivably can be identical for the same set of data. Conversely, the two types of estimates can differ wildly even for the same measurement data. And the real advantage of "G" theory is that the researcher can use the coefficient from the measurement model that matches the actual application of the scores.

Computation of "G" Theory Results

To make the discussion of the "G" theory computation process concrete, let's assume measurement of 10 people ($p = 10$) on a 4-item attitude measure ($i = 4$) using a "0"-to-"9" response scale given on three different occasions ($o = 3$). In ANOVA terminology the design is $10 \times 4 \times 3$. There will be exactly 120 scores produced for this protocol ($10 \times 4 \times 3 = 120$).

If the analyst used only classical test theory, three different Cronbach's alphas could be computed, one for each of the three occasions of measurement. Three different test-retest reliability coefficients could also be computed by correlating total scores from different pairs of measurement occasions (i.e., $r_{1 \times 2}$, $r_{1 \times 3}$, and $r_{2 \times 3}$).

At one extreme the six coefficients might again be at least superficially comforting, perhaps each indicating that only 10% of the observed score variance is measurement error variance. As noted previously:

> Too many classicists would tend to assume that these 10 percents are the same and also tend to not realize that in addition to being unique and cumulative, the sources may also interact to define disastrously large interaction sources of measurement error not considered in classical theory. The effects of these assumptions are all the more pernicious because of their unconscious character. (Thompson, 1991, p. 1072)

At the other extreme the classical coefficients might be wildly different. In this case the researcher may not be sure how to integrate the divergent evidence regarding score quality. Only "G" theory *simultaneously* examines all the measurement influences, and only "G" theory considers interaction effects. Because we usually believe that several sources of measurement error simultaneously intrude in *any* given measurement application, reliability coefficients that honor these premises give us the most accurate estimates for our presumptive model of measurement realities.

Use of ANOVA to Partition Observed Variance

Table 3.2 presents a hypothetical data set for our design. The data can be entered into a conventional statistical package to apply ANOVA to compute and partition score variance.

Table 3.2   Heuristic Data for 10 People on a 4-Item Zero-to-Nine Attitude Measure Given Three Times

Person (p = 10)	Item Scores (i = 4) on Occasion #1 (o = 3)				Item Scores (i = 4) on Occasion #2 (o = 3)				Item Scores (i = 4) on Occasion #3 (o = 3)			
	1	2	3	4	1	2	3	4	1	2	3	4
1.	2	1	2	4	2	2	4	2	3	4	0	1
2.	3	3	3	0	2	4	5	0	4	6	0	0
3.	2	0	2	2	1	2	2	4	5	4	0	7
4.	6	4	4	2	2	0	3	2	4	2	2	4
5.	4	7	4	6	6	4	4	3	2	1	0	0
6.	8	5	4	4	4	2	3	4	5	6	2	0
7.	5	2	6	6	6	4	4	4	6	6	4	1
8.	8	1	8	6	6	6	2	6	1	6	4	2
9.	6	3	6	6	6	5	4	6	4	4	4	3
10.	8	8	7	7	5	5	5	4	7	7	0	0

Entry of the data into a computer package (e.g., SPSS) so that ANOVA could be run would require that 120 rows of data were entered. The first few cases of data can be entered as:

Person	Item	Occasion	Score
1	1	1	2
2	1	1	3
3	1	1	2. . .

The last few cases can be entered as:

Person	Item	Occasion	Score
. . .8	4	3	2
9	4	3	3
10	4	3	0

Table 3.3 presents the results from a measurement analysis of variance of these data. Here tests of statistical significance are irrelevant. As Bird (2002) recently observed,

[M]any experimenters appear to believe that "running an ANOVA" necessarily involves statistical significance testing. If this were true, then it would be difficult or impossible to reform the practice of ANOVA along the lines suggested

Table 3.3 $10 \times 3 \times 4$ Nonfactorial ANOVA With 120 Item Scores as the
Dependent Variable

Effect	Sum of Squares	Degrees of Freedom	Mean Squares
p	127.2416	9	14.1380
o	36.6000	2	18.3000
i	29.4917	3	9.8306
po	96.2333	18	5.3463
pi	77.5917	27	2.8738
oi	61.1333	6	10.1889
poi, e	150.0333	54	2.7784
Sum	578.3250	119	

NOTE: Because the triple interaction requires 54 degrees of freedom ($9 \times 2 \times 3 = 54$), there are no degrees of freedom left for the model error term, and measurement error due to the triple interaction and model error (e) are confounded and cannot be separated.

by the American Psychological Association (APA) Task Force on Statistical Inference (Wilkinson & APA Task Force on Statistical Inference, 1999). (p. 197)

Note that in a generalizability analysis the ANOVA is always "non-factorial." That is, for this problem a factorial analysis would partition observed score variance into eight components: three main effects (p, o, and i), three two-way interaction effects (po, pi, and oi), one three-way interaction (poi), and the model specification error (e). However, these data have only $n - 1$ or $120 - 1 = 119$ degrees of freedom. The estimation of the effects for the three main effects, three two-way interaction effects, and one three-way interaction effect, requires exactly all 119 degrees of freedom.

This means that 0 degrees of freedom are left to separate the highest-order interaction effect from any model-specification error. In any such measurement application of ANOVA the highest-order interaction effect and the model error term are always statistically "confounded" and cannot be separated.

Conversion of Mean Squares Into Score Variance Components

The mean squares from the ANOVA presented in Table 3.3 are the building blocks for the remaining computations. The computations are illustrated here so that they are concrete and not mysterious. However, the variance components for various elements of observed *score* variances can

Table 3.4   Combining Mean Squares to Create Sums Used in Estimating "Variance Components"

Effect	MS_{EFFECT}	+/– Related Interaction				Sum
		$-MS$	$-MS$	$+MS_{(poi,\ e)}$		
p	14.1380	−5.3463	−2.8738	+2.7784	=	8.6963
o	18.3000	−5.3463	−10.1888	+2.7784	=	5.5432
i	9.8306	−2.8738	−10.1888	+2.7784	=	−0.4537
po	5.3463	−2.7784			=	2.5679
pi	2.8738	−2.7784			=	0.0954
oi	10.1889	−2.7784			=	7.4105
poi, e	2.7784				=	2.7784

be easily derived using the following SPSS commands where the scores have been named "x":

```
VARCOMP
x BY person item occasion
/RANDOM = person item occasion
/METHOD = MINQUE (1) /DESIGN
/INTERCEPT = INCLUDE .
```

The process presented here assumes that all the ways of the measurement design are "random" effects (see Frederick, 1999, or Shavelson & Webb, 1991, for detail on "fixed," "random," and "mixed" models). Usually "G" theory presumes that various effects are "random." That is, we typically assume we have sampled from among possible measurement levels for each measurement facet (i.e., assumed that the 4 items are a sample from a large or even infinite universe of equally-admissible pool of items, vs. assuming that the 4 items represent the entire population of all possible items of interest).

The first step in converting ANOVA mean squares into score variance components is illustrated in Table 3.4. Table 3.5 shows the final computations invoking the Table 3.4 intermediate results.

Conversion of Score Variance Components Into Components for Means

The Table 3.5 variance components are estimated for the 120 separate scores. In reality, we wish to aggregate these 120 scores in various ways (e.g., to derive total scores for the whole set of 4 items for each person,

Table 3.5   Computing **Score** Variance Components

Effect	Sum	/	Product				=	Score Variance Component
p	8.6963	/	[(o = 3)	(i = 4)	=	12]	=	0.7247
o	5.5432	/	[(p = 10)	(i = 4)	=	40]	=	0.1386
i	−0.4537	/	[(p = 10)	(o = 3)	=	30]	=	−0.0151
po	2.5679	/	[(i = 4)		=	4]	=	0.6420
pi	0.0954	/	[(o = 3)		=	3]	=	0.0318
oi	7.4105	/	[(p = 10)		=	10]	=	0.7410
poi, e	2.7784						=	2.7784

Table 3.6   Computing **Mean** Variance Components

Effect	Score Variance Component	Frequency	Mean Variance Component	Component Percentage
p	0.7247	1	0.7247	56.35%
o	0.1386	3	0.0462	3.59%
i	0	4	0	0.00%
po	0.6420	3	0.2140	16.64%
pi	0.0318	4	0.0079	0.62%
oi	0.7410	12	0.0618	4.80%
poi, e	2.7784	12	0.2315	18.00%
Sum			1.2861	

rather than continue to consult all 4 scores for each person). To reflect this interest we need to convert the score variance components into variance components for means. This process is illustrated in Table 3.6. These computations can take SPSS score variance components as input into a spreadsheet such as Excel, if the user does not want to do the remaining computations by hand.

Several aspects of these computations warrant explanation. For example, note that the negative score variance component for item (−0.0151) in Table 3.5 has been reset to 0.0 in Table 3.6. Logically, because variance is in a squared metric, negative values for variance components are problematic. If the components are very near zero, it may be reasonable to convert such negative values to 0.0. If negative components are substantially different from zero, the results may call into question whether the basic measurement model is correct (i.e., whether all effects should be included, or whether others might be needed).

The right column of Table 3.6 reports the percentages of the total variance that each mean variance component represents. Note that people (p) produced the majority (56.35%) of the variance. Having variance from people be large is a desirable outcome if our premise in a given study is that people differ as individuals and that it is exactly these differences that we wish to quantify or study.

When we make such an assumption, we are defining people as our "object of measurement." This assumption, in turn, means that we are defining all the variance due to the main effect of people as systematic or true variance, and all other variances as measurement error variances.

If a researcher was conducting a study where all people were, for whatever reason, deemed identical regarding some characteristic, then any variance associated with human individuality would in that case be defined as measurement error variance, and some other main effect would be declared the "object of measurement." Sometimes main effects other than people are legitimate objects of measurement. However, in the social sciences in most studies people are the object of measurement, because we usually assume that people are individually different, and therefore that any differences from people as a main effect are only to be expected and therefore are real or true.

Computation of the Two Reliability Coefficients

As noted previously, in "G" theory we can compute different reliability coefficients depending on whether we are using the scores to make a relative or an absolute decision. However, in both cases we (a) pool together all the relevant measurement error variances (which is determined by the type of decision, and differs for the two decision types) and (b) divide the systematic variance by the sum of the systematic and the measurement error variance to estimate reliability. Because we are dividing one variance by another variance, and variances are in a squared metric, our result is in a squared metric. Indeed, reliability coefficients are *always* in a squared metric, even though the symbols for the estimates may not explicitly contain a square superscript (e.g., α, r_{XX}, generalizability coefficient, measurement phi coefficient).

Reliability for a "Relative" Decision. When we are making a relative decision, we consider only the measurement error variances that could affect the rank orderings of the scores. These are necessarily all but only the interaction effects (here po, pi, and the confounded poi,e) involving the object of measurement (here p). As reported at the bottom of Table 3.7, these measurement error variances for these data sum to 0.4535.

Table 3.7   Computing Systematic and Two Measurement Error Variances From Mean Variance Components

Effect	Mean Variance Component	Systematic Variance	Measurement Error	
			"Relative" Error Variance	"Absolute" Error Variance
p	0.7247	0.7247		
o	0.0462			0.0462
i	0			0
po	0.2140		0.2140	0.2140
pi	0.0079		0.0079	0.0079
oi	0.0618			0.0618
poi, e	0.2315		0.2315	0.2315
Total		0.7247	0.4535	0.5614

For a relative decision the total score variance is estimated to be 1.1782 (0.7247 + 0.4535), as reported in Table 3.8. The ratio of the systematic variance to the total variance (0.7247 / 1.1782) is the reliability estimate for this use of the scores: a generalizability coefficient. As reported in Table 3.8, for these data this reliability estimate is 0.6151.

Reliability for an "Absolute" Decision. When we are making an absolute decision, all the measurement error variances may impact the reliability of the scores interpreted against a standard or cutoff score. Thus, as reported at the bottom of the rightmost column of Table 3.7, all the measurement error variances are added together for this calculation. The result is 0.5614.

Given the general linear model, the numbers differ, but the reliability is still calculated as a ratio of systematic variance (0.7247) to total variance (1.2861 = 0.7247 + 0.5614). The ratio of these variances is the measurement phi coefficient (not to be confused with the correlation coefficient for two dichotomous variables, also called phi, mainly to confuse everybody). For these data this reliability estimate is 0.5635.

Note that the phi coefficient will equal the generalizability coefficient if (and only if) all the measurement error variances uniquely associated with absolute decisions (here o, i, oi) are all 0.0. Otherwise the phi coefficient will be smaller than the generalizability coefficient for the same data, as was true for the Table 3.2 heuristic data. This dynamic only serves to reemphasize the folly of using a classical theory reliability coefficient when evaluating score integrity in the context of making absolute decisions, because classical theory only evaluates measurement error in a relative decision context.

Table 3.8   Computation of Generalizability and Phi Coefficients

	Decision	
Variance	"Relative"	"Absolute"
Systematic	0.7247	0.7247
Measurement Error	0.4535	0.5614
Total Observed	1.1782	1.2861
Ratio	0.6151[a]	0.5635[b]

NOTE: [a]The "generalizability coefficient" is computed by dividing systematic score variance by total score variance (i.e., systematic + measurement error): 0.7247 / [0.7247 + 0.4535] = 0.7247 / 1.1782 = 0.6151.
[b]The "phi coefficient" is computed by dividing systematic score variance by total score variance (i.e., systematic + measurement error): 0.7247 / [0.7247 + 0.5614] = 0.7247 / 1.2861 = 0.5635.

Summary

The previous discussion intimates that generalizability theory is superior to classical theory reliability estimates. Certainly such a view is suggested by Jaeger's (1991) statement referring to the applicability of generalizability analysis: "Thousands of social science researchers will no longer be forced to rely on outmoded reliability estimation procedures when investigating the consistency of their measurements" (p. x).

Only "G" theory accommodates simultaneously (a) multiple sources of measurement error variance, (b) interactions that create additional sources of measurement error variance, and (c) estimation of reliability coefficients in the context of different decisions. The barriers to the use of "G" theory are practical rather than theoretical. In practice only for logistical reasons researchers usually want to estimate score reliability based on a single administration of a single test. That is why internal consistency estimates such as Cronbach's alpha are used so frequently (Hogan, Benjamin, & Brezinksi, 2000).

But more than anything else, generalizability theory is an incredibly powerful "way of thinking" about score reliability. Indeed, generalizability theory can be conceptualized as a way of thinking about score integrity that somewhat merges thinking about score reliability and score validity into a single conceptualization (Brennan, 2001).

Generalizability theory is so conceptually powerful because it forces us to think consciously about (a) our measurement model, (b) our model of reality, and especially (c) whether our measurement model and our model of reality match. A classical theory internal-consistency reliability coefficient considers measurement at only a single point in time. Do we *ever* wish to limit the interpretation of scores to only a single point in time?

A classical test-retest reliability estimate considers measurement using only one measurement, and measurement at only two points in time. Do we ever want to limit the interpretation of our scores to only one set of items or to only these two points in time?

As Cronbach et al. (1972) noted,

> The score . . . is only one of many scores that might serve the same purpose. The [researcher] is almost never interested in the response given to particular stimulus objects or questions, to the particular tester, at the particular moment of the testing. (p. 15)

Similarly, Thompson (1991) emphasized,

> If we virtually always want to generalize over time and over items or tests, then a classical theory approach that never simultaneously considers these two time and item sampling influences, and completely ignores the interactions of these influences, will be quite simply unworkable! (p. 1072)

In short, if possible we should estimate score reliability for situations that interest us. This usually means multiple forms, multiple occasions of measurement, multiple raters, and so forth. And even if we find ourselves unable to model this complex reality, which is the reality we actually presume and wish to explore, at least thinking about this model of reality and realizing that our classical measurement model does not actually honor our model of reality forces us to be more cautious in vesting too much confidence in classical reliability coefficients. Regrettably, these coefficients usually do not unequivocally evaluate dynamics in the score universe that is almost always our real focus.

References

American Educational Research Association, American Psychological Association, and National Council on Measurement in Education. (1999). *Standards for educational and psychological testing.* Washington, DC: American Psychological Association.

Bird, K. D. (2002). Confidence intervals for effect sizes in analysis of variance. *Educational and Psychological Measurement, 62,* 197-226.

Brennan, R. L. (2001). Some problems, pitfalls, and paradoxes in educational measurement. *Educational Measurement: Issues and Practices, 20*(4), 6-18.

Cronbach, L. J. (1957). Beyond the two disciplines of scientific psychology. *American Psychologist, 12,* 671-684.

Cronbach, L. J., Gleser, G. C., Nanda, H., & Rajaratnum, N. (1972). *The dependability of behavioral measures: Theory of generalizability for scores and profiles.* New York: John Wiley.

Dawson, T. E. (1999). Relating variance partitioning in measurement analyses to the exact same process in substantive analyses. In B. Thompson (Ed.), *Advances in social science methodology* (Vol. 5, pp. 101-110). Stamford, CT: JAI Press.

Eason, S. (1991). Why generalizability theory yields better results than classical test theory: A primer with concrete examples. In B. Thompson (Ed.), *Advances in educational research: Substantive findings, methodological developments* (Vol. 1, pp. 83-98). Greenwich, CT: JAI Press.

Frederick, B. N. (1999). Partitioning variance in the multivariate case: A step-by-step guide to canonical commonality analysis. In B. Thompson (Ed.), *Advances in social science methodology* (Vol. 5, pp. 305-318). Stamford, CT: JAI Press.

Hester, Y. C. (2000). An analysis of the use and misuse of ANOVA. (Doctoral dissertation, Texas A&M University, 2000). *Dissertation Abstracts International, 61,* 4332A. (University Microfilms No. AAT9994257)

Hogan, T. P., Benjamin, A., & Brezinksi, K. L. (2000). Reliability methods: A note on the frequency of use of various types. *Educational and Psychological Measurement, 60,* 523-531.

Hoyt, C. J. (1941). Test reliability estimated by analysis of variance. *Psychometrika, 6,* 153-160.

Jaeger, R. M. (1991). Foreword. In R. J. Shavelson & N. M. Webb, *Generalizability theory: A primer* (pp. ix-x). Newbury Park, CA: Sage.

Lindquist, E. F. (1953). *Design and analysis of experiments in education and psychology.* Boston: Houghton Mifflin.

Medley, D. M., & Mitzel, H. E. (1963). Measuring classroom behavior by systematic observation. In N. L. Gage (Ed.), *Handbook of research on teaching* (pp. 247-328). Chicago: Rand McNally.

Rosnow, R. L., & Rosenthal, R. (1989a). Definition and interpretation of interaction effects. *Psychological Bulletin, 105,* 143-146.

Rosnow, R. L., & Rosenthal, R. (1989b). Statistical procedures and the justification of knowledge in psychological science. *American Psychologist, 44,* 1276-1284.

Shavelson, R., & Webb, N. (1991). *Generalizability theory: A primer.* Newbury Park, CA: Sage.

Spearman, C. E. (1904). The proof and measurement of association between two things. *American Journal of Psychology, 15,* 72-101.

Spearman, C. E. (1910). Correlation calculated from faulty data. *British Journal of Psychology, 3,* 271-295.

Thompson, B. (1985). Alternate methods for analyzing data from experiments. *Journal of Experimental Education, 54,* 50-55.

Thompson, B. (1991). Review of *Generalizability Theory: A Primer* by R. J. Shavelson & N. W. Webb. *Educational and Psychological Measurement, 51,* 1069-1075.

Wilkinson, L., & APA Task Force on Statistical Inference. (1999). Statistical methods in psychology journals: Guidelines and explanations. *American Psychologist, 54,* 594-604. [reprint available through the APA Home Page: http://www.apa.org/journals/amp/amp548594.html]

4

Reliability Methods

A Note on the Frequency of Use of Various Types

Thomas P. Hogan
University of Scranton

Amy Benjamin
University of Scranton

Kristen L. Brezinski
University of Scranton

[523]   *Abstract*

This study examined the frequency of use of various types of reliability coefficients for a systematically drawn sample of 696 tests appearing in the APA-published *Directory of Unpublished Experimental Mental Measures*. Almost all articles included some type of reliability report for at least one test administration. Coefficient alpha was the overwhelming favorite among types of coefficients. Several measures treated almost universally in psychological-testing textbooks were rarely or never used. Problems encountered in the study included

Hogan, T. P., Benjamin, A., & Brezinski, K. L. (2000). Reliability methods: A note on the frequency of use of various types. *Educational and Psychological Measurement, 60,* 523-531.

ambiguous designations of types of coefficients, reporting reliability based on a study other than the one cited, inadequate information about subscales, and simply incorrect recording of the information given in an original source.

The APA Task Force on Statistical Inference was appointed by the APA Board of Scientific Affairs in 1996. The recommendations of the Task Force were published in a recent issue of the *American Psychologist* (Wilkinson & APA Task Force on Statistical Inference, 1999). Among its various recommendations, the Task Force emphasized, "*Always* provide some effect-size estimate when reporting a *p* value" (p. 599, italics added). Later, the Task Force also wrote,

> *Always* present effect sizes for primary outcomes.... It helps to add brief comments that place these effect sizes in a practical and theoretical context. ... We must stress again that reporting and interpreting effect sizes in the context of previously reported effects is *essential* to good research. (p. 599, italics added) [524]

However, the Task Force also emphasized that "Interpreting the size of observed effects requires an assessment of the reliability of the scores" (p. 596) being analyzed because score unreliability attenuates detected study effects. And the Task Force explained,

> It is important to remember that a test is not reliable or unreliable. Reliability is a property of the scores on a test for a particular population of examinees (Feldt & Brennan, 1989). Thus, authors should provide reliability coefficients of the scores for the data being analyzed even when the focus of their research is not psychometric. (Wilkinson & APA Task Force on Statistical Inference, 1999, p. 596)

The treatment of reliability is highly standardized in elementary textbooks on educational and psychological testing. All of the textbooks cover test-retest, alternate form, interrater, and internal consistency measures of reliability (cf. Aiken, 1997; Anastasi & Urbina, 1997; Cohen & Swerdlik, 1999; Gregory, 1996; Kaplan & Saccuzzo, 1997; K. R. Murphy & Davidshofer, 1998). Some of these texts also mention generalizability theory without giving it detailed treatment. More advanced treatments of reliability give extensive coverage to generalizability theory; some also include reference to test information functions as a method for expressing reliability (cf. Crocker & Algina, 1986; Feldt & Brennan, 1989; Nunnally & Bernstein, 1994).

These textbooks provide definitions of the various methods of determining reliability, often include basic formulas, and sometimes reference reliability coefficients for selected tests. However, there is usually no indication of the actual frequency of use of the different methods of determining reliability. A student might reasonably infer that the various methods are used about equally or, perhaps, in rough proportion to the amount of space devoted to each method.

Do we know anything, beyond hunches, about the actual frequency of use for the different methods of determining test reliability? We have been unable to find any studies addressing this issue. The current study answered this question within the context of one well-defined population of tests.

Method

The *Directory of Unpublished Experimental Mental Measures,* Volume 7 (Goldman, Mitchel, & Egelson, 1997), a publication of the American Psychological Association, was used to define the population of tests examined in the present study. The most recent directory provided information for 2,078 tests appearing in 37 professional journals from 1991 to 1995. The journals are primarily from the fields of education, psychology, and sociology. The directory provides summary information for the following three items: test name, purpose, and source; and for at least four of the following [525] six characteristics: number of items, time required, format, reliability, validity, and related research. If information on any of the latter six characteristics was not available, that item was not listed in the directory. The tests are categorized into 24 chapters, such as attitudes, creativity, and motivation. The number of entries per chapter varies substantially from as few as 2 to as many as 102. Along with *Tests in Print V* (L. L. Murphy, Impara, & Plake, 1999), *Tests: A Comprehensive Reference for Assessments in Psychology, Education, and Business* (Maddox, 1997), and the Educational Testing Service (ETS) *Test Collection* (e.g., ETS, 1995), the directory serves as one of the most frequently cited sources of information about psychological tests.

From the 2,078 entries in the directory, we drew a systematic sample of every third entry for coding, yielding a sample of 696 tests. For each test in this sample, the following information was coded: (a) test area (i.e., chapter),

Table 4.1   Number of Types of Reliability Coefficients Reported

Number Reported	n	%
None	43	6
One	523	75
Two	117	17
Three	12	2
Four	1	0

(b) type of reliability reported, (c) the reliability coefficient(s), (d) number of items, and (e) number of subscales. If there was more than one type of reliability reported, each type and the corresponding coefficient were coded. When a range of reliabilities was reported, the midpoint of the range was recorded as the reliability coefficient. When two or more reliability coefficients were reported within a single type (e.g., internal consistency coefficients), the simple average (i.e., without conversion via Fisher's z) was recorded.

Results

Table 4.1 summarizes the number of types of reliability reported for each test entry. Reliability information was not reported for 6% of the entries. For the majority of entries (75%), only one type of reliability was reported, whereas 17% reported two types of reliability, and a few cases reported three or four types of reliability. Table 4.2 summarizes the types of reliability coefficients reported; entries are arranged in order of frequency of occurrence. There are a total of 801 entries for the 553 tests for which some type of reliability was reported, because 19% of the tests had more than one type of reliability reported. The "unspecified" category includes entries that reported a reliability [526] coefficient with no indication of its type. Tables 4.1 and 4.2 provide the basic information for answering our question about the frequency of use for various types of reliability methods.

The number of items per test varied considerably, ranging from 2 to 400, but the great majority of tests were in a fairly narrow range centered around the median value of 20. There were a few cases in which we could not determine how many items the test contained. It was also often difficult to determine the number of subscales on a test. If only one reliability coefficient was given, which was the modal case, we assumed there was only one scale. Multiple scales were recorded when there was specific

Table 4.2   Types of Coefficients

Type	n	%
Alpha	533	66.5
Test-retest[a]	152	19.0
Internal consistency[b]	35	4.4
Split-half[c]	33	4.1
KR-20	15	2.5
Interobserver	8	1.0
Interitem	4	0.5
Intercorrelations	4	0.5
Others[d]	3	0.4
Unspecified	14	1.7
Total	801	

NOTE: [a]Includes three cases reported as "stability" coefficients.
[b]Specific type of internal consistency not reported.
[c]Includes one case reported as "Spearman-Brown."
[d]Includes one case each of Guttman, Hoyt, and omega.

reference to separate scales (e.g., by reference to subscale names and/or number of items) or by provision of separate reliability data by subscale. An "indeterminate" category included cases in which there was explicit reference to subscales, but we could not determine from the directory how many such scales there were. We found that 533 (77%) of the measures consisted of a single scale.

Table 4.3 summarizes the actual reliability coefficients recorded. Most coefficients were in the range of .75 to .95. It is difficult to generalize from the data in Table 4.3 because, as noted below, some of the reliability coefficients reported in the directory were not based on the articles covered in the directory but on other sources cited in those articles. The total number of coefficients reported in Table 4.3 is 799, whereas 801 cases are categorized in Table 4.2. We identified 2 cases in which a type of reliability was reported but no reliability coefficient was presented. In one of these cases, the entry stated that "Test-retest was over 80%" and in the other case that "Interrater agreement was 88.7%." [527]

Discussion

Coefficient Selection

The most evident outcome from the study is the overwhelming reliance on coefficient alpha for reporting reliability. It was used for at least two

Table 4.3   Distribution of Coefficient Values

Coefficient	n
.95 to .99	32
.90 to .94	110
.85 to .89	153
.80 to .84	160
.75 to .79	134
.70 to .74	88
.65 to .69	54
.60 to .64	29
.55 to .59	22
.50 to .54	4
.45 to .49	2
.40 to .44	4
.35 to .39	1
.30 to .34	3
.25 to .29	1
.20 to .24	2

NOTE: Range: .20 to .98; median: .81.

thirds of the tests recorded in the directory. Although we could not feasibly verify this for all of the articles represented in this study, we did retrace some ambiguous cases back to the original articles and determined that coefficient alpha was used in other cases in which it was not exactly clear what reliability coefficient was reported in the directory. For example, some coefficients reported in the directory as "internal consistency" were alpha coefficients. It is likely that some of the cases reported as "interitem" or "unspecified" were also alpha coefficients. Thus, if all were known, coefficient alpha was probably used in nearly three quarters of the cases. In his original presentation of alpha, Cronbach (1951) referred to alpha as "a tool that we expect to become increasingly prominent in the test literature" (p. 299). His view seems to have been correct.

In the typical textbook on psychological testing, coefficient alpha generally receives no more treatment and often less treatment than reliability methods such as split-half or KR-20. Of course, alpha is a more general case of the KR-20 formula first presented by the founding editor of *EPM*. Based on our analysis, we recommend that coverage of coefficient alpha be increased [528] substantially. Students should gain a thorough understanding of this coefficient, its strengths, weaknesses, and assumptions, if they are to read the professional literature intelligently.

Indeed, many active researchers, and certainly many graduate students with limited measurement training, may not realize that alpha can be negative, even though alpha estimates a variance-accounted-for statistic. In fact, coefficient alpha can even be less than -1.0 (Reinhardt, 1996)! Perhaps even more surprising than the preponderant use of coefficient alpha was the lack of use of certain types of reliability coefficients that are routinely covered in textbooks on testing. The KR-20, precursor to the more general coefficient alpha, was used in less than 2% of the cases. KR-21 was never encountered in this study; in an era of modern software and hardware, this shortcut estimate is mainly of interest as a conceptual device.

Despite their prominence in the psychometric literature of the past 20 years, we encountered no reference to generalizability coefficients (cf. Eason, 1991) or to the test information functions that arise from item response theory (cf. Fan, 1998). These are surprising results given that the modern coefficients, such as generalizability coefficients, are essential for some applications (Thompson, 1991). As Jaeger (1991) noted, thanks to "this powerful set of techniques . . . thousands of social science researchers will no longer be forced to rely on *outmoded* [classical theory] reliability estimation procedures when investigating the consistency of their measurements" (p. x, italics added).

Test-retest reliability was used with substantial frequency: in almost 20% of the articles. We did not attempt to trace the intertest time intervals for these cases, but it would be interesting to do so in a follow-up study. Interobserver or interrater reliabilities were noted in only 1% of the cases. Of course, this low frequency may be a function of the fact that relatively few investigators are using tests that call for any judgment in the scoring process. We found no instances of alternate form reliability being reported.

Poor Reporting Practices

We encountered a variety of problems in conducting the study. Some of these problems relate to the original articles cited in the directory, whereas others relate to the directory itself. First, although it was encouraging to find that reliability information was reported in the great majority of cases, there were still 6% of the cases in which no reliability information was provided. This disturbing pattern has been confirmed in related studies of reliability reporting practices in selected journals (cf. Thompson & Snyder, 1998; Vacha-Haase, Ness, Nilsson, & Reetz, 1999; Willson, 1980).

One of the most vexing problems we encountered was the imprecise use of the term *internal consistency*. This generic term actually covers a host of [529] specific techniques, including split-half, coefficient alpha, the various Kuder-Richardson formulas, and many techniques based on analysis of variance models. We encountered instances in which the directory recorded the reliability method as internal consistency when the original article cited a more specific method. And we encountered instances in which the original article identified the reliability method as internal consistency. We recommend that journal editors insist that authors identify the specific reliability method employed. We recommend to editors of the directory that if a more specific reliability method is reported in an article, then that method should be recorded in the directory rather than being converted to the more generic "internal consistency" category. Understandably, if the original article is at fault in this regard, there is nothing the directory's editors can do about it.

Another difficulty we encountered is much subtler. In some instances, the reliability reported in the directory is not based on the study cited but on some other source. For example, an entry in the directory may report a test-retest reliability of .85. The article may be based on a sample of 35 cases drawn from elderly hospital patients. However, the reliability may be based an entirely different group of individuals in some other study. The user of the directory might assume that the reliability is based on the article cited in the directory, but this is *not* a safe assumption. Thus, users may employ the directory for an initial scan of instruments that might be relevant for some purpose, but they must carefully examine the original sources to determine exact information about the instruments. It may be possible for compilers of the directory to rectify this difficulty in future editions, but doing so would certainly require additional work.

It is essential for directory users to remember that reliability is a property of scores, not of tests (cf. Joint Committee on Standards for Educational Evaluation, 1994). Thompson and Vacha-Haase (2000) explained these issues in detail. Because score reliability changes with changes in either (a) sample composition or (b) score variability (Crocker & Algina, 1986), potential test users *must* compare the composition and variability of their sample with the composition and the variability associated with any previously reported score reliability coefficient.

Some Directory and Study Limitations

It was curious to find some duplicate entries in the directory. That is, the same test and same article were recorded in different places, sometimes within the same chapter. There was no evident rationale for such duplication.

Finally, we found some instances in which the reliability information recorded in the directory was simply incorrect. We did not systematically check all entries but discovered these errors when retracing other matters, such as whether a report of internal consistency could be more precisely

[530] identified. This point, of course, reemphasizes the need for the user to consult original sources before making final judgments about an instrument identified in the directory. The directory is an outstanding source of information for individuals needing to find an instrument for a particular purpose. However, due diligence must be exercised in its use.

Of course, the present study had two evident limitations. First, the generalizations suggested above are confined to the articles covered in the directory and perhaps somewhat more widely to "unpublished" tests appearing in the broad range of journals in the social and behavioral sciences. If one surveyed "published" tests, a different set of generalizations might emerge. Second, we did not attempt a complete verification of the directory; that is, we did not retrace all entries. Thus, we cannot offer definitive statements about the relative frequency with which certain problems occur in the directory, for example, incorrect information being recorded or specific reliability methods being recorded with a more generic label. We determined that such problems do exist, but we did not conduct retracing in such a systematic manner as to be able to say anything about how common they are.

References

Aiken, L. R. (1997). *Psychological testing and assessment* (9th ed.). Boston: Allyn & Bacon.

Anastasi, A., & Urbina, S. (1997). *Psychological testing* (7th ed.). Upper Saddle River, NJ: Prentice Hall.

Cohen, R. J., & Swerdlik, M. E. (1999). *Psychological testing and assessment: An introduction to tests and measurement* (4th ed.). Mountain View, CA: Mayfield.

Crocker, L., & Algina, J. (1986). *Introduction to classical and modern test theory.* New York: Holt, Rinehart & Winston.

Cronbach, L. J. (1951). Coefficient alpha and the internal structure of tests. *Psychometrika, 16,* 297-334.

Eason, S. (1991). Why generalizability theory yields better results than classical test theory: A primer with concrete examples. In B. Thompson (Ed.), *Advances in educational research: Substantive findings, methodological developments* (Vol. 1, pp. 83-98). Greenwich, CT: JAI Press.

Educational Testing Service. (1995). *The ETS test collection catalog; Vol. 2. Vocational tests and measurement devices* (2nd ed.). Phoenix, AZ: Oryx.

Fan, X. (1998). Item response theory and classical test theory: An empirical comparison of their item/person statistics. *Educational and Psychological Measurement, 58,* 357-381.

Feldt, L. S., & Brennan, R. L. (1989). Reliability. In R. L. Linn (Ed.), *Educational measurement* (3rd ed., pp. 105-146). Washington, DC: American Council on Education/Oryx.

Goldman, B. A., Mitchel, D. F., & Egelson, P. E. (1997). *Directory of unpublished experimental mental measures* (Vol. 7). Washington, DC: American Psychological Association.

Gregory, R. J. (1996). *Psychological testing: History, principles, and applications* (2nd ed.). Boston: Allyn & Bacon.

Jaeger, R. (1991). Forward. In R. J. Shavelson & N. M. Webb (Eds.), *Generalizability theory: A primer* (pp. ix-xi). Newbury Park, CA: Sage.

Joint Committee on Standards for Educational Evaluation. (1994). *The program evaluation standards: How to assess evaluations of educational programs* (2nd ed.). Thousand Oaks, CA: Sage. [531]

Kaplan, R. M., & Saccuzzo, D. P. (1997). *Psychological testing: Principles, applications, and issues* (4th ed.). Pacific Grove, CA: Brooks/Cole.

Maddox, T. (1997). *Tests: A comprehensive reference for assessments in psychology, education, and business* (4th ed.). Austin, TX: Pro-Ed.

Murphy, K. R., & Davidshofer, C. O. (1998). *Psychological testing: Principles and applications* (4th ed.). Upper Saddle River, NJ: Prentice Hall.

Murphy, L. L., Impara, J. C., & Plake, B. S. (1999). *Tests in print.* Lincoln: University of Nebraska Press.

Nunnally, J. C., & Bernstein, I. H. (1994). *Psychometric theory* (3rd ed.). New York: McGraw-Hill.

Reinhardt, B. (1996). Factors affecting coefficient alpha: A mini Monte Carlo study. In B. Thompson (Ed.), *Advances in social science methodology* (Vol. 4, pp. 3-20). Greenwich, CT: JAI Press.

Thompson, B. (1991). Review of generalizability theory: A primer by R. J. Shavelson & N. W. Webb. *Educational and Psychological Measurement, 51,* 1069-1075.

Thompson, B., & Snyder, P. A. (1998). Statistical significance and reliability analyses in recent *JCD* research articles. *Journal of Counseling and Development, 76,* 436-441.

Thompson, B., & Vacha-Haase, T. (2000). Psychometrics *is* datametrics: The test is not reliable. *Educational and Psychological Measurement, 60,* 174-195.

Vacha-Haase, T., Ness, C., Nilsson, I., & Reetz, D. (1999). Practices regarding reporting of reliability coefficients: A review of three journals. *Journal of Experimental Education, 67,* 335-341.

Wilkinson, L., & APA Task Force on Statistical Inference. (1999). Statistical methods in psychology journals: Guidelines and explanations. *American Psychologist, 54,* 594-604. [Reprint available through the APA home page: http://www.apa.org/journals/amp/amp548594.html]

Willson, V. L. (1980). Research techniques in *AERJ* articles: 1969 to 1978. *Educational Researcher, 9*(6), 5-10.

5

Confidence Intervals About Score Reliability Coefficients

Xitao Fan
University of Virginia

Bruce Thompson
Texas A&M University
and
Baylor College of Medicine

[517]   *Abstract*

Confidence intervals for reliability coefficients can be estimated in various ways. The present chapter illustrates a variety of these applications. This chapter was first published as an *EPM* "Guidelines Editorial" promulgating a request that *EPM* authors report confidence intervals for reliability estimates whenever they report score reliabilities, and to note what interval estimation methods they have used. This requirement will reinforce reader understanding that all statistical estimates, including those for score reliability, are

Fan, X., & Thompson, B. (2001). Confidence intervals about score reliability coefficients, please: An *EPM* guidelines editorial. *Educational and Psychological Measurement*, *61*, 517-531.

impacted by sampling error variance. And such requirements may also facilitate understanding that tests are not impregnated with invariant reliability as a routine part of printing.

During recent stewardship of this journal the editors have promulgated a number of "Guidelines Editorials" for prospective authors. These have covered issues such as:

1. *effect sizes*, including explicit requirements that effect sizes be reported along with p values (Thompson, 1994);

2. *score reliability*, including requests that tests not be described as reliable, and that what Cohen (1994) termed "nil" nulls (e.g., H_0: $\alpha = 0$, as opposed to a non-nil null such as $\alpha > .75$) not be used to test reliability or some validity coefficients (Thompson, 1994);

3. *stepwise analyses*, in the form of proscribed reporting of these methods (Thompson, 1995); and [518]

4. *factor analytic methods*, including requests to eschew the use of the ambiguous term, "loading," requests that both factor pattern and factor structure coefficients be reported for correlated factors, and requests that in CFA applications multiple fit indices are reported and that plausible rival models are tested (Thompson & Daniel, 1996).

We have issued these Guidelines Editorials to (a) assist authors in preparing manuscripts by making public our minimal expectations, (b) save referees the time that would otherwise be wasted in reviewing manuscripts not suitable for publication, and (c) facilitate the movement of the field toward more informed practices.

We have also explicitly encouraged authors to consider carefully the recommendations of the APA Task Force on Statistical Inference (Wilkinson & APA Task Force on Statistical Inference, 1999). Regarding reliability, the Task Force noted:

It is important to remember that a test is not reliable or unreliable. Reliability is a property of the scores on a test for a particular population of examinees. . . . Thus, authors should provide reliability coefficients of the scores for the data being analyzed even when the focus of their research is not psychometric. Interpreting the size of observed effects requires an assessment of the reliability of the scores. (Wilkinson & APA Task Force on Statistical Inference, 1999, p. 596)

Unfortunately, empirical studies of articles in various journals suggest that many authors do not understand important measurement concepts (Thompson & Vacha-Haase, 2000). Authors unreasonably induct coefficients from prior studies (Vacha-Haase, Kogan & Thompson, 2000; Whittington, 1998) and presume that reliability is unchanging (Vacha-Haase, 1998; Vacha-Haase, Ness, Nilsson & Reetz, 1999).

These errors occur because many doctoral programs no longer teach students measurement concepts (Aiken, West, Sechrest, & Reno with Roediger, Scarr, Kazdin, & Sherman, 1990; Pedhazur & Schmelkin 1991) [. . .] And as Thompson and Vacha-Haase (2000) argued,

> ignorance about measurement realities creates a self-perpetuating resistance to overcoming misconceptions. We have entered a black-box era in which students with terminal degrees in education and psychology first enter their training based upon scores from a computer-adaptive GRE testing that upon their graduation they could not intelligently explain or evaluate. (p. 180) [519]

Purpose of This "Guidelines Editorial"

The purpose of the present Guidelines Editorial is to ask authors to *report confidence intervals for reliability coefficients whenever these coefficients are reported*. This request is certainly in keeping with the recent recommendations of the APA Task Force. Here and in the related articles in the August 2001 *EPM* issue, methods for computing such confidence intervals are described in more detail.

These requirements will help readers see that all results within the General Linear Model, including measurement partitions of observed score variances, are influenced by sampling error variances (cf. Dawson, 1999). Additionally, the requirements may help readers see that reliability is not an immutable property stamped into tests during the production process.

Heuristic Example

Recent revisions to software and the development of relevant statistical theories make these editorial policies reasonable. The Table 5.1 data can be used to illustrate some of the methods for estimating confidence intervals for reliability coefficients. The tabled data apply an additive constant of −1 to the data reported by Crocker and Algina (1986, p. 162). Because additive constants do not affect variances or ratios of variances (such as reliability [520] coefficients), the reliability computations explained by Crocker and Algina (1986) apply to these data also, as will be illustrated.

Table 5.1   Heuristic Data

Person	Item 1	Item 2	Item 3	Total
1.	1	2	1	4
2.	7	4	6	17
3.	3	1	1	5
4.	3	2	5	10
5.	7	4	4	15
6.	7	4	6	17
7.	5	3	4	12
8.	3	2	2	7
9.	2	1	1	4
10.	0	1	2	3
Mean	3.8	2.4	3.2	9.4
V	6.62222	1.60000	4.17778	30.93333

NOTE: Cronbach's $\alpha = [k / (k - 1)] [1 - (\Sigma V_k / V_{TOTAL})]$. For these data, α is:

$$[3 / 2] [1 - ((6.62222 + 1.60000 + 4.17778) / 30.93333)]$$
$$[1.5] [1 - (12.40000 / 30.93333)]$$
$$[1.5] [1 - .400862]$$
$$[1.5] [0.59914]$$
$$0.89871.$$

ANOVA and Reliability Estimates

Several of the articles in the August 2001 *EPM* issue discuss the computation of confidence intervals in ANOVA and related applications
(cf. Cumming & Finch, 2001; Fidler & Thompson, 2001; Smithson, 2001).
It has long been known that ANOVA results can be employed to compute
reliability coefficients (Hoyt, 1941). Indeed, these basic ideas of applying
ANOVA to estimate reliabilities led to the very "modern" measurement theory called Generalizability theory (Cronbach, Gleser, Nanda, & Rajaratnam,
1972). Accessible explanations of "G" theory and its use of ANOVA are
provided by Eason (1991), Shavelson and Webb (1991), and Webb, Rowley
and Shavelson (1988). Thus, many of the ANOVA confidence interval applications described in the August 2001 *EPM* issue apply to score reliability
estimates as well.

Table 5.2 presents the ANOVA results associated with the Table 5.1
data. Appendices A and B present the data and syntax files that can be used
to obtain these results. Using Hoyt's methods (Crocker & Algina, 1986,
p. 140) yields as a reliability estimate:

Table 5.2   ANOVA Results for the Table 5.1 Data

Source	Sum of Squares	Degrees of Freedom	Mean Squares
People (p)	92.8000	9	10.3111
Items (i)	9.8667	2	4.9333
p*i, and model error (e)	18.8000	18	1.0444
Total	121.4667	29	

NOTE: Because in these applications each cell has only one data entry, there are insufficient degrees of freedom to differentiate the two-way interaction and the model specification error term. Therefore, these two terms are statistically "confounded," and the model is implemented as a two-way nonfactorial analysis in which the interaction is not estimated (see the Appendix B design statement).

$$(MS_{people} - MS_{error}) / MS_{people}$$
$$(10.3111 - 1.0444) / 10.3111$$
$$9.2667 / 10.3111 = .8987.$$

As indicated in the Table 5.1 table note, this results equals Cronbach's alpha.

The result can also be estimated using variance components. The necessary SPSS commands to obtain the variance components are presented in Appendix B. For these data the variance component for persons is 3.089, and [521] for the confounded joint combination of the person*variable interaction and the model specification error is 1.044.

The result can also be estimated using variance components. The necessary SPSS commands to obtain the variance components are presented in Appendix B. For these data the variance component for persons is 3.089, and [521] for the confounded joint combination of the person*variable interaction and the model specification error is 1.044. The estimate may be derived as:

$$[V_{people} / n_p] / [(V_{people} / n_p) + (V_{p*v,e}) / n_p n_v]$$
$$[3.089 / 10] / [(3.089 / 10) + (1.044 / 10(3))]$$
$$.3089 / [.3089 + (1.044 / 30)]$$
$$.3089 / [.3089 + .0348]$$
$$.3089 / .3437 = .8987.$$

Confidence Intervals for Score Reliabilities

Burdick and Graybill (1992, section 6.3.3) presented a method for using ANOVA F values to derive confidence intervals for reliability coefficients. However, their method applies in evaluating the reliability of scores interpreted in the context of (a) an "absolute" decision (i.e., an application evaluating scores using a single pass/fail cutoff) and (b) only one rater or item.

We turn here to methods for constructing confidence intervals for score reliability coefficients involving "relative" decisions (i.e., applications evaluating the stability only of rank orderings of the people or other "objects of measurement", and not of pass/fail decisions). These "relative" decisions are the kinds of applications for which coefficients such as Cronbach's alpha are relevant.

We consider approaches invoking both the "central" F distribution, and those invoking "noncentral" F distributions. Other articles (Cumming & Finch, 2001; Smithson, 2001) provide explanation of "noncentral" distributions, which are old (cf. Fisher, 1931), but less widely known than their "central" counterparts.

Noncentral distributions are not extensively discussed in many textbooks. But Hays (1988) explained that

> Unfortunately, the actual determination of the power for a t test [or F test] against any given true alternative is more complicated than for the normal distribution . . . [W]hen H_0 is false, each t value involves a false expectation; this results in a somewhat different distribution, called the **noncentral** **t distribution**. The probabilities of the various t's cannot be known unless one more parameter, δ, is specified besides . . . [the degrees of freedom]. This is the so-called noncentrality parameter, defined by $\delta = |(\mu_1 - \mu_2) / \sigma_M|$. (p. 304)

In an earlier edition of a related book, Hays and Winkler (1971) further explained that "the determination of the power of a t test [is] considerably more troublesome than for tests using the normal distribution. . . For more accurate [522] work, most advanced texts in statistics give tables of the power function" based on noncentral distributions (p. 430).

In addition to being necessary for many power computations, noncentral distributions are also necessary for accurate calculation of results invoking ratios of estimates to other estimates. Thus, noncentral intervals are needed to compute accurate confidence intervals for standardized effect sizes (cf. Cumming & Finch, 2001).

"Central" Approaches

Confidence Intervals for Cronbach's Coefficient alpha

The sampling distribution for Cronbach's coefficient alpha (α) has been investigated by Kristof (1963) and Feldt (1965, 1980). As discussed by Feldt (1990), Feldt, Woodruff, and Salih (1987), and by Feldt, Woodruff, Salih, and Srichai (1986), for a given *sample* of n examinees taking a test with k items, the upper and lower confidence interval limits for the sample Cronbach coefficient alpha ($\hat{\alpha}$) at the given statistical significance level γ can be constructed as:

$$CI_{upper} = 1 - [(1 - \hat{\alpha}) \times F_{(\gamma/2),df1,df2}], \text{ and}$$

$$CI_{lower} = 1 - [(1 - \hat{\alpha}) \times F_{(1 - \_\gamma/2),df1,df2}],$$

where F represents the values of the F distribution for percentiles $\gamma/2$ and $1-\gamma/2$, respectively, with $df_1 = (n-1)$, and $df_2 = (n-1)(k-1)$.

For the data in Table 5.1, $n=10$ and $k=3$, so $df_1 = 9$, and $df_2 = 18$. If the desired statistical significance level is $\gamma = .05$, the F values needed for constructing the upper/lower limits of the confidence interval are:

$$F_{(.025,9,18)} = 0.27016 \text{ (lower percentile } F \text{ for the } CI_{upper}), \text{ and}$$

$$F_{(.975,9,18)} = 2.92911 \text{ (upper percentile } F \text{ for the } CI_{lower}).$$

Customarily, the F tables in statistics books only list the upper percentiles of $F_{(df1, df2)}$, but not the lower percentiles. It is, however, widely known that the lower percentiles of $F_{(df1,df2)}$ can be obtained as the reciprocal of the upper percentiles of $F_{(df2,df1)}$; note the change of positions of the two degrees of freedom. In other words, the lower percentile $F_{(.025,9,18)}$ can be obtained as:

$$F_{(.025,9,18)} = 1/F_{(.975,18,9)} = 1 / 3.70147 = .27016.$$

Once the two F values are obtained, the 95% confidence interval for the reliability estimate for Table 5.1 data is easily obtained:

$$CI_{lower} = 1 - [(1 - .89871) \times 2.92911] = .70331, \text{ and} \qquad [523]$$
$$CI_{upper} = 1 - [(1 - .89871) \times .27016] = .97264.$$

Statistical Significance Test for Reliability Estimate

As discussed by Feldt (1965), Feldt et al. (1986), and Charter and Feldt (1996), for a sample reliability estimate $\hat{\alpha}$, a statistical significance test can be conducted to test this sample reliability estimate against an hypothesized population reliability α_0 in the following manner:

$$(1 - \alpha_0)/(1 - \alpha_{OBSERVED}) = F_{[df1=n-1,\ df2=(n-1)(k-1)]},$$

where n represents the number of examinees taking the test, and k represents the number of items on the test, as discussed previously. For a given statistical significance level γ and a non-directional test, if the calculated F value is smaller than $F_{(\gamma/2, df1, df2)}$, or larger than $F_{(1-\gamma/2, df1, df2)}$, the null hypothesis ($H_0 : \alpha = \alpha_0$) will be rejected.

It is important to point out that the statistical significance test described here does *not* invoke the "nil" null hypothesis that the score reliability is 0. For scores with *any* reasonable reliability the "nil" null will be rejected with a sample consisting of only a handful of people.

This is why Abelson (1997) commented thusly on statistical tests of measurement results using nil null hypotheses:

> And when a reliability coefficient is declared to be nonzero, that is the ultimate in stupefyingly vacuous information. What we really want to know is whether an estimated reliability is .50'ish or .80'ish. (p. 121)

This is also why our *EPM* editorial policies (Thompson, 1994) specify that:

> Statistical tests of such coefficients in a measurement context make little sense. Either statistical significance tests using the null hypothesis of zero magnitude should be by-passed, or meaningful [i.e., non-nil] null hypotheses should be employed. (p. 844)

For the present data, if the population reliability coefficient is specified to be .70 (i.e., $H_0 : \alpha = .70$), we have the following:

$$F_{calculated} = (1 - .70) / (1 - .89871) = .3 / .10129 = 2.96179.$$

Previously, the critical F values have been obtained: $F_{(.025, 9, 18)} = 0.27016$, and $F_{(.975, 9, 18)} = 2.92911$. Because our $F_{calculated}$ value (2.96179) exceeds the upper critical F value of 2.92911, the null hypothesis is rejected.

The exact p value for $F_{(9,18)} = 2.96179$ is .02386. The exact p value can be obtained through either a spreadsheet program (e.g., Microsoft Excel), or through statistical programs (e.g., SPSS, SAS). For example, in Excel the command is:

$$\text{``=FDIST(2.96179, 9, 18)''}. \qquad \textbf{[524]}$$

We may conclude that the population reliability coefficient is higher than .70; if the population reliability coefficient was .70, it would be very unlikely to have obtained the sample reliability coefficient of .89871.

If a directional (and statistically more powerful) test (H_0: $\alpha \le \alpha_0$; H_a: $\alpha > \alpha_0$) is desired, we can simply compare the $F_{calculated}$ against the upper percentile $F_{(1-\bar{a},df1,df2)}$, instead of $F_{(1-\bar{a}/2,df1,df2)}$. For our data in Table 5.1, the directional critical $F_{(.95,9,18)}$ = 2.45628, which is smaller than the non-directional critical $F_{(.975,9,18)}$ = 2.92911. In Excel, the commands that yield these values respectively are:

$$\text{``=FINV(.05, 9, 18)''}, \text{ and}$$
$$\text{``=FINV(.025, 9, 18)''}.$$

Obviously, the smaller directional critical F value makes it easier to reject the null hypothesis, if the reliability estimate is in the expected direction (i.e., larger than the hypothesized α_0).

Using SPSS for Reliability Confidence Intervals and Tests

SPSS now provides upon request a confidence interval about the reliability estimate based on the procedures discussed above. In addition, it also allows the statistical significance test against a hypothesized reliability value (α_0). The necessary syntax associated with the data being entered as arrayed in Table 5.1 is:

```
reliability variables=v1 to v3/
   scale(TOTAL)=v1 to v3/
   statistics=corr cov/summary=means var total/
   icc=model(random) type(consistency) cin=95 testval=.70/
   model=alpha.
```

The 95% confidence interval obtained through SPSS is, not surprisingly, [0.7033, .9726], as we computed previously. For the present data, if "TESTVAL" is specified to be .70 (i.e., H_0 : α = .70), the $p_{CALCULATED}$ is .0239. If the "nil" null had been employed (i.e., H_0: α = 0), the probability of the sample results instead would be $p < .0001$.

Pearson Correlation Coefficients as Reliability Estimates

In many situations, we may encounter other reliability estimates such as inter-rater or test-retest reliability estimates. Statistically, these reliability estimates are all Pearson correlation coefficients. For a Pearson correlation coefficient, a confidence interval based on Fisher Z transformation can be constructed in a straightforward manner. As explained elsewhere (e.g., Glass & [525] Hopkins, 1996), four steps are involved in constructing a confidence interval for a Pearson correlation coefficient:

1. transform r to Z_r (Fisher Z transformation);
2. compute σ_z: $\sigma_z = 1/(n-3)^{.5}$ (n: number of examinees, or ratees);
3. obtain CI for Z_p: $Z_r \pm 1.96\sigma_z$ (for 95% CI); and
4. transform lower/upper limits back to Pearson r.

As an example, let's assume that we have 20 participants in a study, and two independent raters provide ratings for each participant on some behavior of interest. The inter-rater reliability estimate (i.e., Pearson correlation coefficient between the two raters) is computed to be .80. What is the 90% confidence interval for this inter-rater reliability estimate?

1. $Z_r = .5 \ln [(1+|r|)/(1-|r|)] = .5 \ln (1.8/0.2) = 1.0986$;
2. $\sigma_z = 1/(n-3)^{.5} = 1/17^{.5} = .2425$;
3. 90% CI for Z_r: $1.0986 \pm 1.645 \times .2425 = (.6997, 1.4975)$; and
4. 90% CI for r: lower $Z_r = 0.6997 \rightarrow$ lower r = .6042

   upper $Z_r = 1.4975 \rightarrow$ upper r = .9047.

So the obtained 90% CI for the population inter-rater reliability is [.6042; .9047]. Confidence intervals for other reliability estimates (e.g., test-retest) can be constructed in the same fashion.

Both Fisher Z transformation (from Pearson r to Fisher Z) and back transformation (from Fisher Z to Pearson r) can be easily done in a spreadsheet program (e.g., Microsoft Excel) or a statistics program (e.g., SPSS, SAS). Hand calculation procedures can be found in many introductory statistics textbook, such as Glass and Hopkins (1996).

Reliability Estimate from the Split-Half Approach

In the split-half approach the correlation coefficient between the two halves is first obtained, and the Spearman-Brown "prophecy" formula is then applied to this correlation coefficient to obtain the reliability estimate for the scores of the full test. To construct confidence intervals for the reliability estimate from this approach, the same four steps described in the previous section are applied to the correlation coefficient between the two halves. Once the lower and upper confidence limits for the between-half correlation coefficient are obtained, the Spearman-Brown formula is then applied to these lower and upper limits of the between-half correlation coefficient to obtain confidence interval limits for the reliability estimate of the scores of the full test.

As an example, let's assume that we have obtained the Pearson correlation coefficient of 0.80 between two halves of a test (odd-even split). Applying Spearman-Brown formula to this correlation coefficient, the reliability [526] estimate for the full test scores is .8889 [(2 × .80)/(1 + .80)]. What is the 90% CI for this reliability estimate? Using the results calculated in the previous section, the lower and upper limits (for 90% CI) for the between-half correlation coefficient are .6042 and .9047 respectively. By applying the Spearman-Brown formula to these two limits, we find the 90% CI for the reliability estimate of the full test scores is .7533 [(2 × .6042)/(1 + .6042)] to .9499 [(2 × .9047)/(1 + .9047)].

"Noncentral" Approaches

As explained elsewhere (Cumming & Finch, 2001; Fidler & Thompson, 2001; Smithson, 2001), "noncentral" approaches differ most from their "central" counterparts when (a) degrees of freedom are small or (b) effect size is large. Because the effect size in reliability studies are score reliability coefficients, and we typically expect these to be quite large (cf. Abelson, 1997), noncentral methods may be particularly relevant in constructing confidence intervals for reliability estimates.

Fixed-Effects ANOVA Approach

If a "fixed effects" ANOVA model is invoked (see Fidler & Thompson, 2001; Frederick, 1999), the confidence interval for the reliability can be computed in a series of SPSS analyses. The relevant ANOVA F value is 9.87234 (with 9 and 18 degrees of freedom) for the "person" effect. We may use the Smithson (2001) SPSS syntax to iteratively estimate the confidence interval associated with this effect.

To obtain a 95% confidence interval, as Smithson (2001) explains, "When working with statistics for which 'one-sided' intervals are typically deemed appropriate, $100(1-\alpha)\%$ confidence intervals are computed by declaring 'CONF' to be $1-[2(\alpha)]$ (e.g., use 'CONF'=.90 to obtain a 95% one-sided interval)" (p. 613). However, if we want a two-sided interval we declare "CONF" to be $1-\alpha$ (here .95). The output boundaries on the confidence interval (i.e., variables "R2L" and "R2U") are:

[.47936; .85189].

However, we estimate reliability (a squared statistic in the "domain" or "population" world) as an *unsquared* value computed in a sample (see Thompson & Vacha-Haase, 2000). Therefore, we take the square root of these boundaries, and obtain the interval:

[.69236; .92298].   [527]

Note that we typically treat people as "random," because we usually wish to generalize beyond our sample of people and presume that our sample of people is representative. For most measurement designs we also usually treat most measurement facets (e.g., items, occasions of measurement) as random, because again often we presume they are a subset of possibilities and wish to generalize to a larger domain. Using a random-effects approach may therefore be more relevant, but also will tend to yield wider confidence intervals.

Random-Effects Approach

We might also estimate a reliability confidence interval by using a regression logic and the "R2" computer program developed by Steiger and Fouladi (1992, 1997). The application, "R2," can be downloaded from URL:

http://www.interchg.ubc.ca/steiger/homepage.htm.

For the present purposes we input the squared value of our reliability coefficient (i.e., $.89871^2 = .80768$) as the R^2 value. Because the degrees of freedom for our model are 9 and 18, we input 28 as our n (i.e., in the regression analog $n = df1 + df2 + 1$). We input 10 as the number of variables (i.e., in the regression analog the number of degrees of freedom numerator is the number of predictor variables, plus the single criterion variable).

We input .95 as our confidence value, for the reasons just mentioned, to obtain a two-sided 95% confidence interval. For these data we obtain:

[.40941; .86575].

We then take the square roots of these boundaries to obtain:

$$[.63985; .93046].$$

Note that this interval is wider than that for the fixed-effect approach (i.e., .2906 versus .2306).

Summary

Reliability coefficients for scores can be estimated using a variety of theories. Similarly, intervals for reliability coefficients can be estimated in various ways. We do not expect authors universally to invoke any particular reliability coefficient or any particular confidence interval estimation method. This is similar to our expectation that authors report any effect size estimate (Thompson, 1994) from among the dozens of choices (Kirk, 1996), without declaring that selected effect sizes must be used.

However, we do ask authors to report routinely confidence intervals whenever they report score reliabilities, and to note what estimation methods they have used. This will reinforce reader understanding that all statistical [528] estimates, including those for score reliability, are impacted by sampling error variance. And these requirements may also facilitate understanding that tests are not impregnated with invariant reliability as a routine part of printing/production. [529]

Appendix A   ASCII Text Data File for
ANOVA Estimate of Score Reliability

```
1 1 2
1 2 3
1 3 2
2 1 8
2 2 5
2 3 7
3 1 4
3 2 2
3 3 2
4 1 4
4 2 3
4 3 6
5 1 8
5 2 5
5 3 5
6 1 8
```

```
 6 2 5
 6 3 7
 7 1 6
 7 2 4
 7 3 5
 8 1 4
 8 2 3
 8 3 3
 9 1 3
 9 2 2
 9 3 2
10 1 1
10 2 2
10 3 3
```

Appendix B   SPSS Syntax File for ANOVA Estimate of Score Reliability

```
set printback=listing .
data list file='a:crocker2.dta' records=1/
 person 1-2 item 4 score 6 .
title 'CROCKER2.SPS  ***********************' .
execute .
list variables=all/cases=9999/format=numbered .
subtitle 'RANDOM EFFECTS MODELS ************' .
execute .
UNIANOVA
   score  BY person item
   /RANDOM = person item
   /METHOD = SSTYPE(3)
   /INTERCEPT = INCLUDE
   /PRINT = DESCRIPTIVE
   /CRITERIA = ALPHA(.05)
   /DESIGN = person item .
VARCOMP
   score  BY person item
   /RANDOM = person item
   /METHOD = SSTYPE (3)
   /DESIGN = person item
   /INTERCEPT = INCLUDE .
```

References

Abelson, R. P. (1997). A retrospective on the significance test ban of 1999 (If there were no significance tests, they would be invented). In L. L. Harlow, S. A. Mulaik & J. H. Steiger (Eds.), *What if there were no significance tests?* (pp. 117-141). Mahwah, NJ: Erlbaum.

Aiken, L. S., West, S. G., Sechrest, L., Reno, R. R., with Roediger, H. L., Scarr, S., Kazdin, A. E., & Sherman, S. J. (1990). The training in statistics, methodology, and measurement in psychology. *American Psychologist, 45,* 721-734.

Burdick, R. K., & Graybill, F. A. (1992). *Confidence intervals for variance components.* New York: Marcel Dekker.

Charter, R. A., & Feldt, L. S. (1996). Testing the equality of two alpha coefficients. *Perceptual and Motor Skills, 82,* 763-738.

Cohen, J. (1994). The earth is round ($p < .05$). *American Psychologist, 49,* 997-1003.

Crocker, L., & Algina, J. (1986). *Introduction to classical and modern test theory.* New York: Holt, Rinehart and Winston.

Cronbach, L. J., Gleser, G. C., Nanda, H., & Rajaratnam, N. (1972). *The dependability of measurements.* New York: Wiley and Sons.

Cumming, G., & Finch, S. (2001). A primer on the understanding, use and calculation of confidence intervals that are based on central and noncentral distributions. *Educational and Psychological Measurement, 61,* 532-574.

Dawson, T. D. (1999). Relating variance partitioning in measurement analyses to the exact same process in substantive analyses. In B. Thompson (Ed.), *Advances in social science methodology* (Vol. 5, pp. 101-110). Stamford, CT: JAI Press.

Eason, S. J. (1991). Why generalizability theory yields better results than classical test theory: A primer with concrete examples. In B. Thompson (Ed.), *Advances in educational research: Substantive findings, methodological developments* (Vol. 1, pp. 83-98). Greenwich, CT: JAI Press.

Feldt, L. S. (1965). The approximate sampling distribution of Kuder-Richardson coefficient twenty. *Psychometrika, 30,* 357-370. [530]

Feldt, L. S. (1980). A test of the hypothesis that Cronbach's alpha reliability coefficient is the same for two tests administered to the same sample. *Psychometrika, 45,* 99-105.

Feldt, L. S. (1990). The sampling theory for the intraclass reliability coefficient. *Applied Measurement in Education, 3,* 361-367.

Feldt, L. S., Woodruff, D. J., & Salih, F. A. (1987). Statistical inference for coefficient alpha. *Applied Psychological Measurement, 11,* 93-103.

Feldt, L. S., Woodruff, D. J., Salih, F. A., & Srichai, M. (1986). *Statistical tests and confidence intervals for Cronbach's Coefficient Alpha.* Iowa Testing Programs Occasional Papers Number 33. (ERIC Document Reproduction Service No. ED 291 755)

Fidler, F., & Thompson, B. (2001). Computing correct confidence intervals for ANOVA fixed- and random-effects effect sizes. *Educational and Psychological Measurement, 61,* 575-604.

Fisher, R. A. (1931). Introduction. In J. R. Airey, *Table of Hh functions* (pp. xxvi-xxxv). London: British Association.

Frederick, B. N. (1999). Fixed-, random-, and mixed-effects ANOVA models: A user-friendly guide for increasing the generalizability of ANOVA results. In B. Thompson, B. (Ed.). (1999). *Advances in social science methodology* (vol. 5, pp. 111-122). Stamford, CT: JAI Press.

Glass, G. V, & Hopkins, K. D. (1996). *Statistical methods in education and psychology* (3rd ed.). Boston, MA: Allyn and Bacon.

Hays, W. L. (1988). *Statistics* (4th ed.). New York: Holt, Rinehart and Winston.

Hays, W. L., & Winkler, R. L. (1971). *Statistics: Probability, inference, and decision.* New York: Holt, Rinehart and Winston.

Hoyt, C. J. (1941). Test reliability estimated by analysis of variance. *Psychometrika, 6,* 153-160.

Kirk, R. (1996). Practical significance: A concept whose time has come. *Educational and Psychological Measurement, 56,* 746-759.

Kristof, W. (1963). The statistical theory of stepped-up reliability coefficients when a test has been divided into several equivalent parts. *Psychometrika, 28*, 221-238.

Pedhazur, E. J., & Schmelkin, L. P. (1991). *Measurement, design, and analysis: An integrated approach.* Hillsdale, NJ: Erlbaum.

Shavelson, R. J. & Webb, N. M. (1991). *Generalizability theory: A primer.* Newbury Park, CA: Sage.

Smithson, M. (2001). Correct confidence intervals for various regression effect sizes and parameters: The importance of noncentral distributions in computing intervals. *Educational and Psychological Measurement, 61*, 605-632.

Steiger, J. H. & Fouladi, R. T. (1992). R2: A computer program for interval estimation, power calculation, and hypothesis testing for the squared multiple correlation. *Behavior Research Methods, Instruments, and Computers, 4*, 581-582.

Steiger, J. H. & Fouladi, R. T. (1997). Noncentrality interval estimation and the evaluation of statistical models. In L. Harlow, S. Mulaik & J. H. Steiger (Eds.), *What if there were no significance tests?* (pp. 222-257). Hillsdale, NJ: Erlbaum.

Thompson, B. (1994). Guidelines for authors. *Educational and Psychological Measurement, 54*, 837-847.

Thompson, B. (1995). Stepwise regression and stepwise discriminant analysis need not apply here: A guidelines editorial. *Educational and Psychological Measurement, 55*, 525-534.

Thompson, B., & Daniel, L. G. (1996). Factor analytic evidence for the construct validity of scores: An historical overview and some guidelines. *Educational and Psychological Measurement, 56*, 197-208.

Thompson, B., & Vacha-Haase, T. (2000). Psychometrics *is* datametrics: The test is not reliable. *Educational and Psychological Measurement, 60*, 174-195.

Vacha-Haase, T. (1998). Reliability generalization: Exploring variance in measurement error affecting score reliability across studies. *Educational and Psychological Measurement, 58*, 6-20. [531]

Vacha-Haase, T., Kogan, L. R., & Thompson, B. (2000). Sample compositions and variabilities in published studies versus those in test manuals: Validity of score reliability inductions. *Educational and Psychological Measurement, 60*, 509-522.

Vacha-Haase, T., Ness, C., Nilsson, J., & Reetz, D. (1999). Practices regarding reporting of reliability coefficients: A review of three journals. *Journal of Experimental Education, 67*, 335-341.

Webb, N. M., Rowley, G. L., & Shavelson, R. J. (1988). Using generalizability theory in counseling and development. *Measurement and Evaluation in Counseling and Development, 21*, 81-90.

Whittington, D. (1998). How well do researchers report their measures? An evaluation of measurement in published educational research. *Educational and Psychological Measurement, 58*, 21-37.

Wilkinson, L., & APA Task Force on Statistical Inference. (1999). Statistical methods in psychology journals: Guidelines and explanations. *American Psychologist, 54*, 594-604. [reprint available through the APA Home Page: http://www.apa.org/journals/amp/amp548594.html]

In substantive research we recognize that our sampling methods limit the generalizability of our conclusions. For example, if we conduct a study of teaching methods involving mathematically precocious second graders and find the intervention effective, the reasonable researcher would probably hesitate to conclude that the same teaching method would necessarily be equally effective with mathematically illiterate senior citizens. By the same token, when we estimate the reliability of scores of a self-concept measure written in English and developed for adolescents (see Chapter 10), some caution ought to be demanded in assuming that the same score reliability will result if the measure is used for a mentally-disturbed sample in which participants speak primarily another language.

Even when we estimate score reliability using our own data (as we ought always do), it is important to remember that the computed reliability is not necessarily the exact reliability for all the scores on the measure within the score universe. Confidence intervals can be very useful for estimating, given our data, what might be all the plausible values for the reliability.

To date, confidence intervals are not widely used in either substantive or measurement research (Finch, Cumming, & Thomason, 2001; Kieffer, Reese, & Thompson, 2001), although the new APA (2001) *Publication Manual* emphasizes that confidence intervals "are, in general, *the best* [italics added] reporting strategy" (p. 22). When we construct a confidence interval, we are using procedures to estimate possible parameters in the score universe, given what confidence we desire in capturing the unknown population or universe value. Often researchers use 95% (or 90%, or 67%) as their desired degree of confidence. If a large or infinite number of samples were drawn from the population, and confidence intervals were constructed in the same manner using the same confidence (e.g., 95%), then exactly 95% of the intervals would capture the true parameter, and 5% would not (Cumming & Finch, 2001; Thompson, 2002).

The previous chapter explained how a confidence interval can be computed for coefficient α (or KR-20). Appendix A presents an Excel spreadsheet that automates these various calculations.

Create the spreadsheet in this new Appendix in the same manner that you created the spreadsheet used in Exercise Set 1. When you have successfully computed the spreadsheet, for the input used in row "2" of the Appendix, your output confidence interval should match the one provided in Chapter 5 (i.e., 0.7033, 0.9726).

Confidence Level

Enter a fixed α (e.g., .89871) in column "A" of the spreadsheet across several rows. Also enter a fixed number of people in column "B" of the spreadsheet. And enter a fixed number of items in column "C" of the spreadsheet. Vary the probability (p) value entered in the rows on column "D", using values such as .01, .05, .10, and .33. "Confidence" is one minus whatever this number is (e.g., $1 - .05 = 95\%$ confidence). How does p (or conversely, confidence) impact the width of the confidence intervals for our estimates of score reliability?

Number of People

Enter a fixed α (e.g., .89871) in column "A" of the spreadsheet across several rows. Also enter a fixed number of items in column "C" of the spreadsheet. Enter a fixed value (e.g., .05) for p across the rows in column "D". In column "B" of the spreadsheet enter different samples sizes as regards numbers of people. How does the number of people involved in a study impact the *precision* (i.e., the width of the confidence interval) of our estimates of score reliability?

Number of Items

Enter a fixed α (e.g., .89871) in column "A" of the spreadsheet across several rows. Also enter a fixed number of people in column "B" of the spreadsheet. Enter a fixed value (e.g., .05) for p across the rows in column "D". In column "C" of the spreadsheet enter different numbers of test items. How does the number of items on a measure impact the *precision* (i.e., the width of the confidence interval) of our estimates of score reliability?

Score Reliability

Enter a fixed number of people in column "B" of the spreadsheet. Enter a fixed number of items in column "C" of the spreadsheet. Enter a fixed value (e.g., .05) for p across the rows in column "D". In column "A" enter different values for α (e.g., .95, .70, .50, .20). How does our estimated α

for our own data impact the *precision* (i.e., the width of the confidence interval) of our estimates of score reliability?

References

American Psychological Association. (2001). *Publication manual of the American Psychological Association* (5th ed.). Washington, DC: Author.

Cumming, G., & Finch, S. (2001). A primer on the understanding, use and calculation of confidence intervals that are based on central and noncentral distributions. *Educational and Psychological Measurement, 61,* 532-575.

Finch, S., Cumming, G., & Thomason, N. (2001). Reporting of statistical inference in the *Journal of Applied Psychology*: Little evidence of reform. *Educational and Psychological Measurement, 61,* 181-210.

Kieffer, K. M., Reese, R. J., & Thompson, B. (2001). Statistical techniques employed in *AERJ* and *JCP* articles from 1988 to 1997: A methodological review. *Journal of Experimental Education, 69,* 280-309.

Thompson, B. (2002). What future quantitative social science research could look like: Confidence intervals for effect sizes. *Educational Researcher, 31*(3), 24-31.

Appendix A:

	A	B	C	D	E	F	G	H	I	J	K
	alpha	n	k	p	df1	df2	F Upper	F Lower	CI Lower	CI Upper	CI Width
1											
2	0.89871	10	3	.05	+B2-1	+E2*(C2-1)	=FINV(D2/2,E2,F2)	=FINV(1-(D2/2),E2,F2)	+1-((1-A2)*H2)	+1-((1-A2)*G2)	+J2-I2
3					+B3-1	+E3*(C3-1)	=FINV(D3/2,E3,F3)	=FINV(1-(D3/2),E3,F3)	+1-((1-A3)*H3)	+1-((1-A3)*G3)	+J3-I3
4					+B4-1	+E4*(C4-1)	=FINV(D4/2,E4,F4)	=FINV(1-(D4/2),E4,F4)	+1-((1-A4)*H4)	+1-((1-A4)*G4)	+J4-I4
5											

Part II

The Nature of Reliability

As noted in the Preface, some concepts of reliability are subtle and even philosophical. The readings in this section were selected to facilitate reflection regarding the nature of reliability.

The first reading frames some basic issues in the form of certain author guidelines for *Educational and Psychological Measurement*. The remaining three chapters are a debate regarding whether it is reasonable to speak of "the reliability of the test" or to say "the test is reliable."

The view taken here is that scores (rather than tests) are reliable. Measurement experts have created an unfortunate metaphor suggesting that score reliability, once established, is immutable. To the extent that this unconscious paradigm is adopted, all test users need do to act responsibly is to ensure that reliability experts establish one single time that test scores were once reliable.

If this paradigm were realistic, test users would then be freed from the necessity of any further inquiry regarding score integrity. Furthermore, if test users may simply rely upon a single prior examination of score integrity, then users need not be expected to develop their own expertise to evaluate score integrity.

6

Guidelines for Authors Reporting Score Reliability Estimates

Bruce Thompson
Texas A&M University
and
Baylor College of Medicine

[837]   *Abstract*

EPM was the first journal (a) to formally "require" effect size reporting, or (b) to proscribe description of tests as being reliable, or (c) to proscribe tests of the statistical significance of reliability coefficients, *unless* a "non-nil" null hypothesis was used (e.g., H_0: $r_{xx} < .7$). These author guidelines lay out the rationale as to why these are appropriate analytic practices within contemporary social science.

*E*ducational and Psychological Measurement was founded as a journal more than five decades ago, in 1941. The Founding Editor was G. Frederic Kuder. His colleague, M. W. Richardson, was at that time one

Thompson, B. (1994). Guidelines for authors. *Educational and Psychological Measurement*, *54*, 837-847.

of three Associate Editors. In addition to these well-known figures, members of the journal's first editorial board included luminaries such as Guilford, Lindquist, and Rulon.

In his first editorial, "Presenting a New Journal," Kuder (1941) observed that:

> The interest and activity in the field of the measurement of human character-istics have never been greater than today . . . Educational institutions, govern-ment, and industry are all giving increasing attention to methods of evaluation aimed at determining the status and promise of the individual. Improved methods in measurement are being developed and significant research is being done in many fields. In spite of this rising interest, measurement is still a stepchild. (p. 3)

These words were prescient then, almost 55 years ago, but they remain applicable today.

We are currently experiencing exponential increases in our knowledge of measurement dynamics. Witness continuing developments in generalizability theory, in latent trait measurement, and in structural equation modeling. At the very same time, we see more and more regulatory and legislative mandates for the use of tests in making a variety of high-stakes decisions.

And yet, in at least some respects, measurement does remain something of a stepchild. For example, as Pedhazur and Schmelkin (1991, pp. 2-3) recently noted, "Measurement is the Achilles' heel of sociobehavioral research." [. . .] Thus, "perusal of contemporary psychology journals demonstrates that quantitative reports of scale reliability and validity esti-mates are often missing or [838] incomplete" (Meier & Davis, 1990, p. 113). Similarly, in doctoral dissertations we occasionally even see scores being analyzed that have reliability coefficients that are both negative in sign and large in magnitude (Thompson, 1994a).

All this means that the journal is potentially well-positioned to offer note-worthy leadership to the field at a time when such leadership remains needed. This will require a continued dedication to the traditions of excellence estab-lished by Kuder and his successors. These successors have been: W. Scott Gehman, William B. Michael, and Geraldine Thomas Sheehy. [. . . 839]

Language Use Regarding Score Characteristics

One unfortunate common feature of contemporary scholarly language is the usage of the statement, "the test is reliable" or "the test is valid." Such language is both incorrect and deleterious in its affects on scholarly inquiry, particularly given the pernicious consequences that unconscious paradigmatic beliefs can exact. Although the remaining discussion explicitly deals with score reliability, similar considerations apply with respect to validity.

Too few researchers act on a conscious recognition that *reliability is a characteristic of scores or the data in hand*. Many authorities present this view, but paradigm influences constrain some researchers from actively integrating this presumption into their actual analytic practice.

As Rowley (1976, p. 53, emphasis added) argued, "It needs to be established that an instrument itself is neither reliable nor unreliable. . . . A single instrument can produce *scores* which are reliable, and other *scores* which are unreliable." Similarly, Crocker and Algina (1986, p. 144, emphasis added) argued that, ". . .A test is not 'reliable' or 'unreliable.' Rather, reliability is a property of the *scores* on a test for a *particular* group of examinees."

In another widely respected text, Gronlund and Linn (1990, p. 78, emphasis in original) noted,

> Reliability refers to the *results* obtained with an evaluation instrument and not to the instrument itself. . . . Thus, it is more appropriate to speak of the reliability of the "test scores" or of the "measurement" than of the "test" or the "instrument."

And Eason (1991, p. 84, emphasis added) argued that:

> Though some practitioners of the classical measurement paradigm [incorrectly] speak of reliability as a characteristic of tests, in fact reliability is a characteristic of *data*, albeit data generated on a given measure administered with a given protocol to given subjects on given occasions.

The subjects themselves impact the reliability of scores, and thus it becomes an oxymoron to speak of "the reliability of the test" without considering to whom the test was administered, or other facets of the measurement protocol. Reliability is driven by variance—typically, greater scores variance leads to greater score reliability, and so more *heterogeneous* samples often lead to more *variable* scores, and thus to higher reliability. Therefore, the same measure, when administered to more heterogenous or to more homogeneous sets of subjects, will yield scores with differing reliability. As Dawis (1987, p. 486) observed, ". . .Because reliability is a function of sample as well [840] as of instrument, it should be evaluated on a sample from the intended target population—an obvious but sometimes overlooked point."

Our shorthand ways of speaking (e.g., language saying "the test is reliable") can themselves directly cause confusion and lead to bad practice. As Pedhazur and Schmelkin (1991, p. 82, emphasis in original) observed, "Statements about *the* reliability of a measure are . . . inappropriate and potentially misleading." These telegraphic ways of speaking are not inherently problematic, but they often later become so when we come unconsciously to ascribe literal truth to our shorthand, rather than recognizing that our jargon is sometimes telegraphic and in this case is literally untrue. As noted elsewhere:

> This is not just an issue of sloppy speaking—the problem is that sometimes we unconsciously come to think what we say or what we hear, so that sloppy speaking does sometimes lead to a more pernicious outcome, sloppy thinking and sloppy practice. (Thompson, 1992, p. 436)

Pernicious, unconscious, incorrect assumptions that tests themselves are reliable can lead to insufficient attention to the impacts of measurement integrity on the integrity of substantive research conclusions. For example, with respect to the *American Educational Research Journal*, Willson (1980) reported that:

> . . .Only 37% of the *AERJ* studies explicitly reported reliability coefficients for the data analyzed. Another 18% reported only indirectly through reference to earlier research. [. . .] (pp. 8-9)

More recently, Meier and Davis (1990, p. 115) reported that "the majority [95%, 85% and 60%] of the scales described in the [three *Journal of Counseling Psychology*] JCP volumes [1967, 1977 and 1987] were not accompanied by reports of psychometric properties."

The failure to consider score reliability in substantive research may exact a toll on the interpretations within research studies. For example, we may conduct studies that could not possibly yield noteworthy effect sizes, given that score reliability inherently attenuates effect sizes. Or we may not accurately interpret the effect sizes in our studies if we do not consider the reliability of the scores we are actually analyzing.

These practices may be caused by misperceptions that tests can be reliable or valid. These misperceptions themselves may be caused, or at least reinforced, by the use of telegraphic language that comes to be unconsciously believed as literal truth, and then unconsciously incorporated into paradigms for behavior.

Our language has also been influenced by the language used in professional standards and guidelines. Some standards are inconsistent in their treatment of these issues, or suggest bad logic in service of correct dicta. For [841] example, the test standards of the American Psychological Association (APA), American Educational Research Association (AERA), and National Council on Measurement in Education (NCME) emphasize that, "Because there are many ways of estimating reliability, each influenced by different sources of measurement error, it is unacceptable to say simply, 'The reliability of test X is .90'" (p. 21). Yet, on the same page, these standards speak of "the *reliability of a highly speeded test*" (APA/AERA/ NCME, 1985, p. 21, emphasis added). [One hopes that the test standards, after the on-going revision, will instead emphasize, "It is unacceptable to say, 'The reliability of test X,'" because it is simply untrue that tests are reliable. Reliability is a characteristic of scores, and not of tests."]

Examples of appropriate language use within standards are provided by the Joint Committee on Standard for Educational Evaluation. For example, in these standards reliability is defined thusly: "A generic term, *reliability* refers to the degree of consistency *of the information* obtained from an information gathering process" (Joint Committee, 1994, p. 153, second emphasis added). The Joint Committee also noted that a common error is

> Failing to take into account the fact that the *reliability of* the *scores* provided by an instrument or procedure may fluctuate depending on how, when, and to whom the instrument or procedure is administered. (Joint Committee on Standard for Educational Evaluation, 1994, p. 155, emphasis added)

Based on these considerations, use of wording such as "the reliability of the test" or "the validity of the test" will not be considered acceptable in the journal. Instead, authors should use language such as, "the scores in our study had a classical theory test-retest reliability coefficient of X," or "based on generalizability theory analysis, the scores in our study had a phi coefficient of X." Use of technically correct language will hopefully reinforce better practice.

Statistical Significance Testing

Science is about the business of identifying relationships that recur under stated conditions. Unfortunately, too many researchers, consciously or unconsciously, incorrectly assume that the p values calculated in statistical significance tests evaluate the *probability* that results will replicate (Carver, 1978, 1993). Such researchers often explain what p calculated is by invoking vague and embarrassing amorphisms such as, "p calculated (or statistical significance testing) evaluates whether results were 'due to chance'".

It is true that statistical significance tests do focus on the null hypothesis. It is also true that such tests evaluate sample statistics (e.g., *sample* means, standard deviations, correlations coefficients) in relation to unknowable population parameters (e.g., *population* means, standard deviations, correlations coefficients). [842]

But far too many researchers incorrectly interpret statistical significance tests as evaluating *the probability that the null is true in the population, given the sample statistics for the data in hand*. This would, in fact, be a very interesting issue to evaluate.

If $p_{calculated}$ informed the researcher about the truth of the null in the population, then this information would directly test the replicability of results. Assuming the population itself remained stable, future samples from the population, if representative, should yield similar results. In this case, results for which the null was found to not be true in the population would therefore be likely to be replicated in future samples from the same population where the null would also likely be rejected. Unfortunately, this is *not* what statistical significance tests, and not what the associated $p_{calculated}$ values evaluate.

It is true that the p(robability) values calculated in statistical significance testing, which range from 0 to 1 (or 0% to 100%), do require that a "given" regarding the population parameters must be postulated. The characteristics of the population(s) directly affect what the calculated p values will be, and inescapably must be considered as part of the calculations of p.

For example, if we draw two random samples from two populations, both with equal means, then the single most likely sample statistics (i.e., the sample statistics with the largest $p_{calculated}$ value) will be two equal sample means. These sample results are the most likely for these populations. But these exact same sample statistics would be less likely (i.e., would yield a smaller $p_{calculated}$ value) if the two populations had parameter means that differed by one unit. And the sample statistics involving exactly equal sample means would be still less likely (i.e., would yield a still smaller $p_{calculated}$ value) if the two population means differed by two units.

Indeed, *specific* population parameters *must* unavoidably be assumed even to determine what the $p_{calculated}$ is for the sample statistics. Given that population parameters directly affect the calculated p(robability) of the sample statistics, one must assume *particular* population parameters associated with the null hypothesis being tested (e.g., specific means, medians, standard deviations, correlation coefficients), because there are infinitely many possibilities of what these parameters may be in the population(s).

Only by assuming specific population parameters can a single answer be given to the question, "what is the p(robability) of the sample statistics, assuming the population has certain parameters?" Without the assumption of specific population parameters being true in the population, there are infinitely many plausible estimates of p, and the answers to the question actually posed by statistical significance testing become mathematically indeterminate.

Classically, to get a single estimate of the p(robability) of the sample statistics, the null hypothesis is posited to be exactly true in the population. Thus, statistical significance testing evaluates *the probability of the sample* [843] *statistics for the data in hand, given that null hypothesis is presumed to be exactly true as regards the related parameters in the population.*

Of course, this p is a very different animal than one which evaluates the probability of the population parameters themselves, and the statistical significance testing logic itself means that p evaluates something considerably less interesting than result replicability. As Shaver (1993) recently argued so emphatically:

> [A] test of statistical significance is not an indication of the probability that a result would be obtained upon replication of the study. A test of statistical significance yields the probability of a result occurring under [an assumption of the truth of] the null hypothesis [in the population], not the probability that the result will occur again if the study is replicated. Carver's (1978) treatment should have dealt a death blow to this fallacy. . . (p. 304)

Furthermore, the requirement that statistical significance testing must presume an assumption that the null hypothesis is true in the population is a requirement that an untruth be posited. As Meehl (1978, p. 822) notes, "As I believe is generally recognized by statisticians today and by thoughtful social scientists, the null hypothesis, taken literally, is always false." Similarly, Hays (1981, p. 293) points out that "[t]here is surely nothing on earth that is completely independent of anything else [in the population]. The strength of association may approach zero, but it should seldom or never be exactly zero."

There is a very important implication of the realization that the null is not literally true in the population. The most likely sample statistics for samples drawn from populations in which the null is not literally true are sample statistics that do not correspond to the null hypothesis, e.g., there are some differences in sample means, or r in the sample is not exactly 0. And whenever the null is not *exactly* true in the sample(s), then the null hypothesis will *always* be rejected at some sample size. As Hays (1981, p. 293) emphasizes, "virtually any study can be made to show significant results if one uses enough subjects."

Although statistical significance is a function of at least seven inter-related features of a study (Schneider & Darcy, 1984), sample size is a basic influence on significance. Thus, some researchers (Thompson, 1989, 1993) have advocated interpreting statistical significance tests only within the context of sample size. In any case, as noted elsewhere,

> Statistical significance testing can involve a tautological logic in which tired researchers, having collected data from hundreds of subjects, then conduct a statistical test to evaluate whether there were a lot of subjects, which the researchers already know, because they collected the data and know they're tired. This tautology has created considerable damage as regards the cumulation of knowledge. . . (Thompson, 1992, p. 436)

Statistical significance testing can be a circuitous logic requiring us to invest energy to determine that which we already know, i.e., our sample size. And this energy is not invested in judging the noteworthiness of our [844] effect sizes or the replicability of our effect sizes, since statistical significance testing does not directly evaluate these considerably more impor-tant issues. Decades of effort "to exorcise the null hypothesis" (Cronbach, 1975, p. 124) continue.

These considerations suggest two guidelines as components of editorial policy. First, too often authors say "significant" when they mean "statisti-cally significant." Since statistical significance does not evaluate result importance, *always* using the phrase "statistically significant" when refer-ring to inferential tests helps at least a little to avoid confusing statistical significance with result importance. As Thompson (1993) emphasized:

> Statistics can be employed to evaluate the probability of an event. But impor-tance is a question of human values, and math cannot be employed as an atavistic escape (à la Fromm's *Escape from Freedom*) from the existential human responsibility for making value judgments. If the computer package did not ask you your values prior to its analysis, it could not have considered your value system in calculating p's, and so p's cannot be blithely used to infer the value of research results. Like it or not, empirical science in inescapably a subjective business. (p. 365)

We will follow the admonitions of others against the use of only the words, "significant" or "significance", when referring to statistical significance (e.g., Carver, 1993, p. 288).

Second, too often researchers employ null hypothesis (e.g., $r_{xx} = 0$) statistical significance tests of reliability and validity coefficients. This may be because many computer packages test null hypotheses of zero difference as a default. In any case, Huck and Cormier (1996) explain why testing the statistical significance of reliability coefficients is not sensible:

> When statistically testing reliability coefficients, however, we question whether much is gained simply by saying that a test-retest correlation (or any other kind of reliability coefficient) is significantly different from zero. We say this because it is possible for a researcher to have a very low reliability coefficient turn out to be [statistically] significant, so long as the sample size is large enough.

A one-tailed statistical significance test of an r of roughly .94, even at the $\alpha = .01$ level of statistical significance, will be statistically significant with an n as small as 5! Statistical tests of such coefficients in a measurement context make little sense. Either statistical significance tests using the null hypothesis of zero magnitude should be by-passed, or meaningful null hypotheses should be employed.

Effect Sizes, "What if," and Replicability Analyses

This discussion is not meant to imply that statistical significance testing will not be reported in articles in the journal. However, it is important that these analyses, when reported, are at least supplemented by other analyses. [845]

A series of articles on the limits of statistical significance testing has appeared on a seemingly regular basis in recent editions of even the *American Psychologist* (Cohen, 1990; Kupfersmid, 1988; Rosenthal, 1991; Rosnow & Rosenthal, 1989). And the 1994 APA style manual went so far as to say:

> Neither of the two types of probability values reflects the importance or magnitude of an effect because both depend on sample size. . . . You are encouraged to provide effect-size information. (p. 18)

We will go further. Authors reporting statistical significance will be *required* to both report and interpret effect sizes. However, these effect sizes may be of various forms, including standardized differences, or uncorrected (e.g., r^2, R^2, eta^2) or corrected (e.g., adjusted R^2, omega^2) variance-accounted-for statistics (Snyder & Lawson, 1993).

Authors are also encouraged, but not required, to report "what if" analyses indicating at what different sample size a given fixed effect would become statistically significant, or would have no longer been statistically significant (Snyder & Lawson, 1993; Thompson, 1989). The "Guidelines for Authors" of *Measurement and Evaluation in Counseling and Development* have for many years encouraged just such practices. They note that:

> 8. Authors are encouraged to assist readers in interpreting statistical significance of their results. For example, results may be indexed to sample size. An author may wish to say, "this correlation coefficient would have still been statistically significant even if sample size had been as small as $n = 33$," or "this correlation coefficient would have been statistically significant if sample size had been increased to $n = 138$." (MECD, 1994, p. 143)

Finally, authors will be strongly encouraged to report actual, so-called "external" replication studies, or to conduct "internal" replicability analyses (Thompson, 1993, 1994b). The later include cross-validation, the jackknife, and the bootstrap. Unlike statistical significance tests, these analyses can be employed to inform judgment as to whether detected relationships replicate under stated conditions.

References

American Psychological Association. (1994). *Publication manual of the American Psychological Association* (4th ed.). Washington, DC: Author.

American Psychological Association, American Educational Research Association & National Council on Measurement in Education (APA/AERA/NCME). (1985). *Standards for educational and psychological testing.* Washington, DC: American Psychological Association. [846]

Carver, R. (1978). The case against statistical significance testing. *Harvard Educational Review, 48,* 378-399.

Carver, R. (1993). The case against statistical significance testing, revisited. *Journal of Experimental Education, 61,* 287-292.

Cohen, J. (1990). Things I have learned (so far). *American Psychologist, 45,* 1304-1312.

Crocker, L., & Algina, J. (1986). *Introduction to classical and modern test theory.* New York: Holt, Rinehart and Winston.

Cronbach, L. J. (1975). Beyond the two disciplines of psychology. *American Psychologist, 30,* 116-127.

Dawis, R.V. (1987). Scale construction. *Journal of Counseling Psychology, 34,* 481-489.

Eason, S. (1991). Why generalizability theory yields better results than classical test theory: A primer with concrete examples. In B. Thompson (Ed.), *Advances in educational research: Substantive findings, methodological developments* (Vol. 1, pp. 83-98). Greenwich, CT: JAI Press.

Gronlund, N. E., & Linn, R. L. (1990). *Measurement and evaluation in teaching* (6th ed.). New York: Macmillan.

Hays, W. L. (1981). *Statistics* (3rd ed.). New York: Holt, Rinehart and Winston.

Huck, S. W, & Cormier, W. G. (1996). *Reading statistics and research* (2nd ed.). New York: Harper-Collins.

Joint Committee on Standards for Educational Evaluation. (1994). *The program evaluation standards: How to assess evaluations of educational programs.* Newbury Park, CA: Sage.

Kuder, G. F. (1941). Presenting a new journal. *Educational and Psychological Measurement, 1*(1), 3-4.

Kupfersmid, J. (1988). Improving what is published: A model in search of an editor. *American Psychologist, 43,* 635-642.

Measurement and Evaluation in Counseling and Development. (1994). Guidelines for Authors. *Measurement and Evaluation in Counseling and Development, 27,* 341.

Meehl, P. E. (1978). Theoretical risks and tabular asterisks: Sir Karl, Sir Ronald, and the slow progress of soft psychology. *Journal of Consulting and Clinical Psychology, 46,* 806-834.

Meier, S. T., & Davis, S. R. (1990). Trends in reporting psychometric properties of scales used in counseling psychology research. *Journal of Counseling Psychology, 37,* 113-115.

Pedhazur, E. J., & Schmelkin, L. P. (1991). *Measurement, design, and analysis: An integrated approach.* Hillsdale, NJ: Erlbaum.

Rosenthal, R. (1991). Effect sizes: Pearson's correlation, its display via the BESD, and alternative indices. *American Psychologist, 46,* 1086-1087.

Rosnow, R. L., & Rosenthal, R. (1989). Statistical procedures and the justification of knowledge in psychological science. *American Psychologist, 44,* 1276-1284.

Rowley, G. L. (1976). The reliability of observational measures. *American Educational Research Journal, 13,* 51-59.

Schneider, A. L., & Darcy, R. E. (1984). Policy implications of using significance tests in evaluation research. *Evaluation Review, 8,* 573-582.

Shaver, J. (1993). What statistical significance testing is, and what it is not. *Journal of Experimental Education, 61,* 293-316.

Snyder, P., & Lawson, S. (1993). Evaluating results using corrected and uncorrected effect size estimates. *Journal of Experimental Education, 61,* 334-349.

Thompson, B. (1989). Statistical significance, result importance, and result generalizability: Three noteworthy but somewhat different issues. *Measurement and Evaluation in Counseling and Development, 22,* 2-6.

Thompson, B. (1992). Two and one-half decades of leadership in measurement and evaluation. *Journal of Counseling and Development, 70,* 434-438.

Thompson, B. (1993). The use of statistical significance tests in research: Bootstrap and other alternatives. *Journal of Experimental Education, 61,* 361-377.

Thompson, B. (1994a, April). *Common methodology mistakes in dissertations, revisited.* Paper presented at the annual meeting of the American Educational Research Association, New Orleans. (ERIC Document Reproduction Service No. ED 368 771) [847]

Thompson, B. (1994b). The pivotal role of replication in psychological research: Empirically evaluating the replicability of sample results. *Journal of Personality, 62,* 157-176.

Willson, V. L. (1980). Research techniques in *AERJ* articles: 1969 to 1978. *Educational Researcher, 9*(6), 5-10.

7

Reliability as Psychometrics Versus Datametrics

Shlomo S. Sawilowsky
Wayne State University

[157]   *Abstract*

The present chapter reviews issues regarding *test reliability*, which is psychometric terminology, and *score reliability*, which is score-centric terminology. These issues have arisen, in part, due to some *EPM* editorial policies and Vacha-Haase's "reliability generalization" proposal. The chapter includes (a) a brief historical review of reliability terminology, (b) discussion on the emergence of *datametrics* (loosely defined as the application of psychometry to scores as opposed to an instrument) including a review of textbook authors' uses of psychometric versus datametric terminology, (c) discussion of problems with datametrics, and (d) a critique of Vacha-Haase's proposed meta-analytic reliability generalization via dummy-coded regression. The chapter concludes with a brief summary that presents several suggestions.

Sawilowsky, S. S. (2000). Psychometrics versus datametrics: Comment on Vacha-Haase's "Reliability Generalization" method and some *EPM* editorial policies. *Educational and Psychological Measurement, 60,* 157-173.

The various editorial policies of *Educational and Psychological Measurement* (*EPM*) have been proffered in the form of "Guidelines for Authors" (Thompson, 1994) and in two subsequent "Guidelines Editorials." In the 1994 editorial, in a subsection titled "Language Use Regarding Score Characteristics," Thompson (1994) stated,

> One unfortunate common feature of contemporary scholarly language is the usage of the statement "the test is reliable" or "the test is valid." Such language is both incorrect and deleterious in its effects on scholarly inquiry, particularly given the pernicious consequences that unconscious paradigmatic beliefs can exact. . . .
>
> Too few researchers act on a conscious recognition that reliability is a characteristic of scores or the data in hand. Many authorities present this view, but [158] paradigm influences constrain some researchers from actively integrating the presumption into their actual analytic practice. . . .
>
> Based on these considerations, use of wording such as "the reliability of the test" or "the validity of the test" will not be considered acceptable in the journal. Instead, authors should use language such as "the scores in our study had a classical theory test-retest reliability coefficient of X." (pp. 839, 841)

Subsequently, Vacha-Haase (1998) reiterated these *EPM* editorial policies in her *EPM* article proposing "reliability generalization" (p. 6) as a method to "characterize the mean measurement error variance across studies, and also the sources of variability of these variances across studies" (p. 6).

The purpose of the present chapter is to review the issues regarding *test reliability*, which is psychometric terminology, and *score reliability*, which is score-centric terminology. This chapter is arranged as follows: (a) a brief historical review of reliability terminology, (b) discussion on the emergence of *datametrics* (loosely defined as the application of psychometry to scores as opposed to an instrument) including a review of textbook authors' uses of psychometric versus datametric terminology, (c) discussion of problems with datametrics, and (d) a critique of Vacha-Haase's (1998) proposed meta-analytic reliability generalization via dummy-coded regression. The chapter concludes with a brief summary that presents several suggestions.

Historical Review of Reliability Terminology

Thompson's (1994) editorial echoed a concern raised a half century previously in the literature as regards reference to the reliability of a test.

Some standards are inconsistent in their treatment of these issues. . . . For example, the test standards of the American Psychological Association (APA), American Educational Research Association (AERA), and National Council on Measurement in Education (NCME) emphasize that "because there are many ways of estimating reliability, each influenced by different sources of measurement error, it is unacceptable to say simply, 'The reliability of test X is .90'" (APA/AERA/NCME, 1985, p. 21). Yet, on the same page, these standards speak of *"the reliability of a highly speeded test* [italics added]" (p. 21). (Thompson, 1994, p. 841)

However, the joint standards were specific in recognizing that the problem was due to the "many ways of estimating reliability" (APA/AERA/NCME, 1985, p. 21, quoted in Thompson, 1994). The context of this issue was not the result of discussion on the merits of reliability as it relates to a test versus its scores. Instead, it was the recognition that a statement such as *"the* [italics added} reliability of test X is .90" (APA/AERA/NCME, 1985, p. 21, quoted [159] in Thompson, 1994) is not sufficiently informative, because as many authors have noted, reliability paradigms and their coefficients are simply not interchangeable.

In their *Dictionary of Statistical Terms*, Kendall and Buckland (1971) stated that the reliability coefficient was "introduced by Spearman (1910) into psychology," and it is "the complement of the error variance of the *test* [italics added]" (p. 129). In less than a decade after Spearman's introduction of the concept, Terman (1916, p. 107) discovered that reliability depends on a variety of factors, such as the training of the examiner. Similarly, Monroe, DeVoss, and Kelly (1917, p. 279) pointed out that reliability varies based on variations in the time allowed to take a test, the grading process, or even how the students are approached to take a test. (A relationship between these effects and psychophysical constructs was previously hypothesized by Cattell, 1890.)

Subsequently, Goodenough (1936) was among the first to suggest that the term reliability be relegated to the "limbo of outworn concepts" (p. 177), suggesting that the terminology "reliability in particular seems ill chosen" (Goodenough, 1949, p. 213). Her lament was that "it is still unfortunately common to hear persons who should know better stating 'the reliability of a certain test is thus and so' as if the figure cited were a fixed value" (Goodenough, 1949, p. 214). Her concern, however, was not on the issue of whether a test or its scores can be considered reliable. The concern was with researchers overlooking the fact that reliability can be estimated from different perspectives (e.g., internal consistency, test-retest, Goodenough, 1949, pp. 213-214, footnote 1 to chap. 15) and can be affected by different conditions (e.g., sampling, Goodenough, 1949, pp. 84-85, 106-107, chap. 8, p. 214). Thus, it was argued that statements about the reliability of a certain test must be accompanied by an explanation of what type of reliability was estimated, how it was calculated, and under what conditions or for which sample characteristics the result was obtained.

This point was underscored by J. L. Payne (1975), who noted that "One frequently finds only a passing reference to the effect that 'the reliability coefficient was .92.' How that number was arrived at and what it means are rarely explained" (p. 4); "Is the number a coefficient of correlation? A coefficient of determination? What is the level of chance occurrence in this particular test? What did the original numbers look like? Were they normally distributed?" (p. 5). It could be concluded from Goodenough and Payne that descriptions such as "An estimate of the instrument's reliability was obtained through measures of internal consistency. Cronbach alpha, obtained from the administration of the survey to the sample described below, was .92" (Hillman & Sawilowsky, 1991, p. 116) are meaningful and should be acceptable in any scholarly journal. [160]

Psychometrics Versus Datametrics in Textbook Treatments

Thompson (1994) and Vacha-Haase (1998) used phrases such as the reliability of the data at hand, and hence I coined the term datametrics. Datametrics emerges when reliability and other desirable characteristics are considered to be concomitant with the scores or data at hand instead of being a property of the instrument or its use.

An Early Datametrician?

In retrospect, there might have been other datametricians prior to Rowley (1976), who was the earliest citation from Thompson (1994) and Vacha-Haase (1998). In his textbook, for example, Ebel (1972) wrote that

> The reliability coefficient for a set of scores from a group of examinees is the coefficient of correlation between that set of scores and another set of scores on an equivalent test obtained independently from the members of the same group. (p. 410)

However, this definition appeared in a chapter titled, "How to Estimate, Interpret, and Improve *Test Reliability* [italics added]." Ebel used phrases such as "the reliability of the test" frequently throughout the chapter (see J. L. Payne, 1975, p. 22, for additional comments).

Textbooks Cited by Thompson (1994) and Vacha-Haase (1998)

Thompson (1994) marshaled several sources and citations in defense of the claim that it is the scores that are reliable as opposed to the instrument itself. The references (which were repeated by Vacha-Haase, 1998) included (a) Pedhazur and Schmelkin (1991), (b) Crocker and Algina (1986), and (c) Gronlund and Linn (1990).

Pedhazur and Schmelkin (1991). These authors cited Tryon (1957), who noted that the preceding 50 years of psychological testing resulted in confusion regarding reliability of measures because of the "array of different formulations" (p. 229). This was the same point previously mentioned by Goodenough (1936, 1949) and subsequently mentioned by J. L. Payne (1975). Pedhazur and Schmelkin amplified this idea (see further their comments on p. 88) in noting that

> different approaches to reliability estimation attend to different sources of errors. Thus, what is viewed as random error from the perspective of one approach may be viewed as systematic error or ignored altogether from another [161] perspective. Statements about the reliability of a measure are, therefore, inappropriate and potentially misleading. (p. 82)

Pedhazur and Schmelkin (1991) did not promote the notion of the reliability of scores; rather, they reiterated the position that a reliability coefficient obtained via one paradigm constitutes different information than that from a reliability coefficient obtained via a different paradigm of measurement. This position was reiterated throughout their chapter on reliability. For example, in their review of classical measurement theory, they stated

$$r_{XT}^2 = r_{XX} = \sigma_T^2 / \sigma_X^2 \tag{5.8}$$

where r_{XX} = reliability of measure x. *This, then, is the definition of reliability of a measure: It is the ratio of true-score variance to observed-score variance.* (p. 85)

Note the phrases "reliability of measure x" and "reliability of a measure" as opposed to "scores reliability." Indeed, they used the phrase "reliability of the measure" frequently, such as on pages 81, 82, 83, 86, 87, 88, 89, 90, 94, 97, 100, 110, and 115; the phrase "reliability of an instrument," such as on pages 91, 92, and 101; and the phrase "reliability of the test" on page 116. They also used the phrase "unreliability of the measure" on pages 113 and 114.

Pedhazur and Schmelkin (1991) clarified their position:

> Earlier, it was pointed out that, because one may attend to different sources of error when estimating reliability, it is more appropriate to use the term reliability generically. Now that it was shown that reliability estimates are essentially squared correlation coefficients, there is another sense in which one should avoid speaking of *the* [italics added] reliability of a given instrument, *without specifying the population from which the sample used for its estimation was drawn* [italics added].
>
> As was pointed out in Chapter 3, the correlation coefficient is population specific. It follows that, the same instrument may be more or less reliable, depending on the variability of the population of interest. (p. 86)

Pedhazur and Schmelkin's conclusion provides a reasonable approach to citing reliability information:

> Researchers who bother at all to report reliability estimates for the instruments they use (many do not) frequently report only reliability estimates contained in the manuals of the instruments or estimates reported by other researchers. Such information may be useful for comparative purposes, *but it is imperative to recognize that the relevant reliability estimate is the one obtained for the sample used in the study under consideration* [italics added]. It is this reliability coefficient that has to be used when calculating other statistics (e.g., standard errors of measurement; see below), and it is this estimate that may help explain certain findings (e.g., lower than expected correlation between variables under study). (p. 86) **[162]**

Crocker and Algina (1986). Crocker and Algina stated "that a test is not 'reliable' or 'unreliable.' Rather, reliability is a property of the scores on a test for a particular group of examinees" (p. 144) and used the phrases "reliability of scores on the test under various conditions" (p. 152) and "reliability coefficient for a set of scores" (p. 131). However, they also used the phrases "the reliability coefficient for an instrument" (p. 127), "test reliability" (pp. 142, 144), and "Coefficient alpha . . . is a characteristic of a test" (p. 142). Their reasoning for using both sets of terminology alluded to the problem mentioned by Tryon (1957), as Crocker and Algina (1986) stated, "Using test data, it is possible to estimate *the* [italics added] reliability coefficient for an instrument in several different ways" (p. 127).

Gronlund and Linn (1990). These two authors indicated that "Reliability refers to the results obtained with an evaluation instrument, not to the instrument itself" (p. 78) and used the phrases "scores' reliability" (p. 83) and "reliability of test scores" (p. 85). Nevertheless, they also used the phrases "reliability of a full test" (p. 83), "in comparing the reliability coefficients of two or more tests" (p. 93), "we would want to favor the test with the largest reliability coefficient" (p. 93), "In general, the longer the test is, the higher its reliability will be" (p. 93), and "teacher-made test of relatively low reliability" (p. 100).

More important, however, is the remarkable revelation contained in the very next paragraph after the citation from Thompson (1994) and Vacha-Haase (1998):

> A closely related point is that an estimate of reliability always refers to a particular type of consistency. *Test scores are not reliable in general* [italics added]. They are reliable (or generalizable) over different periods of time, over different samples of questions, over different raters, and the like. It is possible for test scores to be consistent in one of these respects and not in another. (Gronlund & Linn, 1990, p. 78)

The proponents of the phrase "scores reliability" or "reliability for the data in hand" should carefully reread the above-cited selection from Gronlund and Linn (1990; also Linn & Gronlund, 1995, p. 82). The same argument made and reasons given in the editorial policy of *EPM* and by Vacha-Haase (1998) are used to preclude test scores as being referred to as being reliable!

Broader Survey of Textbook Treatments of Reliability

Thompson (1994) stated that "Many authorities present this view" (p. 839) that "reliability is a characteristic of scores or the data at hand" (p. 839), and this statement was endorsed by Vacha-Haase (1998). In the current chapter, I [163] present an independent perusal of 63 measurement and evaluation textbooks. These textbooks were published since 1986, the earliest date for the textbooks cited by Thompson and Vacha-Haase.

Textbook authors' terminology fell into three categories, as compiled in Table 7.1. There were contemporary authors who discussed or defined reliability as a (a) property of the test or measure; (b) property of the test, but reliability was also mentioned in relation to scores; or (c) property of the scores, but reliability was also discussed in relation to the test. A total of 44 (69.8%) textbook authors by definition, statement, or implication (e.g., chapter titled "Test Reliability") considered reliability to be a property

Table 7.1   Reliability Terminology Used by 63 Contemporary Educational and
Psychological Measurement and/or Evaluation Textbook Authors
(1986-2000)

Group 1:   *Reliability is a property of the test* (*n* = 44; 69.8%) Aiken (1997, p. 58), Bott
(1996, p. 39), Cangelosi (1990, p. 29; 1991, pp. 29, 34), Carey (1994, p. 80),
Evans, Evans, and Mercer (1986, p. 20), Gay and Airasian (2000, p. 627),
Gellman (1995, p. 4), Gillford (1993), Gredler (1996, pp. 109, 117), Gregory
(1996, pp. 84, 85, 100), Gronlund (1993, pp. 34, 35), Hanna (1993, p. 421),
Hart (1994, p. 112), Hopkins (1998, p. 108), Hopkins and Antes (1989,
p. 180), Hopkins, Stanley, and Hopkins (1990, p. 117), Howell, Fox, and
Morehead (1993, p. 97), Hoy and Gregg (1994, p. 70), Kaplan and Saccuzzo
(1993, p. 103), Kelley (1999, p. 127), Kubiszyn and Borich (1996, p. 311),
Lyman (1991, p. 159), Mehrens and Lehmann (1987, pp. 101, 122),
R. Mitchell (1992, p. 23), Nunnally and Berstein (1994, pp. 229, 256),
Oosterhof (1990, pp. 50, 51; 1996, p. 53), D. A. Payne (1992, pp. 268, 558),
Pedhazur and Schmelkin (1991, p. 82), Popham (1990, pp. 121-123; 1993,
p. 120), Puckett and Black (1994, p. 278), Salvia and Hughes (1990, p. 67),
Salvia and Ysseldyke (1988, pp. 109, 117), Silverman (1993, p. 148), Thissen
(1990, p. 162), Thorndike, Cunningham, Thorndike, and Hagen (1991, p. 91),
Traub (1994, p. 44), Tuckman (1988, p. 6; 1994, p. 180), Wallace, Larsen,
and Elksnin (1992, p. 38), Walsh and Betz (1995, p. 47), Wise (1989, p. 73),
Worthen, Borg, and White (1993, p. 65)

Group 2:   *Reliability is a property of the test but also mention reliability of the scores
or data* (*n* = 8; 12.7%) Airasian (1991, p. 246), Chase (1999, p. 54),
Cunningham (1986, p. 358), Drummond (1996, pp. 45, 51-52), Gallagher
(1993, p. 74), McDaniel (1994, p. 46), Thorndike (1997, p. 96), Weiss
(1998, p. 146)

Group 3:   *Reliability is a property of the scores but also mention reliability of the test
or measure* (*n* = 11; 17.5%) Crocker and Algina (1986, p. 127), Gredler
(1999, p. 51), Gronlund (1998, pp. 208, 215, 216), Gronlund and Linn (1990,
pp. 93, 97, 269), Hopkins and Antes (1990, pp. 287, 549), Linn and Gronlund
(1995, pp. 106, 489), McMillan (1997, p. 61), Nitko (1996, p. 55), Sax (1989,
p. 269), Suen (1990, p. 33), Worthen, White, Fan, and Sudweeks (1999, p. 95)

NOTE: Page numbers in parentheses for Groups 1 and 2 are references to an implicit
definition or explicit use of reliability in reference to the test. Page numbers for Group 3 are
examples in which the author(s) used reliability in reference to the test despite referring
reliability to scores.

of the test. An additional 8 authors (12.7%) presented similar definitions but
also occasionally referred to the reliability to scores. Eleven (17.5%) authors
explicitly or implicitly defined reliability as a characteristic of scores.

Problems Inherent With Datametrics

A number of problems arise when taking a data-centric perspective on reliability. In this section, linguistic inconsistencies, which occur frequently,

are first examined. For example, Gronlund (1998) wrote about how to "build in" (p. 26; also see Gronlund, 1988, p. 33) reliability. This makes sense in terms of building reliability into a test, but how is it possible to build in reliability into a score or group of scores? Second, the meaning and use of the standard error of measure(ment) (SEM) is discussed, and then third, issues are raised related to the selection of tests.

Terminology

Thompson (1994) and Vacha-Haase (1998) refer to "score characteristics," "score reliability," "score measurement," "score quality," and "score integrity." The singular form (score vs. scores) is potentially misleading, as Stanley (1971) noted that "the concept of *reliability coefficient* is not applicable to a single individual. . . . One can ask meaningfully, What is the reliability coefficient of this test for my seventh-graders? but not, What is the *reliability coefficient* of this test for a particular student" (p. 373).

Moreover, datametrics obviate many well-known measurement terms. Some terminology differences between the psychometric and datametric approaches are compiled and presented without further comment in Table 7.2.

Concept and Use of SEM

Gronlund and Linn (1990), who were cited as proponents of datametrics, gave two procedures for using the SEM. The first procedure was to use the SEM reported in the test manual that accompanied the standardized test. If [164] the SEM was not reported, they proposed to estimate it from their Table 4.3 (p. 91), which is entered via the standard deviation (σ) and reliability coefficient (r_{XX}) obtained "from the test manual" (p. 89). Neither of these approaches is consistent with a datametric perspective, in which the SEM should be calculated from the data at hand (i.e., scores from the examinees in the sample).

Apparently, Gronlund and Linn (1990) connected the SEM with the instrument. To support this view, they noted, "The standard error is likely to remain fairly constant from group to group. This is not true of the reliability coefficient, which is highly dependent on the spread of scores in the group tested" (p. 92). It is not clear how they came to this conclusion. The SEM is estimated with the formula [165]

$$SEM = \sigma_X (1 - r_{XX})^{.5}$$

Table 7.2   A Comparison of Measure(ment) Terminology for Psychometrics
Versus Datametrics

Psychometrics	Datametrics
Psychometric properties of the test	Datametric properties of the scores
Classical test theory	Classical scores theory
Theory of parallel tests	Theory of parallel scores
Reliability study	Scores study
Test reliability	Scores reliability
Instrument reliability	Scores reliability
Internal consistency reliability	Internal scoring pattern
Test-retest reliability	Scores-rescores reliability
Alternate forms reliability	Alternate scores reliability
Parallel forms reliability	Parallel scores reliability
Reliability and test length	Reliability and number of scores
Reliability and time to take the test	Reliability and time taken to produce scores
Interrater reliability	Interrater scoring pattern
Standard error of measure	Standard error of measurement
Test standardization	Scores standardization
Norm group	Data at hand
Norm scores	Scores at/in hand
Test development process	Scores development process
Reliability generalization	Scores generalization

According to the "scores reliability" policy of *EPM*, and box-and-whisker plots from Vacha-Haase (1998), r_{XX} varies sufficiently to preclude associating it with the instrument. This implies that σ_X, obtained from either the norm group or the sample at hand, must have the remarkable ability to fluctuate in such a fashion so that, regardless of the many values of r_{XX}, the SEM remains "constant from group to group" (Gronlund & Linn, 1990, p. 92).

Traub (1994) noted that an important "use for reliability coefficients is in comparing the relative merits of two or more instruments being considered for the same application" (p. 44), which, of course, is only pertinent if the reliability coefficient pertains to the instrument. Gronlund (1988) agreed, although the preference was stated in favor of the SEM:

> For the test user, the standard error of measurement is probably more useful than the reliability coefficient. Although reliability coefficients can be used in evaluating the quality of a test and in comparing the relative merits of different tests, the standard error of measurement is directly applicable to the interpretation of individual test scores. (p. 148)

Nevertheless, Gronlund and Linn (1990) admitted that "The main difficulty encountered with the standard error occurs when we want to compare two tests that differ in length, or that use different types of scores. [166] Here, the reliability coefficient is the only suitable measure" (p. 93). Therefore, in practice, psychometry prevails over datametrics, even to these two datametricians.

Test Selection

If reliability only relates to the set of scores that a test publisher obtained in a pilot, field test, or norming procedure, then what role do the *Mental Measurement Yearbook* (Kramer & Conoley, 1992), *Tests in Print* (J. V. Mitchell, 1983), *Tests* (Sweetland & Keyser, 1986), or textbooks such as Drummond (1996) serve? Do consumers intend to purchase the set of scores obtained during the test development process from a test publisher?

An interesting phenomenon surfaced in the minority of textbooks mentioned above in which "reliability" was used to refer to the scores instead of the test. Sections devoted to the selection of tests covered a variety of topics (e.g., recency of the norming process, degree of overlap in content, and objectives covered), but conspicuously absent was the consideration of reliability information. The reason appears self-evident; if reliability does not refer to the test, why should it be considered when choosing a standardized test?

Validity, the degree that a test measures what it purports to measure, relates to the use of the test as opposed to the test itself. If there is evidence of validity, the consumer benefits in administering the test to the extent that the consumer is interested in making a similar measurement. In other words, the test is a common focal point because both test developer and consumer have the same measurement interest. The caveat, of course, is that the test is useful only to the extent that the consumer's intended use overlaps with the evidence supporting the purported use of the test.

In contradistinction, reliability from a datametric perspective leaves no common focal point between the test developer and the consumer. Because the consumer desires the test, and not the test developer's scores, there is little interest in the reliability of the scores obtained from examinees not within the consumer's population. Thus, Hopkins, Stanley, and Hopkins (1990) noted that "rarely is our primary interest in the test scores themselves" (p. 144) but rather with the reliability of the test.

Criticisms of Vacha-Haase's (1998) Meta-Analysis

As noted above, Terman (1916) and Monroe et al. (1917, p. 279) found that testing conditions bring about slight variation in reliability estimates for a test, regardless of which reliability coefficient is employed. Presumably, it is this variation that prompted the datametric perspective. This argument is persuasive to some textbook authors. For example, Gredler (1996, p. 109) [167] initially referred to test reliability (p. 109), yet she recapitulated and asserted that "reliability refers to the results of an assessment and not the assessment itself" (Gredler, 1999, p. 50). However, she echoed Gronlund and Linn's (1990, p. 78; Linn & Gronlund, 1995, p. 82) revelation that even scores cannot be considered reliable because they, too, are affected by "temporary conditions, such as the student's physical well-being, his or her motivation and/or anxiety, and testing conditions, such as an overheated classroom" (p. 51).

Nevertheless, Vacha-Haase (1998) conducted a meta-analysis to (a) investigate the "reliability of scores for a given test across studies," (b) determine the amount of variation of reliability estimates, and (c) determine the sources of variation. The criticism with regard to (a) is that the design of her study does not contribute to supporting the datametric perspective. This is because she did not focus on scores. That is, she did not study an individual's *score* or a group's *set of scores* on the same test used in different studies. Instead, she cataloged and analyzed reliability coefficients obtained for a test that was used by researchers in independently conducted studies.

With regard to (b) and (c), many textbook authors identify and discuss factors that influence reliability. The factors that were included as independent variables (IVs) in the dummy-coded regression in Vacha-Haase (1998) were obtained from her data set (personal communications) and are presented in Table 7.3. An immediate problem that arises is the confounding of IVs. For example, gender appears twice. As one IV, it is coded as all female = 1, not = 0; and as another IV, it is coded as mixed = 1, all males or females = 0. Similarly, the IV of student status is confounded. It appears as an IV of student = 1, not student = 0; and as a separate IV as college student = 1, other = 0.

The absence of descriptive statistics accompanying Vacha-Haase's (1998) regression table is disconcerting, as it obscured the fact that only 3 of the 87 studies were test-retest, whereas the remaining 97% of the examples were measures of internal consistency. The importance of descriptive

Table 7.3   Independent Variables in Vacha-Haase (1998)

Variable	N	Percentage
Reliability type		
Cronbach/Kuder-Richardson	84	96.6
Test-retest	3	3.4
Bem Sex Role Inventory form		
Short	47	54.0
Long	21	24.1
Gender (1 and 2)		
Male	8	9.2
Female	18	20.7
Mixed	61	70.1
Language		
English	59	67.8
Other	28	32.2
Referent		
Me	81	93.1
Not me	6	6.9
Article type		
Measurement	19	21.8
Substantive	68	78.2
Sample (1 and 2)		
College student	51	58.6
Non-college student	13	14.9
Nonstudent	23	26.4
Likert-type scale		
7-point	n/a	
Other	n/a	

NOTE: Likert-type scale data did not appear on Vacha-Haase's coding sheets.

statistics was emphasized by textbook authors as early as Rugg (1917), who noted that "statistical material must be interpreted by descriptive material" (p. 313). Although dummy-coded regression easily handles unequal sample sizes, Pedhazur and Schmelkin (1991) pointed out that the "situation is radically different when [in addition to unequal sample sizes] . . . randomization and/or sampling is [also] abrogated" (p. 473), a topic to be discussed further.

It is a statistical artifact of measures of internal consistency that their correlational engine is less stable when the range is restricted. The most commonly cited distortion is in terms of traits or characteristics of the sample, which is referred to as the problem of group homogeneity. This depresses reliability, expressed as $1 - (\sigma_{Error}^2 / \sigma_{Scores}^2)$, because σ_{Scores}^2 decreases with homogeneity.

Group homogeneity is of particular importance in considering Vacha-Haase's (1998) analysis. Failure to consider this factor certainly leads to a

Table 7.4   Breakdown If Random Versus Nonrandom Sampling in 58 Studies in Vacha-Haase's (1998) Meta-Analysis

Study ID	Status
7, 14, 18(1/2), 20	Random = 3 1/2 (7.1%)
13	Possibly random, not enough information = 1 (2.0%)
1, 2, 6, 15, 16, 17, 18(1/2), 21, 23, 25, 26, 30, 31, 34, 35, 36, 37, 38, 40, 41, 43, 48, 49, 50, 55, 56*	Convenience = 26 1/2 (54.1%)
4, 10, 11, 19, 22, 24, 28, 29, 44, 54	Self-selected = 10 (20.4%)
3, 5, 8, 9, 42, 45, 46, 47	No information = 8 (16.3%)

NOTE: 18 (1/2) indicates that one group in Study 18 was random, and one group was a convenience sample. The study marked "*" refers to Levit (1991), which was included in her meta-analysis but inadvertently not asterisked in Vacha-Haase's reference list. Some articles contained multiple studies.

[168] misspecified dummy-coded regression. The IV that would address this issue is whether the studies collected for analysis by Vacha-Haase were based on a random or a nonrandom sample. I was able to obtain 49 of the 57 articles cited in Vacha-Haase's meta-analysis. They were examined and categorized as being random or nonrandom. The results are compiled in Table 7.4. Vacha-Haase indicated studies included in the meta-analysis by the asterisk (*) symbol. The entry under the column "Study ID" refers to the ith study with the * in her reference section. Eighty-nine percent (36.5 of 41) of the studies in which descriptions of the sampling plan were given were found to be based on nonrandom samples.

There are a variety of other statistical issues that should be raised with Vacha-Haase's (1998) analysis. Wood (1991) noted that, "It is also necessary to remember that the reliability coefficient is a correlation coefficient and, as such, is calibrated on a non-linear scale" (p. 140). Textbook authors as long ago as 1935 noted that it is "unsafe" to analyze correlations "unless the means [169] and the standard deviations of the different groups are the same" (O'Dell, 1935, p. 207). Therefore, they should be subjected to Fisher's Z transformation prior to analysis. (For a recent example, see Baker, Plasencia-Peinado, & Lezcano-Lytle, 1998, p. 194.) Although it is inappropriate with some measures of internal consistency (e.g., Kuder-Richardson or Cronbach's alpha), other measures of estimates of reliability (e.g., test-retest) are ordinary Pearson product-moment coefficients of correlation (even though conceptually they refer to "an r between observed and true scores," Suen, 1990, p. 33, and unlike Pearson's 1; the r^2 does not suffer from the skewed distribution problem). Other statistical issues pertain to the absence of considering underlying assumptions, such as homogeneity of regression slopes and normality.

The box plot of reliability coefficients presented by Vacha-Haase (1998) certainly suggested that there was some dispersion in reliability estimates among the studies in her meta-analysis. There were 84 values recorded representing either Cronbach alpha or Kuder-Richardson statistics. However, consider traditional descriptive information on the Bem Sex Role Inventory (BSRI), which she did not report. The mean estimate of reliability for the F Scale was .807, and the 95% confidence interval for the mean was .791 to .823. The standard deviation was .07. The estimate of reliability for the M Scale was .846, and the 95% confidence interval for the mean was .837 to .854. The standard deviation was .04. These are remarkably narrow confidence bands for applied research.

Conclusion

Suen (1990) stated that "having more than one reliability coefficient with the classical theory is inherently self-contradictory" (p. 37). However, for the following two reasons, the existence of varying reliability estimates for a single [170] instrument is not surprising nor should its existence result in an editorial policy to proscribe the phrase test reliability.

First, as Nunnally and Bernstein (1994) noted, "it is meaningful to think of a test as having a number of different reliability coefficients, depending on which sources of measurement error are considered" (p. 256). This reflects the history on this issue according to Goodenough (1936, 1949), Tryon (1957), and J. L. Payne (1975).

Second, as Traub (1994) noted,

> reliability coefficients are almost always calculated from the measurements taken of samples of persons, not whole populations. Thus the usual reliability experiment provides a sample estimate of the reliability coefficient for the population. Had a different sample of persons participated in the experiment, the reliability coefficient obtained would almost certainly have been a different number. (p. 66)

This view reiterates the position of Pedhazur and Schmelkin (1991) and too many other authors to cite.

The collection of reliability estimates in the literature certainly did not originate with Vacha-Haase (1998). For example, more than 25 years ago, Nuttall and Wilmott (1972) reported on a collection of studies on the

British General Certificate of Education (GC). The GC had reliability estimates in the range of .80 to .90 based on "selected populations" (p. 113). On this note, Wood (1991) stated,

> The point about selected populations is well taken. Like all correlation measures, reliability is indeed a function of the range and distribution of the variables involved. That is why there is no point in talking about the reliability of a test or examination, *unless it is in terms of a strictly defined population* [italics added]. (p. 139)

Indeed, the purpose for using a nationally representative scientifically selected random sample when conducting reliability studies during the test construction process is to obtain *the* reliability estimate of a test for general purposes. In my view, authors ought always to report these reliability coefficients from manuals and other sources along with the reliability estimate obtained from, and a description of, the researcher's own sample.

References

Aiken, L. R. (1997). *Psychological testing and assessment* (9th ed.). Boston: Allyn & Bacon.

Airasian, P. W. (1991). *Classroom assessment.* New York: McGraw-Hill.

Baker, S. K., Plasencia-Peinado, J., & Lezcano-Lytle, V. (1998). The use of curriculum-based measurement with language-minority students. In M. R. Shinn (Ed.), *Advanced applications of curriculum-based measurement* (pp. 175-213). New York: Guilford. [171]

Bott, P. A. (1996). *Testing and assessment in occupational and technical education.* Boston: Allyn & Bacon.

Cangelosi, J. S. (1990). *Designing tests for evaluating student achievement.* New York: Longman.

Cangelosi, J. S. (1991). *Evaluating classroom instruction.* New York: Longman.

Carey, L. M. (1994). *Measuring and evaluating school learning* (2nd ed.). Boston: Allyn & Bacon.

Cattell, J. M. (1890). Mental tests and measurements. *Mind, 15,* 373-381.

Chase, C. I. (1999). *Contemporary assessment for educators.* New York: Longman.

Crocker, L., & Algina, J. (1986). *Introduction to classical and modern test theory.* Fort Worth, TX: Holt, Rinehart & Winston.

Cunningham, G. K. (1986). *Educational and psychological measurement.* New York: Macmillan.

Drummond, R. J. (1996). *Appraisal procedures for counselors and helping professionals* (3rd ed.). Englewood Cliffs, NJ: Merrill.

Ebel, R. L. (1972). *Essentials of educational measurement* (2nd ed.). Englewood Cliffs, NJ: Prentice Hall.

Evans, S. S., Evans, W. H., & Mercer, C. D. (1986). *Assessment for instruction.* Boston: Allyn & Bacon.

Gallagher, J. D. (1993). *Classroom assessment for teachers.* Upper Saddle River, NJ: Merrill.

Gay, L. R., & Airasian, P. (2000). *Educational research* (6th ed.). Upper Saddle River, NJ: Prentice Hall.

Gellman, E. S. (1995). *School testing: What parents and educators need to know.* Westport, CT: Praeger.

Gillford, B. R. (1993). *Policy perspectives on educational testing.* Boston: Kluwer Academic.

Goodenough, F. L. (1936). A critical note on the use of the term "reliability" in mental measurement. *Journal of Educational Psychology, 27,* 173-178.

Goodenough, F. L. (1949). *Mental testing: Its history, principles, and applications.* New York: Rinehart.

Gredler, M. E. (1996). *Program evaluation.* Englewood Cliffs, NJ: Prentice Hall.

Gredler, M. E. (1999). *Classroom assessment and learning.* New York: Longman.

Gregory, R. J. (1996). *Psychological testing: History, principles, and applications* (2nd ed.). Boston: Allyn & Bacon.

Gronlund, N. E. (1988). *How to construct achievement tests* (4th ed.). Englewood Cliffs, NJ: Prentice Hall.

Gronlund, N. E. (1993). *How to make achievement tests and assessments* (5th ed.). Boston: Allyn & Bacon.

Gronlund, N. E. (1998). *Assessment of student achievement* (6th ed.). Boston: Allyn & Bacon.

Gronlund, N. E., & Linn, R. (1990). *Measurement and evaluation in teaching* (6th ed.). New York: Macmillan.

Hanna, G. S. (1993). *Better teaching through better measurement.* Fort Worth, TX: Harcourt Brace jovanovich.

Hart, D. (1994). *Authentic assessment: A handbook for educators.* Menlo Park, CA: Addison-Wesley.

Hillman, S. B., & Sawilowsky, S. S. (1991). Multidimensional differences between adolescent substance abusers and users. *Psychological Reports, 68,* 115-122.

Hopkins, K. D. (1998). *Educational and psychological measurement and evaluation* (8th ed.). Boston: Allyn & Bacon.

Hopkins, K. D., & Antes, R. L. (1989). *Classroom testing construction* (2nd ed.). Itasca, IL: F. E. Peacock.

Hopkins, K. D., & Antes, R. L. (1990). *Classroom measurement and evaluation* (3rd ed.). Itasca, IL: F. E. Peacock.

Hopkins, K. D., Stanley, J. C., & Hopkins, B. R. (1990). *Educational and psychological measurement and evaluation* (7th ed.). Englewood Cliffs, NJ: Prentice Hall.[172]

Howell, K. W., Fox, S. L., & Morehead, M. K. (1993). *Curriculum-based evaluation: Teaching and decision making.* Pacific Grove, CA: Brooks/Cole.

Hoy, C., & Gregg, N. (1994). *Assessment: The special educator's role.* Pacific Grove, CA: Brooks/Cole.

Kaplan, R. M., & Saccuzzo, D. P. (1993). *Psychological testing: Principles, applications, and issues* (3rd ed.). Pacific Grove, CA: Brooks/Cole.

Kelley, D. L. (1999). *Measurement made accessible: A research approach using qualitative, quantitative, and quality improvement methods.* Thousand Oaks, CA: Sage.

Kendall, M. G., & Buckland, W. R. (1971). *A dictionary of statistical terms* (3rd ed.). Edinburgh, UK: Oliver & Boyd.

Kramer, J. J., & Conoley, J. C. (1992). *The eleventh mental measurement yearbook.* Lincoln, NE: Buros Institute of Mental Measurement.

Kubiszyn, T., & Borich, G. (1996). *Educational testing and measurement* (5th ed.). New York: Harper-Collins.

Levit, D. B. (1991). Gender differences in ego defenses in adolescence: Sex roles as one way to understand the differences. *Journal of Personality and Social Psychology, 61,* 992-999.

Linn, J. E., & Gronlund, M. A. (1995). *Measurement and assessment in teaching* (7th ed.). Englewood Cliffs, NJ: Merrill.

Lyman, H. B. (1991). *Test scores & what they mean* (5th ed.). Englewood Cliffs, NJ: Prentice Hall.

McDaniel, E. (1994). *Understanding educational measurement.* Madison, WI: WCB Brown & Benchmark.

McMillan, J. H. (1997). *Classroom assessment: Principles and practice for effective instruction.* Boston: Allyn & Bacon.

Mehrens, W. A., & Lehmann, I. J. (1987). *Using standardized tests in education* (4th ed.). New York: Longman.

Mitchell, J. V. (1983). *Tests in print III. An index to tests, test reviews, and the literature on specific tests.* Lincoln, NE: Buros Institute of Mental Measurement.

Mitchell, R. (1992). *Testing for learning: How new approaches to evaluation can improve American schools.* New York: Free Press.

Monroe, W. S., DeVoss, J. C., & Kelly, F. J. (1917). *Educational tests and measurements.* Boston: Houghton Mifflin.

Nitko, A. J. (1996). *Educational assessment of students.* Englewood Cliffs, NJ: Merrill.

Nunnally, J. C., & Bernstein, I. H. (1994). *Psychometric theory* (3rd ed.). New York: McGraw-Hill.

Nuttall, D. L., & Wilmott, A. S. (with Backhouse, J. K., & Morrison, R. B.). (1972). *British examinations: Techniques of analysis.* Slough, UK: National Foundation for Educational Research in England and Wales.

O'Dell, C. W. (1935). *Statistical method in education.* New York: Appleton-Century.

Oosterhof, A. (1990). *Classroom applications of educational measurement.* Columbus, OH: Merrill.

Oosterhof, A. (1996). *Developing and using classroom assessments.* Englewood Cliffs, NJ: Prentice Hall.

Payne, D. A. (1992). *Measuring and evaluating educational outcomes.* New York: Merrill.

Payne, J. L. (1975). *Principles of social science measurement.* College Station, TX: Lytton.

Pedhazur, E. J., & Schmelkin, L. P. (1991). *Measurement, design, and analysis: An integrated approach.* Hillsdale, NJ: Lawrence Erlbaum.

Popham, W. J. (1990). *Modern educational measurement: A practitioner's perspective* (2nd ed.). Englewood Cliffs, NJ: Prentice Hall.

Popham, W. J. (1993). *Educational evaluation* (3rd ed.). Boston: Allyn & Bacon.

Puckett, M. B., & Black, J. K. (1994). *Authentic assessment of the young child: Celebrating development and learning.* New York: Merrill. [173]

Rowley, G. L. (1976). The reliability of observational measures. *American Educational Research Journal, 13,* 51-59.

Rugg, H. 0. (1917). *Statistical methods applied to education: A textbook for students of education in the quantitative study of school problems.* Boston: Houghton Mifflin.

Salvia, J., & Hughes, C. (1990). *Curriculum-based assessment: Testing what is taught.* New York: Macmillan.

Salvia, J., & Ysseldyke, J. E. (1988). *Assessment: In special and remedial education* (4th ed.). Boston: Houghton Mifflin.

Sax, G. (1989). *Principles of educational and psychological measurement and evaluation* (3rd ed.). Belmont, CA: Wadsworth.

Silverman, D. (1993). *Interpreting qualitative data: Methods, for analysing talk, text, and interaction.* London: Sage.

Stanley, J. C. (1971). Reliability. In R. L. Thorndike (Ed.), *Educational measurement* (2nd ed., pp. 356-442). Washington, DC: American Council on Education.

Suen, H. K. (1990). *Principles of test theories.* Hillsdale, NJ: Lawrence Erlbaum.

Sweetland, R. C., & Keyser, D. J. (1986). *Tests: A comprehensive reference for assessment in psychology, education and business* (2nd ed.). Kansas City, MO: Test Corporation of America.

Terman, L. M. (1916). *The measurement of intelligence: An explanation of and a complete guide for the use of the Stanford revision and extension of the Binet-Simon Intelligence Scale.* Boston: Houghton Mifflin.

Thissen, D. (1990). Reliability and measurement precision. In H. Wainer (Ed.) with N. J. Dorans, R. Flaugher, B. F. Green, R. J. Mislevey, L. Steinberg, & D. Thissen, *Computerized adaptive testing: A primer* (pp. 161-186). Hillsdale, NJ: Lawrence Erlbaum.

Thompson, B. (1994). Guidelines for authors. *Educational and Psychological Measurement, 54,* 837-847.

Thorndike, R. M. (1997). *Measurement and evaluation in psychology and education* (6th ed.). Upper Saddle River, NJ: Merrill.

Thorndike, R. M., Cunningham, G. K., Thorndike, R. L., & Hagen, E. P. (1991). *Measurement and evaluation in psychology and education* (5th ed.). New York: Macmillan.

Traub, R. E. (1994). *Measurement methods for the social sciences—Reliability for the social sciences: Theory and applications* (Vol. 3). Thousand Oaks, CA: Sage.

Tryon, R. C. (1957). Reliability and behavior domain validity: Reformulation and historical critique. *Psychological Bulletin, 54,* 229-249.

Tuckman, B. W. (1988). *Testing for teachers* (2nd ed.). San Diego, CA: Harcourt Brace Jovanovich.

Tuckman, B. W. (1994). *Conducting educational research* (4th ed.). Fort Worth, TX: Harcourt Brace.

Vacha-Haase, T. (1998). Reliability generalization: Exploring variance in measurement error affecting score reliability across studies. *Educational and Psychological Measurement, 58*, 6-20.

Wallace, G., Larsen, S. C., & Elksnin, L. K. (1992). *Educational assessment of learning problems: Testing for teaching* (2nd ed.). Boston: Allyn & Bacon.

Walsh, W. B., & Betz, N. E. (1995). *Tests and assessment* (3rd ed.); Englewood Cliffs, NJ: Prentice Hall.

Weiss, C. H. (1998). *Evaluation* (2nd ed.). Upper Saddle River, NJ: Prentice Hall.

Wise, P. S. (1989). *The use of assessment techniques by applied psychologists.* Belmont, CA: Wadsworth.

Wood, R. (1991). *Assessment and testing: A survey of research commissioned by the University of Cambridge Local Examinations Syndicate.* Cambridge, UK: Cambridge University Press.

Worthen, B. R., Borg, W. R., & White, K. R. (1993). *Measurement and evaluation in the school.* New York: Longman.

Worthen, B. R., White, K. R., Fan, X., & Sudweeks, R. R. (1999). *Measurement and assessment in schools* (2nd ed.). New York: Longman.

8

Psychometrics *Is* Datametrics

The Test Is Not Reliable

Bruce Thompson
Texas A&M University
and
Baylor College of Medicine

Tammi Vacha-Haase
Colorado State University

[174]   *Abstract*

The present chapter responds to selected criticisms of some *EPM* editorial policies and Vacha-Haase's (1998) "reliability generalization" (RG) meta-analytic methods. However, the treatment is more broadly a manifesto regarding the nature of score reliability, and what are reasonable expectations for psychometric reporting practices in substantive inquiries. The consequences of misunderstandings of score reliability are explored. It is suggested that paradigmatic misconceptions regarding psychometric issues feed into a spiral of

Thompson, B., & Vacha-Haase, T. (2000). Psychometrics *is* datametrics: The test is not reliable. *Educational and Psychological Measurement*, 60, 174-195.

123

presumptions that measurement training is unnecessary for doctoral
students, which then in turn further reinforce misunderstandings of
score integrity issues.

P rofessor Sawilowsky (2000) has presented thoughtful criticisms of both
selected *Educational and Psychological Measurement* (*EPM*)
editorial policies (cf. Thompson, 1994) and Vacha-Haase's (1998) *EPM*
delineation of proposed "reliability generalization" (RG) meta-analytic
methods. In this response to Sawilowsky's comments our primary focus
will not be defending ourselves or our editorial policies and our analytic
proposals from all criticisms or all critics. Instead, as in our original work,
here our clear and present purpose remains moving the field toward more
reflective practices as regards measurement.

Therefore, we focus on those criticisms of Professor Sawilowsky that we
believe are immediately relevant to our determined (albeit ambitious) focus.
We especially hope that our major emphases will not be lost within a [175]
litany of minor concerns; we avoid this possibility by addressing here only the
issues most relevant to our objectives, and demur from comment otherwise.

Our Use of Quotations

Here, as in our previous work, we again make use of numerous quotations. We do so out of stylistic preference, out of affection for either the
words or the ideas and metaphors in cited references.

We do not intend to suggest that the present argument should be resolved
on the basis of *ethos* rather than logic or *logos*. Nor has it been our intention
to rely on such quotations to suggest that all textbook authors agree with our
views.

Indeed, although Sawilowsky's summary of views in various measurement
textbooks does not present a complete or a random representation, we believe
that his portrayal is nevertheless reasonably accurate. Although there are
clearly exceptions, as Sawilowsky's Table 1 suggests, measurement textbooks
on the whole do poorly at accurately communicating fundamental measurement concepts to our graduate students, at least as regards score reliability.

Of course, equally disturbing patterns also have been noted regarding
typical textbook treatments of other methodological issues. For example,
Carver (1978), citing examples, long ago noted that "generations of
students have been misdirected by textbook writers into the . . . erroneous
interpretation of statistical significance" (p. 384).

Organization

We have previously argued (Thompson, 1994; Vacha-Haase, 1998) that it is incorrect to say "the test is reliable" or to speak of "the reliability of the test." These statements may have combinations of three distinct meanings which here we explicitly distinguish in our remaining discussion:

1. "*the* reliability of the test," dealing with the proposition of whether a given measure may be characterized by only a single class of reliability estimates;

2. "the reliability of the *test*," dealing with the proposition of whether reliability is a property that inures to a given measure *per se*, solely as a function of the test; and

3. "the reliability of *the* test," dealing with the proposition of whether reliability estimates should be thought of as applying to a measurement in hand or instead to the universe (or domain or population) of all real or hypothetical parallel measures.

Regarding the first proposition, we agree with Sawilowsky that "because there are many ways of estimating reliability, each influenced by [176] different sources of measurement error, it is unacceptable to say simply, 'The reliability of test X is .90'" (AERA/APA/NCME, 1985, p. 21). The measurement theory used to estimate score reliability may itself impact the estimate. Therefore, any specification of an estimate should always specify the theory or model used to derive a particular estimate. And it should not be assumed that other models would yield the same estimate.

Given our agreement with Sawilowsky on these point, we focus our remaining discussion on the last two propositions. Specifically, we address four issues: (a) tests qua tests are not reliable, (b) the nature of reliability, (c) "rules" for RG analyses, and (d) reasonable expectations for reliability reporting practices. We end with a brief summary of our views.

Tests qua Tests Are Not Reliable!

Regarding the second meaning of the phrase "the reliability of the *test* (i.e., the proposition that reliability is a property that inures to a given measure *per se*) we emphatically reiterate once again our conviction that this proposition asserts an obvious and pernicious fallacy. The fallacy of this view remains unaltered by counts of how many textbook (or article) authors unconsciously or unintentionally assert the patently false proposition that reliability is solely an unchanging function of a given test *per se*.

A Somewhat Simplified Theory of Reliability

At the turn of the century, Spearman (1904) first articulated a coherent measurement theory, sometimes called "true score theory," but now often called "classical theory," merely because this theory is older than some of the "modern" measurement theories. Spearman (1910) also popularized use of the term "reliability" itself. Spearman's ideas were soon adopted and extended by others (cf. Thorndike, 1904).

In classical measurement theory reliability deals with the *consistency* with which individuals (presuming here that people are what some modern theorists would call the "object of measurement") are *rank ordered* by measurement across parallel test forms, repeated measurements, and so forth. Upon reflection it should be clear that the people measured themselves affect the consistency of their rank orderings on a given measure (i.e., that score reliability is not solely a function of the test).

Specifically, the degree of homogeneity of the scores (i.e., SD_X) directly affects the consistency (e.g., stability) of the score orderings. As Cunningham (1986) explained, [177]

> [W]hen scores are bunched together, a small [random measurement error] change in raw score will lead to large changes in relative position. If scores are spread out (variability is high), it is more likely that the relative position in the group will remain stable across the two forms of the test and the correlation coefficient will be relatively large. (p. 114)

In other words, "greater differences between the scores of individuals reduce the possibility of shifting positions" (Linn & Gronlund, 1995, p. 101).

The fact that the homogeneity or the heterogeneity of the scores of the people being measured directly impacts score reliability obviously means that reliability is not indelibly and unalterably stamped into test booklets during the printing process. Score reliability changes as a measure is administered to different samples, partially as a function of the score standard deviation in a given group (Guilford & Fruchter, 1978, p. 431).

Example Illustrating That the Test qua Test Is Not Reliable

The most extreme case of score homogeneity would involve giving an attitude measure to people who felt the same about a referent, or a cognitive test to examinees who had no knowledge in a subject area. We now expand upon a concrete heuristic example presented by Hopkins (1998, p. 110) to emphasize the point that tests *per se* are not reliable.

Presume that Riverwater Publishing Company has invested awe-inspiring resources to develop three equivalent forms of the "Mandarin Vocabulary Test" (MVT). Each MVT form consists of 100 multiple-choice questions each with five alternative answers. The MVT is designed to measure general knowledge of Mandarin Chinese vocabulary.

In rigorous standardization, all three MVT forms were administered in counterbalanced orders to a normative sample of 5,000 15-65 year olds drawn from the area of China where Mandarin is commonly spoken. The normative sample was carefully selected to match closely the demographic profile of this population, as reported in a recent census. Using MVT scores from the normative sample, a variety of classical reliability coefficients (e.g., stability, equivalence) were then computed. Every coefficient was greater than .95.

If the *test* is reliable, you could repeatedly administer any form of the MVT to any sample of 50 United States undergraduate students, with perfect assurance, because during production every MVT test booklet has been impregnated with both ink and this superior reliability, that the scores in your sample would be equally reliable. Of course, the same provisos would afford you the assurance that you could also obtain reliable scores by allowing two-year-old [178] toddlers to use pencils to complete adult standardized IQ tests, or blind adults to respond to visually-presented progressive matrices tasks.

The present example presents an extreme of score homogeneity. Presuming none of your 50 undergraduate students speaks even a smattering of Mandarin, and that there are no practice or motivation change effects, on each re-administration of each form the group's MVT means will randomly and fairly narrowly fluctuate around the "chance score" of 20.

Furthermore, the rank orderings of individual's scores across forms and administrations will be extremely inconsistent, because even though the homogeneous scores of individuals may change very little, the closeness of the scores will mean that small random fluctuations will alter rank orderings. Given the relatively small *SD* of the scores, the rank order of your favorite student, Wendy, may bounce all over the place throughout the range of rank orderings. So will the rank orderings of all the other students. That is, the reliability of these Mandarin Vocabulary Test scores will be very poor, notwithstanding the exemplary features of the Riverwater production process and the extraordinary quality of the scores when the test is used in China!

Etiology of Endemic Misspeaking About Reliability

It seems obvious to us that on its face "reliability is not a property of a test in itself but rather when that instrument is applied to a particular group of examinees" (Ebel, 1979, p. 275). This point was emphasized in Linn and Gronlund's (1995) bold-faced "general point #1" (p. 82), and by Sax with Newton's (1997) bolded and shaded-box statement (p. 276). Similarly, as Guilford and Fruchter (1978) emphasized, "Note that it is *measurements* that . . . [are] said to have the property of reliability rather than the measuring instruments" (p. 408, emphasis in original).

Why do so many authors, unlike these, so routinely assert patent untruth about reliability, as we interpret Professor Sawilowsky's Table 7.1 to document? We can identify two dynamics that may explain this distressing phenomenon: (a) a tendency to speak telegraphically, and (b) ignorance spirally reinforced by paradigmatic influences.

Telegraphic Speaking. We believe that some people use the phrase "the reliability of the test" as a telegraphic shorthand in place of truthful but longer statements (e.g., "the reliability of the test scores"). This tendency is understandable, but deleterious.

As Sawilowsky notes, some textbook authors do alternate between describing scores and tests as reliable. For example, Mehrens and Lehmann (1991) in the first paragraph of their chapter on reliability noted that, [179] "Technically speaking, *data* should be reliable, and the inferences we draw from the data should be valid" (p. 248, emphasis added). And subsequently they remind the reader that technically it is scores that are reliable: "How reliable should a test (more technically speaking, any set of scores) be in order to be useful?" (Mehrens & Lehmann, 1991, p. 263).

Similarly, Worthen, White, Fan, and Sudweeks (1999) emphasized that speaking of "the reliability of the test" is sinful:

> Up to now, we have taken a bit of literary license, sometimes writing as if reliability refers to the measurement instrument itself. Not so. Technically, reliability refers to the consistency of the *results* obtained, not to the instrument itself. . . . Not surprisingly, many have adopted the shorthand of speaking of the *test's* reliability, a sin that can probably be forgiven as long as you understand this critical distinction. (p. 95, emphasis in original)

Of course, how easily the sin might be forgiven is a function of the perceived consequences of the sin.

Ignorance Spirally Reinforced by Paradigmatic Influences. Although many authors who speak of "the reliability of the test" may not seriously mean what they say, there is always the off chance that some naive reader may not expect authors to be gratuitously misleading. As Carver (1993) noted in the context of other misspeaking,

> When trying to emulate the best principles of science, it seems important to say what we mean and to mean what we say. . . . Why be unnecessarily confusing when clarity should be most important? (p. 288)

As noted by Thompson (1992), "the problem is that sometimes we unconsciously come to think what we say or what we hear, so that sloppy speaking does sometimes lead to a more pernicious outcome, sloppy thinking and sloppy practice" (p. 436). In other words, naive readers of telegraphic discussion of reliability may instantiate paradigms incorporating erroneous precepts. These then will tend to go uncorrected, because their influence is unconscious.

As defined by Gage (1963, p. 95), "Paradigms are models, patterns, or schemata. Paradigms are not the theories; they are rather ways of thinking or patterns for research." Tuthill and Ashton (1983) noted that

> A scientific paradigm can be thought of as a socially shared cognitive schema. Just as our cognitive schema provide us, as individuals, with a way of making sense of the world around us, a scientific paradigm provides a group of scientists with a way of collectively making sense of their scientific world. (p. 7)

But scientists may be unable consciously to recognize the influence of their paradigms. As Lincoln and Guba (1985) noted: [180]

> If it is difficult for a fish to understand water because it has spent all its life in it, so it is difficult for scientists . . . to understand what their basic axioms or assumptions might be and what impact those axioms and assumptions have upon everyday thinking and lifestyle. (pp. 19-20)

Even though researchers are usually unaware of paradigm influences, paradigms are nevertheless potent influences in that they tell us what we need to think about, and also the things *about which we need not think.* As Patton (1975) suggested,

> Paradigms are normative, they tell the practitioner what to do without the necessity of long existential or epistemological consideration. But it is this

aspect of a paradigm that constitutes both its strength *and* its weaknesses—its strength in that it makes action possible; its weakness in that the very reason for action is hidden in the unquestioned assumptions of the paradigm. (p. 9)

Once we have entered a mindspace in which tests *per se* are unalterably reliable, it becomes wasteful to allocate doctoral curriculum to teach students anything more sophisticated than how rotely to cite the unalterable reliability coefficients reported in a test manual. Thus, misconceptions regarding reliability are propagated in part because

[a]lthough most programs in sociobehavioral sciences, especially doctoral programs, require a modicum of exposure to statistics and research design, few seem to require the same where measurement is concerned. Thus, many students get the impression that no special competencies are necessary for the development and use of measures . . . (Pedhazur & Schmelkin, 1991, pp. 2-3)

An empirical description of doctoral curricula in education and psychology programs throughout the country confirms this disturbing portrayal (Aiken, West, Sechrest, & Reno with Roediger, Scarr, Kazdin & Sherman, 1990). An updated description is nearing completion, but probably will yield similarly distressing results.

Thus, ignorance about measurement realities creates a self-perpetuating resistance to overcoming misconceptions. We have entered a black-box era in which students with terminal degrees in education and psychology first enter their training based upon scores from a computer-adaptive GRE testing that upon their graduation they could not intelligently explain or evaluate. Nor could they intelligently evaluate the score integrity from related protocols they will then use with their own future students and clients!

Nature of Reliability

We also wish to argue the proposition that reliability estimates should be thought of as applying to the universe (or domain or population) of all real or hypothetical parallel measures rather than to a measurement in hand (e.g., [181] Form 1 of the MVT consisting of 100 specific items). In other words, we are also philosophically opposed to speaking of "the reliability of *the* test."

Our objections can only be presented by exploring both (a) classical and (b) modern measurement theories a bit more deeply. Unfortunately, as Cunningham (1986) noted, "Despite its being relatively easy to compute, there are few subjects in the field of measurement more difficult to understand than reliability" (p. 101).

To make our discussion more accessible we will somewhat simplify distinctions between measurement models that are "strictly parallel," "tau-equivalent," "essentially tau-equivalent," "congeneric," or "multi-factor congeneric" (Feldt & Brennan, 1989, pp. 110-111; Lord & Novick, 1968, pp. 47-50). The fit of these various measurement models can be evaluated using structural equation modeling (SEM), as explained by Jöreskog and Sörbom (1989, pp. 76-96).

Classical Theory View of Score Reliability

Classical test theory (Spearman, 1904) is largely built on the conceptualization that each observed score has two independent score components, a "true" score and a random "measurement error" score. A true score can be conceptualized as "the mean of an infinitely large sample of repeated measurements of an individual" presuming no practice or changing motivation effects (Guilford & Fruchter, 1978, p. 408).

The concept of parallel tests is also commonly invoked as part of classical measurement theory. In this context a true score represents "the average score a person would obtain on an infinite number of parallel forms of a test, assuming that the person is not affected by taking the tests (i.e., assuming no practice or fatigue [or motivation] effect)" (Hopkins, 1998, p. 114).

The reliability coefficient (e.g., r_{XX}) "is logically defined as the proportion of the variance that is true variance" (Guilford & Fruchter, 1978, p. 408). More specifically, the reliability coefficient "is defined as the squared correlation ρ_{XT} between observed score[s] and true score[s]" (Lord & Novick, 1968, p. 61).

Construction of Parallel Tests. The notion of parallel tests can be more concretely communicated by again adapting an example presented by Hopkins (1998, pp. 110-112). The senior author's cherished 1968 Webster's dictionary contains roughly 142,000 words. We might define these words as the population (or universe or domain) of all possible items for a 100-item English vocabulary test. Here each "supply"-format item presents a target vocabulary word and examinees are then asked to write a brief definition. Obviously, there are a huge (but finite) number of parallel test forms that we could create by drawing different random samples of 100 items. [182]

In other cases there are literally infinitely many potential parallel test forms. For example, if the domain consisting of multiplying the number 2.0 times possible real numbers between 0.0 and 10.0, there would be infinitely many possible 100-item parallel tests, because there are infinitely many real numbers between 0.0 and 10.0.

Of course, in practice there may not be as many parallel tests, because we usually do not wish to randomly sample all possible combinations of items. Instead, we often elect to sample items from within sampling frames using a more restrictive "table of specifications" (Sax with Newton, 1997, pp. 73-74), requiring, for example, 10 one-digit addition problems, 10 three-digit addition problems, and 10 multiplication problems involving two-digit integers. Furthermore, as Cunningham (1986) pointed out,

> The usual practice is to construct a test, rather than draw the items randomly from the domain. . . . The normal procedures of [non-random item selection partially based on] item analysis . . . use[s] the degree to which items correlate with the total score as a criterion for evaluating [and selecting] items . . . (p. 105)

Nevertheless, the concept of numerous or infinite parallel tests administered infinitely many times pervades classical views of reliability. Of course, as Feldt and Brennan (1989) explained,

> In practice, test forms do not exist in unlimited numbers. . . . Thus, measurement concepts such as true score and error variance are conceptual notions only . . . [C]learly this infinity is only a useful fiction. (p. 109)

But an important point is that when we estimate score reliability we are estimating characteristics of scores in the universe (or domain or population), and not the reliability only for a single test form. As Crocker and Algina (1986) explained,

> According to the classical true score model, the reliability coefficient was defined as the correlation between strictly parallel tests. The reliability coefficient was shown also to be equivalent to the proportion of observed score variance that is attributable to variance in examinees' true scores. . . . [Thus a] reliability coefficient for a set of scores can never be determined exactly; it can, however, be *estimated* for a given sample of individuals responding to a given sample of test items. (p. 131)

Estimation of Parallel Form Equivalence. In a substantive inquiry, we do not want the scores on the 100-item cognitive achievement posttest to characterize only achievement at that instant, ignoring achievement in the few preceding instants or the scores that would be obtained on the same measure in the next few moments. Furthermore, we usually are interested not only in the scores on only these 100 items, but also in the scores on parallel measures in the same domain. Consequently, we are usually *not* interested in evaluating [183] "the reliability of *the* test." Fortunately, we also are *not* estimating "the reliability of *the* test."

Thus, Stanley (1971) emphasized that, "The test score has practical significance insofar as it is representative of the individual's ability to respond to *all* of the tasks in the universe which it undertakes to sample" (p. 407, emphasis added). And Hills (1981) noted that, though classical theory may provide various flavors of estimates (e.g., internal consistency, stability), "None of these [classical] ways of estimating reliability is inherently better than the others. Ideally we would like to know all of them . . ." (p. 150).

Modern Theory View of Score Reliability

The modern measurement theory called "generalizability theory" makes these points even more obvious. "G" theory was articulated by Cronbach, Gleser, Nanda, and Rajaratnum (1972; also see Brennan, 1983). Accessible treatments are provided by Shavelson and Webb (1991) and Webb, Rowley, and Shavelson (1988). Generalizability theory offers a model for obtaining better characterizations of score reliability than those offered by classical theory. But "G" theory also offers a powerful paradigm for more clearly *thinking* about score reliability.

Generalizability theory *simultaneously* considers all possible main effect sources of measurement error and all possible interactions of these measurement errors. As Feldt and Brennan (1989) emphasized, "It is an acknowledged principle in reliability estimation that the best estimate of the [reliability] coefficient and the standard error [of measurement] is one that reflects the impact of *all* sources of measurement error" (p. 109, emphasis added). This is *not* a matter of mere statistical nit-picking (Thompson, 1992).

In an *EPM* book review Thompson (1991) argued:

I believe that most measurement classicists *unconsciously* presume that their error variance sources (a) substantially overlap each other and (b) do not interact to create additional new error variance. Thus, a practitioner may do classical internal consistency, test-retest, and equivalent forms reliability analyses, and may find in all three that measurement error comprises 10% of score variance. Too many classicists would tend to assume that these 10 percents are the same and also tend to not realize that in addition to being unique and cumulative, the sources may also interact to define disastrously large interaction sources of measurement error not considered in classical theory. The effects of these assumptions are all the more pernicious because of their unconscious character. (pp. 1071-1072)

Thus, "G" theory is important (a) analytically in that the theory allows the estimation of score reliability in a manner "that reflects the impact of *all* sources of measurement error" (Feldt & Brennan, 1989, p. 109), and (b) conceptually in that the theory allows us to understand that measurement error influences cumulate and may interact to produce even more error variance. [184]

As very important as are the analytical advantages of "G" theory mentioned (and also other important advantages unmentioned) here, the way that "G" theory offers a conceptually clarifying "way of thinking" about score reliability is in some respects even more important. As Thompson (1991) noted,

too few researchers recognize that in all analyses we inherently invoke both a presumptive model of reality and an analytic model. When the two don't match, the analysis doesn't help us understand the reality we believe exists. If we virtually always want to generalize over time and over items or tests, then a classical theory approach that never simultaneously considers these two time and item sampling influences, and completely ignores the interactions of these influences, will be quite simply unworkable! (p. 1072)

That is, in reliability analyses we should estimate the score reliabilities within the score universe for all the measurement and substantive facets (e.g., time, item sets, the interaction of time with items) over which we wish generalize. Thus, we are interested in more than "the reliability of *the* test" in hand at one instant in time, even if in our substantive work we actually only measured once, or in a single form consisting of a single item set, even if in our work we only have a single item set.

In our substantive work, we use samples of people that are carefully drawn so that we may generalize to similar persons. In experiments, we may use samples of conditions so that we may generalize to a larger range of experimental conditions, using "random effects" analytic models (Clark, 1973). In a similar fashion, in "G" theory we invariably treat items as random effects, thus honoring our wish to generalize across the domain of parallel forms (Shavelson & Webb, 1991). "G" theory forces us to think about and acknowledge this choice, thus making our wish conscious.

"Rules" for RG Analyses

Professor Sawilowsky criticizes some of the analytic choices made by Vacha-Haase (1998). For example, he suggests that too little description was provided of the distribution shapes of the dummy-coded variables. Of course, more descriptive information is always better than less information as long as journal space is not a consideration.

However, it is important to remember that "RG" studies are a meta-analytic characterization of what is hoped is a population of previous reports. We may not like the ingredients that go into making this sausage, but the "RG" chef can only work with the ingredients provided by the literature. Obviously, at some extreme the literature may not be sufficient to conduct an "RG" study, just as can happen in both "validity generalization" and in substantive meta-analysis studies.

However, as the field moves toward better understanding of reliability, and score reliability coefficients are more frequently reported even in substantive [185] studies, the ingredients going into a given "RG" recipe will improve. As Vacha-Haase (1998) suggested,

> if authors of empirical studies routinely report reliability coefficients, even in substantive studies, the field will cumulate more evidence regarding the psychometric integrity of scores. Such practices would provide more fodder for reliability generalization analyses focusing upon the differential influences of various sources of measurement error. (p. 14)

We also want to emphasize that we do not see "RG" as involving always a single genre of analyses. For example, some authors will use box-and-whisker plots, others regression, some ANOVA. Some authors will focus on reliability coefficients, while others may examine standard errors of measurement. We now briefly consider two "RG" methodology issues, from among the many that could be elaborated.

Conversion of Reliability Coefficients Using *z*

Professor Sawilowsky suggests that at least some reliability coefficients should be subjected to Fisher's *r*-to-*z* transformation prior to conducting meta-analysis. We will argue that a Z transformation of reliability coefficients is not necessary prior to RG meta-analysis.

To present this view, a somewhat more technical treatment of reliability is now unavoidable. Specifically, it will be necessary to distinguish the *way* we estimate score reliability from *what* we are estimating.

In classical test theory the reliability coefficient (e.g., ρ_{XX}) is the ratio of true score variance to total observed score variance (cf. MacDonald, 1999, p. 66; Mehrens & Lehmann, 1991, p. 251; Sax with Newton, 1997, p. 274):

$$\rho_{XX} = \sigma_T^2 / \sigma_X^2.$$

Note that the variance ratio formula for reliability is the direct analog of the classical algorithm for estimating an uncorrected variance-accounted-for effect size (Snyder & Lawson, 1993) in substantive analysis:

$$r^2 = R^2 = \eta^2 = SD_{YHAT}^2 / SD_Y^2.$$

Of course, because the numerator and the denominator variances both involve division by $n-1$, and these cancel out, the values in the squared r family can also be computed as:

$$r^2 = R^2 = \eta^2 = SOS_{YAHT}^2 / SOS_Y^2.$$

These comparisons suggest that a reliability coefficient may be in an r^2 metric, even though ρ_{XX} is not presented with an exponent. Such a view would be consistent with Nunnally's (1978) definition of r_{XX} as "the [186] estimated square of the correlation of scores on a collection of items with true scores" (p. 211).

Of course, doubtless "it seems odd to some students that reliability [without an exponent] is defined as the *square* of the correlation between X_f and T" (Feldt & Brennan, 1989, p. 109). Similarly, MacDonald (1999) noted that

> We would not normally expect a variance ratio to equal a correlation coefficient [i.e., r_{XX} or ρ_r]. This seems less strange when it is noted that
>
> $$\rho_r = \rho_{YT}^2 = \rho_{Y'T'}^2, \qquad (5.12)$$
>
> that is, the reliability coefficient is the square of the correlation between Y [observed scores] and T [true scores] . . . (p. 66)

Thus, what we are estimating is a population (or universe or domain) variance-accounted-for statistic, the reliability coefficient. But the universe is not directly observable. How can this population value be estimated? We do so correlating or estimating the correlation of sampled parallel test forms.

The variance-accounted-for universe reliability coefficient (ρ_{XX}, ρ_r in these various notations) is estimated by computing (or estimating) the *unsquared* correlation between scores on observed parallel tests, or on a single test administered twice. As Lord and Novick (1968) explained,

> The square of the correlation between observed scores and true scores is equal to the correlation between parallel measurements. Thus, assuming at least one pair of parallel measurements can be obtained, we have succeeded in expressing an unobservable [universe] quantity ρ_{XT}^2 in terms of $\rho_{XX'}$, a parameter of a (bivariate) observed-score distribution. (pp. 58-59)

In other words, often the *way* we estimate score reliability is by computing unsquared r values. But by doing so, nevertheless *what* we are estimating is variance-accounted-for universe values (i.e., reliability coefficients). For example, if in a test-retest situation $\rho_{XX'}$ equalled .81,

> the following interpretations would be appropriate. First, we may say that [$\rho_{XX'}$] 81% of the observed score variance is attributable to true score variance for this examinee group. . . . Second, we may say that ($.81^2$), or [$\rho_{XX'}^2 =$] 65%, of the observed score variance on the second test could be predicted by the variance of the observed scores on the first test. (Crocker & Algina, 1986, p. 116)

The bottom line is that we believe the direct use of reliability coefficients in RG studies is appropriate, because variance-accounted-for statistics are intervally comparable. We must distinguish *what* we are estimating from *how* we formulate the estimates. As Worthen, White, Fan and Sudweeks (1999) noted,

> Readers with good statistical knowledge may notice that the correlation coefficient should be squared for the purpose of such interpretation in terms of [187] percentage of variance. . . . Although, in [a] statistical sense, reliability coefficient is a correlation coefficient in many situations, psychometrically, it is different. For interpretive purposes, [the] reliability coefficient is *directly* interpretable as percentage of variance without being squared. (p. 113, emphasis in original)

Of course, it would also be reasonable to take the square root of reliability coefficients, and apply the Fisher transformation. The important concerns are that the values are apples and apples across the various reports and that the values are intervally scaled so that the RG analysis can invoke parametric statistics when desired.

RG Analysis of Reliability Coefficients Versus SEM

To further emphasize that we do not see RG as invoking a monolithic methodological approach, we now mention briefly an alternative focus. An RG study could reasonably look at the standard error of the measurement (SEM) across studies using a given measure.

Conceptually, the SEM might be defined as the standard deviation of a given individual's scores on infinitely many administrations of infinitely parallel measures. As Feldt and Brennan (1989) explained, "Because such repeated assessments are presumed to vary only because of measurement error, the standard deviation reflects the potency of random error sources" (p. 105).

In practice, we often estimate the SEM as $SD_X (1 - r_{XX})^{.5}$ (cf. Linn & Gronlund, 1995, p. 96). For example, if the estimated score reliability for an IQ test was .9, and SD_X equalled 15, the SEM would be estimated to be:

$$= 15 (1 - .9)^{.5}$$
$$= 15 (.1)^{.5}$$
$$= 15 (.316)$$
$$= 4.743.$$

However, this estimate of SEM is rather crude, because this is an estimate of *individual* observed score variation in the population, and the estimate assumes the untruth that this intraindividual variance induced by measurement error is constant across individuals (Thompson, 1992). In truth, when a single test form is administered to a group of examinees, "obtained scores above the mean tend to have positive errors of measurement (e's) and scores below the mean tend to have negative e's. In addition, very high and very low obtained scores tend to have larger e's than scores near the center of the distribution" (Hopkins, 1998, p. 118).

This is why Thorndike, Cunningham, Thorndike, and Hagen (1991), for example, argued that "The meticulous test constructor will report [188] the standard error of the measurement for the test at different score levels" (p. 106). These are called "conditional SEMs."

RG researchers might reasonably find all prior studies that reported score reliability for a given measure, and compute the SEM (or even conditional SEMs for selected score ranges) by applying the SEM formula using the sample reliability estimate and the sample SD_X. Then these values would become the meta-analytic focus. This would have the advantage that "the error of measurement is independent of the variability of the group on which it is computed" (Anastasi, 1988, p. 134).

However, this can be done *only* when the RG study focuses on a single measure with a scoring protocol that does not itself lead to a different range of scores. For example, an RG analysis of SEMs across studies would not be reasonable when the meta-analysis looked at variations in score quality in a range of measures (e.g., a pool of self-concept studies involving three different measures of self-concept). Nor would an SEM focus be appropriate even when a single measure was investigated, if both short and long forms were used in the prior studies, as was the case in the Vacha-Haase (1998) RG study. As Feldt and Brennan (1989) emphasized, "Because the standard error is scale specific, however, it cannot be compared from one instrument to another or from one scoring procedure to another. For such comparisons, the 'unitless' reliability coefficient is clearly more useful" (p. 106). Finally, we also note that in previous *EPM* articles some have argued SEM is essentially only a function of test length, which for an RG study involving a single measure would be a fixed constant (Lord, 1957, 1959; Swineford, 1959).

Expectations for Reliability Reporting Practices

The present discussion suggests a set of expectations that should be imposed on those conducting scholarly inquiry. First, regarding test developers and test publishers,

> The number and nature of persons on whom reliability was checked should likewise be reported. With such information, test users can predict whether the test will be about equally reliable for the group with which they expect to use it, or whether it is likely to be more or less reliable. (Anastasi, 1988, p. 28)

Second, scholars conducting either substantive (i.e., non-measurement focused) or measurement research should be expected to report explicit and direct evidence of score integrity in their sample.

Empirical studies indicate that a distressing large number of researchers do not even mention score reliability evidence (perhaps "thinking" that their test booklets have been indelibly impregnated with reliability), and that distressing few researchers compute reliability estimates using their own data [189] (Meier & Davis, 1990; Thompson & Snyder, 1998; Vacha-Haase, Ness, Nilsson, & Reetz, 1999; Willson, 1980). Strikingly, 20 years ago Willson (1980) noted that

> Only 37% of the *AERJ* studies explicitly reported reliability coefficients for the data analyzed. Another 18% reported only indirectly through reference to

earlier research. . . . That reliability . . . is unreported in almost half the published research is . . . inexcusable at this late date. . ." (pp. 8-9)

Consequences of Bad Practice

That so many substantive researchers fail even to mention score reliability, and that others only vaguely cite a related reliability reference for an independent sample, is disturbing because the potential effects of poor score reliabilities are so noteworthy. Conducting substantive analyses involving scores with low reliability both (a) lessens power against Type II error and (b) directly attenuates effect sizes.

Of course, in the APA (1994) publication guidelines effect size reporting is "encouraged" (p. 18), and the editorial policies of *EPM* (Thompson, 1994) and other journals (cf. Heldref Foundation, 1997; Murphy, 1997) *require* effect size reporting. And the recent recommendations of the APA Task Force on Statistical Inference[1] emphasized, "*Always* provide some effect-size estimate when reporting a *p* value" (Wilkinson & APA Task Force on Statistical Inference, 1999, p. 599, emphasis added). Later the Task Force also wrote,

> *Always* present effect sizes for primary outcomes. . . . We must stress again that reporting and interpreting effect sizes in the context of previously reported effects is *essential* to good research. (p. 599, emphasis added)

As noted in the *EPM* author guidelines (Thompson, 1994),

> The failure to consider score reliability in substantive research may exact a toll on the interpretations within research studies. For example, we may conduct studies that could not possibly yield noteworthy effect sizes, given that score reliability inherently attenuates effect sizes. Or we may not accurately interpret the effect sizes in our studies if we do not consider the reliability of the scores we are actually analyzing. (p. 840)

As Pedhazur and Schmelkin (1991) argued:

> Researchers who bother at all to report reliability estimates for the instruments they use (many do not) frequently report only reliability estimates contained in the manuals of the instruments or estimates reported by other researchers. Such information may be useful for comparative purposes, but it is imperative to recognize that the *relevant reliability estimate is the one obtained for the sample used in the [present] study under consideration.* (p. 86, emphasis in original) [190]

Because these consequences are serious, the Joint Committee on Standards for Educational Evaluation (1994)[2], which developed the first standards for professional conduct that were ever certified as American standards by the American National Standards Institute (ANSI), emphasized that, "the generalizability of previous favorable reliability results may not be simply assumed. Reliability information should be collected that is directly relevant to the groups and ways in which the information gathering procedures will be used . . ." (p. 154).

Minimally Acceptable Practice

The crudest and barely acceptable minimal evidence of score quality in a substantive study would involve an *explicit* and *direct* comparison (Thompson, 1992) of (a) relevant sample characteristics (e.g., age, gender), whatever these may be in the context of a particular inquiry, with the same features reported in the manual for the normative sample or in earlier research and (b) the sample score *SD* with the *SD* reported in the manual or in other earlier research. In short, as Crocker and Algina (1986) suggested,

> . . . [R]eliability is a property of the scores on a test for a particular group of examinees. Thus, potential test users need to determine whether reliability estimates reported in test manuals are based on samples similar in *composition* and *variability* to the group for whom the test will be used. (p. 144, emphasis added)

Given empirical evidence that score reliability is unmentioned in a large percentage of articles, and that in many other cases authors consider score reliability only to the extent of citing a test manual or earlier study reporting reliability for an independent sample (Meier & Davis, 1990; Thompson & Snyder, 1998; Vacha-Haase, Ness, Nilsson & Reetz, 1999; Willson, 1980), one might question what percentage of authors only citing previous independent reports *explicitly* and *directly* compared the "*composition* and *variability*" (p. 144, emphasis added) of the previous sample with those features of the group for whom the measure is being used. An empirical inquiry addressing this question is currently underway. The problem with failure to *explicitly* and *directly* compare the *composition* and *variability* of a normative sample with the related features of a given sample, by merely citing a test manual, is that researchers may (a) finesse via vagueness the quality of the previous results and/or (b) generalize previous results to samples where similar favorable results are unlikely.

Better Practice

Of course, we believe the better practice would be to estimate score reliability for one's own data. After all, this is usually not difficult to do with [191] modern software. This is the acid test of sample-to-normative-sample match as regards reliability.

Large discrepancies between reliability estimates reported in the manual and those obtained in a given study alert the researcher to the possibility that the normative sample and the research sample may represent discrete populations, and thus such comparisons even may bear somewhat upon the generalizability of substantive results. This is a real possibility in most studies. Although many normative samples are very carefully drawn (e.g., matched to census profiles), roughly 95% of published inquiries are based on samples of convenience not invoking random sampling (Ludbrook & Dudley, 1998), and therefore may not be representative of identifiable populations.

Discrepancies between reliability estimates for samples and those of normative samples reported in test manuals can also occur when the normative sample was employed to select final items from a large item pool by consulting item analysis results in the sample. Because these item analysis statistics (e.g., discrimination) may capitalize on the sampling error in the normative sample, the items may then not perform as well in future samples, and therefore score reliability in future samples may "shrink" from the estimates reported in manuals (Lord & Novick, 1968, pp. 334, 350).

Empirical Evidence

On the other hand, some might argue that with a "representative sample of 300 or more persons" (Nunnally, 1978, p. 206) and "even when tests have as few as 10 items, reliability estimates are rather precise" (p. 208), and that therefore reliability coefficients for a measure should theoretically be very stable. Too few authors are currently reporting score reliability for their own data (e.g., Vacha-Haase et al., 1999; Willson, 1980), and too few RG studies have yet been done, to test empirically whether such a theoretical view holds up.

But Vacha-Haase's (1998) results seem to suggest that reliability coefficients may vary more than we might expect. In a related vein, Shaddish, Bootzin, Koller, and Brownell (1981) examined reliability estimates for 24 total and subtest scores on four measures when applied in somewhat novel settings and found that in one measurement model the estimated reliabilities of these scores went down an average of 21.6% ($SD = 14.0$%) and in another measurement model went down an average of 25.5% ($SD = 18.5$%).

Wood and Lilienfeld (1999) examined interrater reliabilities of scores on the Exner Comprehensive System scoring of the Rorschach test. The manual claims reliabilities that are quite high. However, Wood and Lilienfeld (1999) suggested that interrater reliability computed as intraclass correlation coefficients for various scores for both normal and clinical samples actually range from below .2 to 1.0. [192]

Crowley and Taylor (1994) computed alpha coefficients, which are lower bound estimates of reliability (Crocker & Algina, 1986, p. 139), for their samples and compared their results with those presented in original reports involving three measures. They found some striking discrepancies. For example, on one Family Support Scale subscale, alpha deteriorated by 25% in their sample of fathers, even though they collected data from 922 parents from 17 sites around the country. On a subscale for a different test, alpha went from the .81 estimate presented in the original report to −.16. The only solace was that their estimated alpha was not less than −1.0, because such values are indeed possible for alpha.

On the other hand, Campbell et al. (1999) conducted a stability reliability study in which they computer administered various measures, including 46 psychological scales, and compared their test-retest reliability estimates with those obtained in matched samples from the literature in which conventional administration had been used. They found that "the stability of the Computer administration condition exceeded the TR values in the [conventional administration] literature in 35 of 46 cases (77%) for the psychological tests" (p. 29).

And variations in score reliability may not be as easily understood or predicted as we might expect. For example, Feldt and Qualls (1999) studied reliabilities of scores in 170 school districts on seven subscales of the Iowa Tests of Educational Development. They found that "subpopulations that are almost always more homogeneous than larger normative sample groups will, with rare exception, yield lower levels of observed-score variance. However, smaller values of α_x^2 cannot automatically be assumed to lower reliability estimates" (p. 380).

Ultimately, a series of RG studies may reveal that either (a) reliability estimates for most measures fluctuate only to a trivial extent across samples or (b) these variations can not readily be systematically explained or predicted, at which point this meta-analytic method will and should be abandoned. However, we do not anticipate this demise.

Summary

In our view, we believe that social scientists should avoid the "common error" of

> Failing to take into account the fact that the *reliability of the scores* provided by an instrument or procedure may fluctuate depending on how, when, and to whom the instrument or procedure is administered. (Joint Committee on Standards for Educational Evaluation, 1994, p. 155, emphasis added)

We also believe that investigation of these dynamics is interesting.

We must remember that score unreliability tends to attenuate effect sizes. As Stanley (1971) emphasized some three decades ago, [193]

> One can make no worthwhile prediction of a completely unreliable criterion, or of a perfectly reliable criterion with quite unpredictable predictors; and in an experiment one can demonstrate no improvement with a measure of performance which depends entirely upon [measurement error] chance factors. . . . Data on reliability of predictors and criteria are necessary if the research worker is to be able to interpret the extent to which imperfect corre-lation between predictors and criteria is due to lack of overlapping function (or common variance) and the extent to which it is due to lack of precision in the measures. (p. 358)

Or, in the more recent words of the APA Task Force on Statistical Infer-ence, we believe that

> It is important to remember that a test is not reliable or unreliable. Reliability is a property of the scores on a test for a particular population of examinees (Feldt & Brennan, 1989). Thus, authors should provide reliability coefficients of the scores for the data being analyzed even when the focus of their research is not psychometric. Interpreting the size of observed effects requires an assess-ment of the reliability of the scores. (Wilkinson & APA Task Force on Statis-tical Inference, 1999, p. 596)

We concur.

References

Aiken, L. S., West, S. G., Sechrest, L., & Reno, R. R., with Roediger, H. L., Scarr, S., Kazdin, A. E., & Sherman, S. J. (1990). The training in statistics, methodology, and measurement in psychology. *American Psychologist, 45,* 721-734.

American Educational Research Association, American Psychological Association, & National Council on Measurement in Education (AERA/APA/NCME). (1985). *Standards for educational and psychological testing.* Washington, DC: American Psychological Association.

American Psychological Association. (1994). *Publication manual of the American Psychological Association* (4th ed.). Washington, DC: Author.

Anastasi, A. (1988). *Psychological testing* (6th ed.). New York: MacMillan.

Brennan, R. L. (1983). *Elements of generalizability theory.* Iowa City, IA: American College Testing Program.

Campbell, K. A., Rohlman, D. S., Storzbach, D., Binder, L. M., Anger, W. K., Kovera, C. A., Davis, K. L., & Grossman, S. J. (1999). Test-retest reliability of psychological and neurobiological tests self-administered by computer. *Assessment, 6,* 21-32.

Carver, R. (1978). The case against statistical significance testing. *Harvard Educational Review, 48,* 378-399.

Carver, R. (1993). The case against statistical significance testing, revisited. *Journal of Experimental Education, 61,* 287-292. [194]

Clark, H. H. (1973). The language-as-fixed-effect fallacy: A critique of language statistics in psychological research. *Journal of Verbal Learning and Verbal Behavior, 12,* 335-359.

Crocker, L., & Algina, J. (1986). *Introduction to classical and modern test theory.* New York: Holt, Rinehart and Winston.

Cronbach, L. J., Gleser, G. C., Nanda, H., & Rajaratnum, N. (1972). *The dependability of behavioral measures: Theory of generalizability for scores and profiles.* New York: Wiley.

Crowley, S. L., & Taylor, M. J. (1994). Mothers' and fathers' perceptions of family functioning in families having children with disabilities. *Early Education and Development, 5,* 213-225.

Cunningham, G. K. (1986). *Educational and psychological measurement.* New York: Macmillan.

Ebel, R. L. (1979). *Essentials of educational measurement* (3rd ed). Englewood Cliffs, NJ: Prentice-Hall.

Feldt, L. S., & Brennan, R. L. (1989). Reliability. In R.L. Linn (Ed.), *Educational measurement* (3rd ed., pp. 105-146). Phoenix, AZ: Ornyx.

Feldt, L. S., & Qualls, A. L. (1999). Variability in reliability coefficients and the standard error of measurement from school district to district. *Applied Measurement in Education, 12,* 367-381.

Gage, N. L. (1963). Paradigms for research on teaching. In N.L. Gage (Ed.), *Handbook of research on teaching* (pp. 94-141). Chicago: Rand McNally.

Guilford, J. P., & Fruchter, B. (1978). *Fundamental statistics in psychology and education* (6th ed.). New York: McGraw-Hill.

Joint Committee on Standards for Educational Evaluation. (1994). *The program evaluation standards: How to assess evaluations of educational programs* (2nd ed.). Newbury Park, CA: Sage.

Heldref Foundation. (1997). Guidelines for contributors. *Journal of Experimental Education, 65,* 95-96.

Hills, J. R. (1981). *Measurement and evaluation in the classroom* (2nd ed.). Columbus, OH: Merrill.

Hopkins, K. D. (1998). *Educational and psychological measurement and evaluation* (8th ed.). Boston: Allyn and Bacon.

Jöreskog, K. G., & Sörbom, D. (1989). *LISREL 7: A guide to the program and applications* (2nd ed.). Chicago: SPSS.

Lincoln, Y. S., & Guba, E. G. (1985). *Naturalistic inquiry.* Beverly Hills, CA: Sage.

Linn, R. L., & Gronlund, N. E. (1995). *Measurement and assessment in teaching* (7th ed.). Englewood Cliffs, NJ: Prentice-Hall.

Lord, F. M. (1957). Do tests of the same length have the same standard error of measurement? *Educational and Psychological Measurement, 17,* 501-521.

Lord, F. M. (1959). Tests of the same length have the same standard error of measurement? *Educational and Psychological Measurement, 19,* 233-239.

Lord, F. M., & Novick, M. R. (1968). *Statistical theories of mental test scores.* Reading, MA: Addison-Wesley.

Ludbrook, J., & Dudley, H. (1998). Why permutation tests are superior to t and F tests in medical research. *The American Statistician, 52,* 127-132.

MacDonald, R. P. (1999). *Test theory: A unified treatment.* Mahwah, NJ: Erlbaum.

Mehrens, W. A., & Lehmann, I. J. (1991). *Measurement and evaluation in education and psychology* (4th ed.). Fort Worth, TX: Holt, Rinehart and Winston.

Meier, S. T., & Davis, S. R. (1990). Trends in reporting psychometric properties of scales used in counseling psychology research. *Journal of Counseling Psychology, 37,* 113-115.

Murphy, K. R. (1997). Editorial. *Journal of Applied Psychology, 82*, 3-5.

Nunnally, J. C. (1978). *Psychometric theory* (2nd ed.). New York: McGraw-Hill.

Patton, M. Q. (1975). *Alternative evaluation research paradigm.* Grand Forks: University of North Dakota Press.

Pedhazur, E. J., & Schmelkin, L. P. (1991). *Measurement, design, and analysis: An integrated approach.* Hillsdale, NJ: Erlbaum. [195]

Sawilowsky, S. S. (2000). Psychometrics vs. datametrics: Comment on Vacha-Haase's "Reliability Generalization" method and some *EPM* editorial policies. *Educational and Psychological Measurement, 60*, 157-173.

Sax, G., with Newton, J. W. (1997). *Principles of educational and psychological measurement* (4th ed.). Belmont, CA: Wadsworth.

Shaddish, W. R., Jr., Bootzin, R. R., Koller, D., & Brownell, L. (1981). Psychometric instability of measures in novel settings: Use of psychiatric rating scales in nursing homes. *Journal of Behavioral Assessment, 3*, 221-232.

Shavelson, R., & Webb, N. (1991). *Generalizability theory: A primer.* Newbury Park, CA: SAGE.

Snyder, P., & Lawson, S. (1993). Evaluating results using corrected and uncorrected effect size estimates. *Journal of Experimental Education, 613* , 334-349.

Spearman, C. E. (1904). The proof and measurement of association between two things. *American Journal of Psychology, 15*, 72-101.

Spearman, C. E. (1910). Correlation calculated from faulty data. *British Journal of Psychology, 3*, 271-295.

Stanley, J. C. (1971). Reliability. In R. L. Thorndike (Ed.), *Educational measurement* (2nd ed., pp. 356-442). Washington, DC: American Council on Education.

Swineford, F. (1959). Note on "Tests of the same length do have the same standard error of measurement". *Educational and Psychological Measurement, 19*, 241-242.

Thompson, B. (1991). Review of *Generalizability Theory: A Primer* by R. J. Shavelson & N. W. Webb. *Educational and Psychological Measurement, 51*, 1069-1075.

Thompson, B. (1992). Two and one-half decades of leadership in measurement and evaluation. *Journal of Counseling and Development, 70*, 434-438.

Thompson, B. (1994). Guidelines for authors. *Educational and Psychological Measurement, 54*, 837-847.

Thompson, B., & Snyder, P. A. (1998). Statistical significance and reliability analyses in recent *JCD* research articles. *Journal of Counseling and Development, 76*, 436-441.

Thorndike, E. L. (1904). *An introduction to the theory of mental and social measurements.* New York: Science Press.

Thorndike, R. M., Cunningham, G. K., Thorndike, R. L., & Hagen, E. P. (1991). *Measurement and evaluation in psychology and education* (5th ed.). New York: MacMillan.

Tuthill, D., & Ashton, P. (1983). Improving educational research through the development of educational paradigms. *Educational Researcher, 12*(10), 6-14.

Vacha-Haase, T. (1998). Reliability generalization: Exploring variance in measurement error affecting score reliability across studies. *Educational and Psychological Measurement, 58*, 6-20.

Vacha-Haase, T., Ness, C., Nilsson, J., & Reetz, D. (1999). Practices regarding reporting of reliability coefficients: A review of three journals. *Journal of Experimental Education, 67*, 335-341.

Webb, N., Rowley, G., & Shavelson, R. (1988). Using generalizability theory in counseling and development. *Measurement and Evaluation in Counseling and Development, 21*, 81-90.

Wilkinson, L., & APA Task Force on Statistical Inference. (1999). Statistical methods in psychology journals: Guidelines and explanations. *American Psychologist, 54*, 594-604. [reprint available through the APA Home Page: http://www.apa.org/journals/amp/amp548594.html]

Willson, V.L. (1980). Research techniques in *AERJ* articles: 1969 to 1978. *Educational Researcher, 9*(6), 5-10.

Wood, J. M., & Lilienfeld, S. O. (1999). The Rorschach Inkblot Test: A case of overstatement? *Assessment, 6*, 341-351.

Worthen, B. R., White, K. R., Fan, X., & Sudweeks, R. R. (1999). *Measurement and assessment in schools.* New York: Addison Wesley Longman.

Notes

1. The senior author is a member of the APA Task Force on Statistical Inference.

2. The senior author was the NCME representative to the Joint Committee on Standards for Educational Evaluation from 1992 to 1996.

9

Reliability: Rejoinder to Thompson and Vacha-Haase

Shlomo S. Sawilowsky
Wayne State University

[196]   *Abstract*

Thompson and Vacha-Haase (in the previous chapter) examined the statement "*the* reliability of *the test* with emphasis on the following three words: (a) the first "the," (b) "test," and (c) the second "the." I focus instead on the word *reliability*.

J. L. Payne (1975) noted that the "vocabulary of social science epistemology presents us with certain problems. We find many terms which are poorly defined" (p. 1). Indeed, "the term 'reliability' as it is generally used has gotten completely out of hand" (p. 126). In one of the first measurement textbooks, Thorndike (1919) used the term reliability without giving the reader the benefit of a definition; a half century later, both the Joint Committee of the American Psychological Association (APA), American Educational

Sawilowsky, S. S. (2000). Reliability: Rejoinder to Thompson and Vacha-Haase. *Educational and Psychological Measurement*, *60*, 196-200.

Research Association (AERA), and National Council on Measurement in Education (NCME) (Technical Recommendations, 1954) and the APA Committee on Test Standards (APA, 1966, p. 25) maintained it "is a generic term." Here, we continue the debate on its meaning and usage.

Many definitions of test reliability have been offered in the literature. Most of them are either theoretical, such as the proportion of true score variance to total variance, or descriptions of procedures of how reliability evidence is obtained. For example, the statement that reliability is the correlation of the scores on the test with the scores on the retest is a description of one process and its associated coefficient that provides evidence supporting one paradigm of test reliability. It is not a definition of what is reliability.

Otis (1922) stated that reliability is the consistency that a test measures what it *does* measure. The unfortunate appearance of the word *does* in this definition, and subsequent statements to the same effect by others (e.g., Goodenough, 1936), have led to the present situation that "most test experts [197] consider reliability to be a part of validity" (D. A. Payne, 1968, p. 121). As mentioned in my antecedent chapter [Chapter 7], validity refers to the use of the test and not the test itself; hence, by this understanding reliability (being a part of validity) also would not refer to the test itself but rather to its scores. This is the datametric perspective.

D. A. Payne (1968), among many others, demurred. He differentiated between the question of "does the test measure consistently?" (p. 121) with "does the test measure what I want it to measure?" (p. 121). He related the former to reliability and the latter to validity. This makes it clear why reliability is the "sine qua non of measurement" (J. L. Payne, 1975, p. 4), because "unless independent determinations on the same reality can be shown to yield congruent results, one cannot say that anyone thing is being measured. If a measure is reliable, then we can say that it measures some thing" (p. 14). Reliability is therefore a necessary (although insufficient) condition and precursor to validity, because without reliability, "one cannot proceed to ask whether 'it' is what was intended" to be measured because "there is no 'it'" (p. 15). Thus, test reliability is defined as "the consistency that a test measures whatever it measures" (as opposed to what it purports to measure). Evidence of consistency is made manifest by many methods: internal homogeneity; repeated measurement by retest or alternate or parallel forms; studies of equivalence, stability, or equivalence and stability; and so forth. This is the psychometric perspective.

Consider measurements with a physical scale. If three independent measures of an object yield values of 120, 770, and 18, there is no point discussing whether the scale is measuring pounds or kilograms. The values are not even similar to the same power of 10. Because there is no consistency, there is no evidence of reliability. Therefore, the question of what the scale is measuring, or the purpose for using it, is moot.

In contradistinction, suppose another scale yields values of 12.99, 13.01, and 13.00. These values are more consistent in comparison with the previous scale. The consistency via repeated measures is one type of evidence that indicates that the scale is reliable in measuring whatever it measures. Because the scale is reliable it can be certified for use in trade. Objects measured on it can be stamped with their values.

The question of validity becomes germane only on receipt of reliability evidence. Does this scale purport to measure weight in pounds or mass in kilograms? Is it intended for liquid or dry measure? If it measures dry weight in pounds, does it do so in U.S. or British units? Does it produce values according to the Avoirdupois or the Troy weight systems? Is it accurate in the valley, on the mountaintop, or on the moon? These questions relate to validity of use and require evidence external to the reliability information.

Because even the person taking a test may affect its reliability, social and behavioral science scales are not entirely analogous to the weight scale from [198] the physical sciences. Factors such as temperature, air pressure, humidity, spring tension, battery condition, and the levelness of the floor may affect the weight scale but are readily discernible and compensated. There are, however, an infinite number of disconcerting factors that may arise in measuring straightforward variables such as achievement and how much more so for complex educational and psychological constructs such as aptitude. Even those that are known cannot be easily compensated for, potentially mitigating the consistency evidence. My antecedent article gave references who observed ad hoc factors affecting consistency. There are many more than these (e.g., Thorndike, 1949, p. 73), including such subtleties as the use of the separate answer sheet as opposed to the answer in booklet format (Muller, Calhoun, & Orling, 1972). Symonds (1928) was among the first to begin cataloging the factors influencing test reliability in a systematic fashion.

If a review of a test's use in the literature revealed it was used frequently in violation of random selection, in the absence of considerations of designed experiments, or even in violation of the test manufacturer's standardized administration and scoring procedures, then it would not be surprising to find some dispersion of the reliability estimates in these studies. (See Sawilowsky, 2000, regarding the consequences of violating these conditions on research outcomes.) Nevertheless, note that none of the 22 factors enumerated by Symonds (1928) that affect reliability prompted him to abandon the position that reliability refers to the test in favor of its scores.

Four Specific Disagreements With Thompson and Vacha-Haase

First, throughout the literature, authors refer to reliability as the consistency that a test measures whatever it measures (e.g., Ary, Jacobs, & Razavieh, 1990, p. 268; Magnusson, 1966, p. 60). I disagree with the opinion of Thompson and Vacha-Haase (2000 [the previous chapter]) and their cited references on this. I do not believe that when authors referred to a test's reliability estimate (a) their proclamation constituted a sin; (b) their words were patently or perniciously false; (c) their writings were offered telegraphically, sloppily, ignorantly, or unconsciously; or (d) their statements confused doctoral students. It remains a question to the editors and the editorial boards of academic journals as to why the importance of citing a test's reliability estimate for the sample in the study, as well as from the test manual, has not been emphasized.

Second, many of Thompson and Vacha-Haase's (2000) comments are predicated on the notion of what happens "once we have entered a mind space in which tests per se are *unalterably* [italics added] reliable." It has been acknowledged throughout the literature that tests' reliability estimates are "alterable." [199]

Third, reconsider the case of Wendy and her cohorts' score of 20 via guessing on a 5-choice 100-item test. The Binomial Test demonstrates how "narrowly" repeated measures will fluctuate in obtaining either more or less than 20 correctly by guessing. Which 20 questions she and her cohorts get correct will change from administration to administration of different forms of the test, but the test will be remarkably consistent and hence reliable (.95) in producing values in a near neighborhood of 20.

The "rank ordering" of examinees whose performance is based on chance is governed by sampling error, which Thompson and Vacha-Haase (2000) exploit in their example. In terms of rank ordering, Cronbach (1949) noted that, "Tests, no matter how reliable, give inaccurate measures for pupils whose scores are near the chance level" (p. 63). Moreover, it has been publicized for half a century (Cronbach, 1949, p. 60; see also Ary et al., 1990, p. 281) that reliability coefficients pertain to the consistency of the entire test, not a particular point on its scale. Nunnally and Bernstein (1994, pp. 327-332) describe an iterative phi coefficient approach to discriminate at a cut point and the construction of an equidiscriminating test whose reliabilities are optimal at different levels of the test. Livingston's (1972) and Brennan and Kane's (1977) indices also indicate the dependability of a test at a cut point, although their intended use is for criterion-referenced tests and a more informative part of the scale than the expected score due to chance.

Fourth, I noted the importance of an (inter)nationally representative sample. This was violated in Thompson and Vacha-Haase's (2000) exposition of the Mandarin Vocabulary Test (MVT), which was applied to a group that was unlike the norm group. All of the current testing standards committees and their publications have broadened their purview beyond technical aspects of a test. Standards now cover test construction, selection, use, and even the manual and user's guides on to whom and how to administer the test. The testing professional who administered the MVT to Wendy and her cohorts should review these standards; the testing expert who administered "visually-presented progressive matrices tasks" to "blind adults" should consult the Americans with Disabilities Act of 1990 and the ethical standards of the profession. The courts certainly will.

References

American Psychological Association. (1966). *Standards for educational and psychological tests and manuals.* Washington, DC: Author.

Ary, D., Jacobs, L. C., & Razavieh, A. (1990). *Introduction to research in education* (4th ed.). Fort Worth, TX: Holt, Rinehart & Winston.

Brennan, R. L., & Kane, M. T. (1977). An index of dependability for mastery tests. *Journal of Educational Measurement, 14,* 277-289.

Cronbach, L. J. (1949). *Essentials of psychological tests.* New York: Harper & Brothers. [200]

Goodenough, F. L. (1936). A critical note on the use of the term "reliability" in mental measurement. *Journal of Educational Psychology, 2,* 173-178.

Livingston, S. A. (1972). Criterion-referenced applications of classical test theory. *Journal of Educational Measurement, 9,* 13-26.

Magnusson, D. (1966). *Test theory* (H. Mabon, Trans.). Reading, MA: Addison-Wesley.

Muller, D., Calhoun, E., & Orling, R. (1972). Test reliability as a function of answer sheet mode. *Journal of Educational Measurement, 9,* 321-324.

Nunnally, J. C., & Bernstein, I. H. (1994). *Psychometric theory* (3rd ed.). New York: McGraw-Hill.

Otis, A. S. (1922). *The Otis self-administering test of mental ability.* Yonkers-on-Hudson, NY: World Book.

Payne, D. A. (1968). *The specification and measurement of learning outcomes.* Waltham, MA: Blaisdell.

Payne, J. L. (1975). *Principles of social science measurement.* College Station, TX: Lytton.

Sawilowsky, S. S. (2000). Quasi-experimental design: The legacy of Campbell and Stanley. In B. D. Zumbo (Ed.), *Social indicators/quality of life research methods: Methodological developments and issues, Yearbook 1999.* Norwell, MA: Kluwer Academic.

Symonds, P. M. (1928). Factors influencing test reliability. *Journal of Educational Psychology, 19,* 73-87.

Technical recommendations for psychological tests and diagnostic techniques. (1954). *Psychological Bulletin, 51*, 28.

Thompson, B., & Vacha-Haase, T. (2000). Psychometrics *is* datametrics: The test *is* not reliable. *Educational and Psychological Measurement, 60*, 174-195.

Thorndike, R. L. (1919). *An introduction to the theory of mental and social measurements.* New York: Teachers College, Columbia University.

Thorndike, R. L. (1949). *Personnel selection.* New York: John Wiley.

Part III

Reliability Induction and Reporting Practices

In substantive (nonmeasurement) research, efforts to generalize intervention effects from troubled, urban adolescents to a geriatric, nonclinical sample would probably be met with serious scrutiny. Yet, in a measurement context, many researchers seem prepared to invoke prior psychometric results without any *explicit* comparison of (a) composition and (b) variability of a current sample with the sample from which prior reliability coefficients (e.g., a test manual) are being inducted.

Indeed, in a striking preponderance of studies reliability is never mentioned, even though scores are never perfect, and measurement error attenuates effect sizes and lessens power against Type II error. The three chapters in this section suggest that contemporary practices in published research as regards measurement are often incomplete, inappropriate, or both.

10

Sample Compositions and Variabilities in Published Studies Versus Those in Test Manuals

Validity of Score Reliability Inductions

Tammi Vacha-Haase
Colorado State University

Lori R. Kogan
Colorado State University

Bruce Thompson
Texas A&M University
and
Baylor College of Medicine

[509]

Abstract

As measurement specialists, we have done a disservice to both ourselves and our profession by habitually referring to "the reliability

Vacha-Haase, T., Kogan, L. R., & Thompson, B. (2000). Sample compositions and variabilities in published studies versus those in test manuals: Validity of score reliability inductions. *Educational and Psychological Measurement*, 60, 509-522.

of the test," or saying that "the test is reliable." This has created a mindset implying that reliability, once proven, is immutable. More importantly, practitioners and scholars need not know measurement theories if they may simply rely upon the reliability purportedly intrinsic within all uses of established measures. The present study investigated empirically exactly how dissimilar in both composition and variability samples inducting reliability coefficients from prior studies were from the cited prior samples from which coefficients were generalized.

The 1994 APA *Publication Manual* "encouraged" (p. 18) effect size reporting in all articles. However, a recent summary of 11 empirical studies of reporting practices in one or two post-1994 volumes of 23 journals indicated that this "encouragement" has had no or little effect (Vacha-Haase, Nilsson, Reetz, Lance, & Thompson, 2000). In part, the "encouragement" may have been so ineffective because only "encouraging" effect size reporting sends

> a self-canceling mixed-message. To present an "encouragement" in the context of strict absolute standards regarding the esoterics of author note placement, [510] pagination, and margins is to send the message, "these myriad requirements count, this encouragement doesn't." (Thompson, 1999, p. 162)

Consequently, editors at several journals now "require" effect size reporting. These journals include: *Educational and Psychological Measurement, Journal of Agricultural Education, Journal of Applied Psychology, Journal of Consulting and Clinical Psychology, Journal of Early Intervention, Journal of Experimental Education, Journal of Learning Disabilities, Language Learning*, and *The Professional Educator*. Of course, editors at additional journals are also considering the adoption of similar requirements.

The APA Task Force on Statistical Inference also went further than a mere "encouragement," suggesting "*Always* provide some effect-size estimate when reporting a *p* value" (Wilkinson & APA Task Force on Statistical Inference, 1999, p. 599, emphasis added). Later the Task Force also wrote,

> *Always* present effect sizes for primary outcomes. . . . It helps to add brief comments that place these effect sizes in a practical and theoretical context. . . . We must stress again that reporting and interpreting effect sizes in the

context of previously reported effects is *essential* to good research. (p. 599, emphasis added)

Reliability Attenuates Effects

However, the APA Task Force also noted that "Interpreting the size of observed effects requires an assessment of the reliability of the scores" (p. 596), because score unreliability attenuates effect size. And it was emphasized that:

> It is important to remember that a test is not reliable or unreliable. Reliability is a property of the scores on a test for a particular population of examinees. . . . Thus, authors should provide reliability coefficients of the scores for the data being analyzed even when the focus of their research is not psychometric. (p. 596)

Thompson and Vacha-Haase (2000) explored these issues in considerable detail; Sawilowsky (2000) offered the contrary viewpoint.

Although it is scores, not tests, that are reliable or unreliable (Thompson, 1994; Vacha-Haase, 1998), many authors continue mistakenly to refer to the "reliability of the test." As Gronlund and Linn (1990) emphasized, "Reliability refers to the *results* obtained with an evaluation instrument and not to the instrument itself. Thus it is more appropriate to speak of the reliability of 'test scores' or the 'measurement' than of the 'test' or the 'instrument'" (p. 78, emphasis in original).

Such telegraphic misspeaking may provide an efficient shorthand for communicating, but the downside is that listeners and readers may believe that we really mean tests are reliable *per se*, because they may presume that scholars would never gratuitously misspeak even in the service of a [511] communication shorthand (Thompson, 1992). Given these dynamics, it is not so surprising that less and less space is allocated for measurement training in doctoral curricula (Aiken, West, Sechrest, & Reno, with Roediger, Scarr, Kazdin, & Sherman, 1990), and that many people do not understand score reliability (Mittag & Thompson, 2000).

Factors Affecting Reliability Inductions

Within any study, reliability is influenced by the instrument utilized, but also by sample *composition* and *variability* (Dawis, 1987). Thus, it is critical to report reliability coefficients for the actual data collected. That is, analyzing the reliability of one's own data, even in substantive (i.e., non-measurement) studies, is crucial to assessing measurement error and its impacts on one's detected effects (Vacha-Haase, 1998). However, the reporting of reliability coefficients for the data in hand is often the exception rather than the norm (cf. Meier & Davis, 1990; Thompson & Snyder, 1998; Vacha-Haase, Ness, Nilsson, & Reetz, 1999).

Too many researchers erroneously assume that their scores will be as reliable as previously reported reliabilities. For example, when investigating three counseling or psychology journals published between 1990 and 1997 (i.e., *Journal of Counseling Psychology*, *Psychology and Aging*, and *Professional Psychology: Research and Practice*), Vacha-Haase et al. (1999) found that only 35.6% of articles from these journals provided reliability coefficients for the data actually analyzed in the study. Twenty-three percent mentioned reliability from previous studies, 3.8% supplied only a citation when referring to reliability, and 36.4% made no mention of reliability whatsoever.

Similarly, in her comprehensive *EPM* study Whittington (1998) found that 54% of articles using existing measures cited score reliability from a prior study, but provided insufficient information to determine whether the samples were reasonably comparable, and that 56% of the articles reporting development of a measure as part of an inquiry provided no evidence of score reliability for the new measure. In the same vein, some two decades ago Willson (1980) stated, "That reliability . . . is unreported in almost half the published research is . . . inexcusable at this late date" (p. 9).

Purpose of the Present Chapter

Citing reliability coefficients for scores collected from a prior administration of a measure is better than not even mentioning reliability. Such citations at least implicitly acknowledge that poor score reliability attenuates effect sizes, and thus must be considered even in substantive studies. However, researchers may not recognize or consider the factors that make reasonable the induction of prior reliability coefficients to a current sample. [512]

Crocker and Algina (1986) emphasized,

> Reliability is a property of the scores on a test for a particular group of examinees. Thus, potential test users need to determine whether reliability estimates reported in test manuals are based on samples similar in *composition* and *variability* to the group for whom the test will be used. (p. 144, emphasis added)

Thus, two questions arise. First, in studies inducting reliability coefficients from prior reports, such as test manuals, how many of these inductions were justified by *explicit* and *direct* comparisons of sample composition and variability with those in the prior reports? Second, in studies inducting reliability coefficients from prior reports, indeed how similar were the sample compositions and variabilities with those in the prior reports? Here these questions were addressed by examining reliability induction practices as regards two measures.

Definition of Reliability Induction

Vacha-Haase (1998) used the term, "reliability generalization (RG)," as a label for a measurement meta-analytic method characterizing (a) the typical score reliability associated with a given measure, (b) the variability in score reliability across samples and administration protocols for a given measure, and (c) which measurement protocol facets predict or explain variations in score reliability for a given measure. To avoid confusion with RG, here a different term, "reliability induction," is used to refer to the practice of *explicitly* referencing the reliability coefficients from *prior* reports as the sole warrant for presuming the score integrity of entirely *new* data. This practice is inductive, because such researchers reason from a particular set of facts to a broader conclusion.

Reliability Induction of the Bem Sex Role Inventory

Background on the BSRI

The Bem Sex Role Inventory (BSRI; Bem, 1974, 1981) is one of the most widely used instruments for research in the area of gender orientation. The BSRI, first published in 1974 (Bem, 1974), assesses masculine and feminine sex-role orientation. The BSRI's development can be traced to Constantinople (1973), who argued that stereotypically masculine and stereotypically feminine psychological traits are distinct dimensions. Persons can possess varying amounts of the two traits in any combinations, regardless of physical gender. For example, persons who are *both* masculine and feminine in their psychological outlook are termed "androgynous." [513]

Bem (1979) explained that the BSRI was "designed to assess the extent to which the culture's definitions of desirable female and male attributes are reflected in an individual's self-description" (p. 1048). The long version of the instrument consists of 60 adjectives or short phrases: 20 items that are "Masculine," 20 considered "Feminine," and 20 items that are described as being "Neutral." A short form of the Bem Sex-Role Inventory (Bem, 1981) consists of only 10 items associated with each of the "Masculine," "Feminine," and "Neutral" traits.

The BSRI illustrates the fact that scores, not tests, are reliable. Thompson (1990) noted, "Notwithstanding erroneous folkwisdom to the contrary, sometimes scores from shorter tests are more reliable than scores from longer tests" (p. 586). In fact, the 20-item short-form feminine scale of the Bem generally yields more reliable scores (r_{xx} ranging from .84 to .87) than does the 40-item feminine scale long-form (r_{xx} ranging from .75 to .78) (Bem, 1981).

The BSRI has been the focus of considerable debate (Bem, 1979; Pedhazur & Tetenbaum, 1979) and continues to stimulate research interest in both substantive and psychometric studies. In fact, so many exploratory factor analytic (EFA) studies have been conducted that Thompson (1989) developed, applied, and reported a method of EFA meta-analysis that was illustrated using previous BSRI EFA reports.

Studies Invoking Reliability Induction

Vacha-Haase (1998) identified 628 articles that included an administration of the BSRI and were published from 1984 to July, 1997. These 628 articles were divided into three separate categories:

- authors of 413 articles (65.8%) did not provide *any* information regarding score reliability for the data in hand, or score reliability from previous studies or from the manual;
- authors of 82 articles (13.1%) provided reliability coefficients from the data actually analyzed in the article, as now recommended by the APA Task Force; and
- authors of 92 articles (14.6%) presented specific reliability coefficients from either the manual (Bem, 1974, 1981) or previous studies while authors of 41 articles (6.5%) merely referenced reliability as having been previously reported elsewhere, although the specific coefficients being inducted were not presented.

The present study focused on those articles in the last category.

So that we could compare the sample (a) compositions and (b) variabilities with those in the original study from which the prior reliability coefficients were being explicitly inducted, we could only consider inductive [514] reports that presented descriptions of their own sample compositions and variabilities. A subset of 20 articles inducting prior reliability coefficients provided these necessary details. These 20 studies invoked

Table 10.1   BSRI Score Standard Deviations From the Inducted Reports

	Inducted Report	
Scale/Form	1974	1981
Masculine		
Short	—	.80
Long	.69	.68
Feminine		
Short	—	.79
Long	.56	.59

NOTE: The BSRI short form was not presented until the 1981 manual was published.

reliability inductions for a total of 164 BSRI scores. In inducting these reliability coefficients from prior reports, in no cases were these 164 inductions justified by *explicit* and *direct* comparisons of sample composition and variability with those in the prior reports.

Most of the 164 reliability inductions invoked either Bem's 1974 article ($n = 96$; 58.5%) or the 1981 BSRI manual ($n = 58$; 35.4%). Apparently, both these studies involved samples that were all Caucasian. In the first study, the breakdown of the sample by gender was .612 male, and .388 female. In the second study, the breakdown of the sample by gender was .583 male, and .417 female. Table 10.1 characterizes the score variabilities from these two previous reports from which the reliability coefficients were inducted.

Deviations From Inducted Sample Composition. Regarding *age*, both Bem (1974, 1981) studies involved only college undergraduates as participants. Of the 154 coefficients that were inducted from these two original studies, 66 (42.8%) of the coefficients also involved college student samples. However, 18 (11.7%) instances inducted reliabilities from the original college samples to adolescent or high school samples. And 70 (45.5%) instances inducted reliabilities from the original college samples to adult samples.

Deviations from the proportions (0.0 to 1.0) of sample compositions as regards *gender* and *ethnicity* were computed using as baselines whichever proportions (0.0 to 1.0) characterized the samples from which the reliability coefficients were being inducted. For example, the proportion of males in the Bem (1981) study was .583. If a study inducted the reliability for BSRI scores by citing the Bem (1981) study, the proportion of males in the study [515] (e.g., .683) was subtracted from the original study proportion of males (e.g., .583 − .683 = −.100) to create a deviation score.

Table 10.2   Deviations in Gender and Ethnicity Proportions of Samples From the BSRI Inducted Samples

| | Statistic | | | |
Composition Variable	Minimum	Maximum	Mean	SD
Gender				
Male	−.42	.61	.27	.45
Female	−.61	.42	−.27	.45
Ethnicity				
Caucasian	.00	1.00	.28	.38
African American	−1.00	.00	−.04	.15
Hispanic	−1.00	.00	−.02	.14
Asian American	−1.00	.00	−.03	.14
International	−1.00	.00	−.08	.27

If a study invoking a reliability induction exactly matched the demographic proportions (e.g., proportion males, proportion Caucasians) in the cited original study, all proportion deviations would be zero. Thus, a positive proportion deviation (e.g., .583 − .483 = .100) indicates that there was a lower proportion (e.g., .483) in the new study in comparison with the study from which reliability was inducted (e.g., .583). A negative proportion indicates that there was a higher proportion (e.g., .683) in the new study in comparison with the study from which reliability was inducted (e.g., .583). Descriptive statistics for these deviations of sample proportional makeups as regards gender and ethnicity are presented in Table 10.2.

Deviations From Inducted Sample Score Variabilities. As explained by Thompson and Vacha-Haase (2000) and others, the variability of scores itself tends to affect score reliability. Table 10.1 presented the score standard deviations for the two inducted sources. Again, deviation scores were computed using the inducted studies as baselines.

For example, as reported in Table 10.1, the *SD* of the scores in Bem (1981) for the BSRI long-form masculine scale was .80. If a study inducted the reliability coefficient on this scale from Bem (1981), and the standard deviation in the study for the long-form masculine scale was 1.70, then the deviation *SD* was computed to be −.90 (i.e., .80 − 1.70). Thus, studies with greater score variability than the *SD* in the original cited reference had negative deviation *SD*s, while studies with less score variability than that in the original cited study had positive deviation *SD*s. Table 10.3 [516] presents the deviations of the sample *standard deviations* from those reported in the inducted score reports.

Table 10.3   Deviations in the Sample BSRI Score Variabilities From the
Variabilities in the Inducted Prior Reports

	Statistic			
BSRI Scale	*Minimum*	*Maximum*	*Mean*	*SD*
Masculine	−.42	.45	−.04	.14
Feminine	−.78	.28	−.04	.16

Reliability Induction of the Rosenberg

Background on the Rosenberg

The Rosenberg Self-Esteem Instrument (RSEI; Rosenberg, 1965) was designed to measure global positive or negative attitudes toward one's self. Rosenberg (1965) explained, "An instrument was required which would enable us to rank people along side a continuum ranging from those who had very high to those who had very low self-esteem" (p. 16). Rosenberg emphasized that in the construction of the instrument he "especially attempted to select items which openly and directly dealt" (p. 17) with self-esteem.

The Rosenberg scale consists of 10 items, each answered on a 4-point Likert scale, ranging from "strongly agree" to "strongly disagree." Examples of items include "On the whole I am satisfied with myself" and "I feel I do not have much to be proud of." Positive and negative items are presently alternatively to reduce the effects of response set.

Studies Invoking Reliability Induction

Simmelink and Vacha-Haase (1999) identified all the studies ($n = 416$) appearing in the PsycINFO database between the years of 1958 and 1998 that contained the words "Rosenberg Self-Esteem Instrument/Scale." Those appearing in books ($n = 9$), foreign languages ($n = 34$), or were false hits ($n = 15$) or unable to be located ($n = 5$) were excluded.

The remaining 353 reports were classified into the following categories:

– 131 (37.1%) made *no* mention of reliability;
– 85 (24.1%) provided reliability coefficients for the data analyzed in the study; and [517]
– 137 (38.8%) explicitly inducted the reliability coefficients from previous works (Fleming & Courtney, 1984; Rosenberg, 1965; Silber & Tippett, 1965; Simons, Rosenberg, & Rosenberg, 1973).

Table 10.4   RSEI Gender and Ethnicity Proportions and Score Standard Deviations From the Inducted Reports

	Study From Which Reliability Inducted			
Variable/ Category	Fleming & Courtney (1984)	Rosenberg (1965)	Silber & Tippett (1965)	Simons et al. (1973)
Gender				
Male	.4286	.4840	.5227	.5000[a]
Female	.5714	.5160	.4773	.5000[a]
Ethnicity				
Caucasian	.8190	.9109	1.0000	.3700[a]
African American	.0603[a]	.0845		.6300
Hispanic	.0603[a]	.0003		
Asian American	.0603[a]	.0028		
Native American		.0010		
Other		.0006		
SD	—	—	1.84	—

NOTE: Only Silber and Tippett (1965) reported the SD in their study. The sample ethnicity was not reported by Rosenberg (1965) for his sample of state of New York high school students, drawn to represent census data. These proportions were derived here by consulting 1960 census data for the high school students in the state.
[a]Inferred.

Of the articles in the last category, only 34 provided the standard deviations on the Rosenberg for the sample in the study. In no cases were these inductions justified by *explicit* and *direct* comparisons of sample composition and variability with those in the prior reports.

These 34 articles involved the induction of prior reliability coefficients as regards 91 scores. Table 10.4 describes the sample compositions in the four prior studies from which most of these 91 explicit inductions of previous reliabilities were invoked.

Deviations from Inducted Sample Composition. Regarding *age*, as reported in Figure 10.1, only 11 of the 91 scores for which reliability was inducted from a previous study involved a match between sample compositions. However, 7 of these 11 instances involved induction of reliabilities reported for a sample of "disturbed" college students (Silber & Tippett, 1965) to normal college students. Thus, only 4 of 91 inductions (4.4%) involved true matches.

Deviations from the proportions of sample compositions as regards *gender* and *ethnicity* were again computed using as baselines whichever

New Sample Invoking Induction

Original Inducted Sample	adolesc.	College students	adults	elderly	other	Total Row
high school	**4** **4.4%**	23	14	6	2	49 53.8
dist college	15	7	8			30 33.0
psyc fresh	8					8 8.8
grades 3-13	4					4 4.4
Column Total	31 34.1	30 33.0	22 24.2	6 6.6	2 2.2	91 100.0

Figure 10.1   Cross-Tabulation of Original Inducted Sample Types by Sample Type in the New Samples

NOTE: The cells in which original and the inducted sample types exactly match are presented in **bold**.

Table 10.5   Deviations in Gender and Ethnicity Proportions of Samples From the RSEI Inducted Samples

| Composition Variable | Statistic | | | |
	Minimum	Maximum	Mean	SD
Gender				
Male	−.50	.52	.18	38
Female	−.52	.50	−.18	.38
Ethnicity				
Caucasian	−.55	1.00	.37	.53
African American	−.92	.62	−.06	.41
Hispanic	−1.00	.00	−.08	.27
Asian American	−.10	.00	−.01	.03

proportions characterized the samples from which the reliability coefficients were [518] being inducted. Descriptive statistics for the deviations of sample proportional makeups as regards gender and ethnicity are presented in Table 10.5.

Deviations From Inducted Sample Score Variabilities. Of the four previous studies from which previous RSEI score reliability coefficients were inducted, only Silber and Tippett (1965, p. 1046) provided the SD for the sample yielding the reliability coefficient that they reported. Thus, 61 of the 91 inducted reliabilities involved initial reports for which authors could not conceivably have judged whether the variabilities of their own data were even remotely similar to those in the original inducted reports!

For the 28 other inductions, the mean deviation the *SD*s in the studies from the *SD* in the inducted report was 1.10 (*SD* = .46). The deviations of the *SD*s from the original *SD* ranged from a minimum of −.36 to a maximum of 1.55.

Discussion

Crocker and Algina (1986) emphasized that sample composition and variability impacts score reliability. Logically, when one explicitly inducts the reliability coefficient from a prior study to a new sample, without computing score reliability for the new data, this induction turns upon the pivotal requirement that both samples are comparable as regards both *composition* and score *variability*.

The present study was undertaken to compare the compositions and variabilities of samples from which reliabilities were inducted to these same two features of the new samples. The study focused only on reports in which (a) this induction was explicitly invoked, and (b) reliability was not computed [519] for the data actually in hand. The present study examined such reports for 133 prior BSRI studies and for 137 prior RSEI studies.

The present study addressed two research questions. First, in studies inducting reliability coefficients from prior reports, such as test manuals, how many of these inductions were justified by *explicit* and *direct* comparisons of sample composition and variability with those in the prior reports? Second, in studies inducting reliability coefficients from prior reports, indeed how similar were the sample compositions and variabilities with those in the prior reports?

Conclusions

Certainly the present study is delimited by only investigating practices regarding reliability induction of scores from two measures. However, both measures have been widely used for decades. And parallel work is currently underway as regards the reliability induction of other measures.

As Vacha-Haase (1998) reported for the BSRI, and as Simmelink and Vacha-Haase (1999) reported for the RSEI, 65.8% and 37.1%, respectively, of the articles employing these measures made *no* mention of reliability. Only 13.1% and 24.1% of the reports presented reliability coefficients for the data actually being analyzed, as now recommended by the APA Task Force (Wilkinson & APA Task Force on Statistical Inference, 1999). Thus, the preponderance of the 981 reports explicitly invoked an induction of previously reported reliability coefficients, as if reliability was an immutable and unchanging characteristic of a measure *per se*.

Regarding these reports, three conclusions seem warranted by our results: [520]

1. **None** of the 270 articles explicitly invoking a reliability induction **explicitly compared** the composition and the variability of their sample with those of the prior report from which reliability was being inducted.

2. Only 54 of the 270 articles in which a prior reliability was inducted even provided enough information with which the reader might evaluate whether the induction was plausible.

3. When sufficient information was reported with which one might evaluate the induction, in many instances the induction seemed starkly implausible.

Sample Composition. Regarding *age*, for the BSRI, 57.2% of the reliability inductions generalized coefficients from studies of college undergraduates (Bem, 1974, 1981) to either younger or older non-college student samples. And, as reported in Figure 10.1, only 4.4% of the inducted reliabilities for the RSEI involved samples that were similar as regards age and sample normalcy.

The *gender* compositions in the new BSRI and RSEI samples differed by as much as 27% and 18% from those in the inducted studies, as reported in Tables 2 and 5. As regards *ethnicity*, 14 BSRI and 9 RSEI reports inducted prior reliability coefficients from U.S. Caucasian samples to samples that were exclusively non-U.S. or non-Caucasian. While 21 RSEI reports inducted prior reliability coefficients from U.S. Caucasian samples to samples that were ethnically mixed, 136 BSRI reports made this same induction.

Sample Variability. As regards sample comparability of score variance in the inducted and the new reports, differences were again quite striking. For the BSRI, as reported in Table 10.1, score standard deviations in the two original reports ranged from .56 to .80. As reported in Table 10.3, deviations in the SDs in the new versus the inducted original studies ranged from SDs that were as much as .78 lower or as much as .45 higher. For the RSEI, as noted previously, the deviation of SDs in the studies from the SD in the inducted report ranged from a minimum of $-.36$ to a maximum of $+1.55$ ($M = 1.10$; $SD = .46$).

Etiology of Bad Practice

The present study documents empirically exactly how dissimilar in both composition and variability samples inducting reliability coefficients from prior studies were from the cited prior samples from which the coefficients were inducted. The picture is certainly not pretty.

As measurement specialists, we have done a disservice to both ourselves and our profession by habitually referring to "the reliability of the test," or saying that "the test is reliable." This has created a mindset implying that reliability, once proven, is immutable. More importantly, practitioners and scholars need not know measurement theories if they may simply rely upon the reliability purportedly intrinsic within all uses of established measures. [521]

Once this mindset has been communicated, measurement training becomes less relevant for doctoral curriculum (Aiken et al., 1990; Thompson & Vacha-Haase, 2000). Misconceptions regarding reliability flourish in part because

> [a]lthough most programs in sociobehavioral sciences, especially doctoral programs, require a modicum of exposure to statistics and research design, few seem to require the same where measurement is concerned. Thus, many students get the impression that no special competencies are necessary for the development and use of measures . . . (Pedhazur & Schmelkin, 1991, pp. 2-3)

We can and should do better in formulating the implicit and explicit measurement messages we communicate to our students and our readers.

In summary, researchers should report the reliabilities of their own scores, even in non-measurement substantive studies (Wilkinson & APA Task Force on Statistical Inference, 1999). Second, citing reliability coefficients from prior studies as the basis for concluding that new scores are reliable is only modestly plausible only if the compositions and variabilities of the two samples are *explicitly* and *directly* compared. Readers should expect to see those researchers inducting the reliability coefficients from prior studies acknowledge explicitly that the induction is being made, and explicitly to defend the attempted inductions.

References

Aiken, L. S., West, S. G., Sechrest, L., Reno, R. R., with Roediger, H. L., Scarr, S., Kazdin, A. E., & Sherman, S. J. (1990). The training in statistics, methodology, and measurement in psychology. *American Psychologist, 45*, 721-734.

American Psychological Association. (1994). *Publication manual of the American Psychological Association* (4th ed.). Washington, DC: Author.

Bem, S. L. (1974). The measurement of psychological androgyny. *Journal of Consulting and Clinical psychology, 42*, 155-162.

Bem, S. L. (1979). Theory and measurement of androgyny: A reply to the Pedhazur-Tetenbaum and Locksley-Colten critiques. *Journal of Personality and Social Psychology, 37*, 1047-1054.

Bem, S. L. (1981). *Bem Sex-Role Inventory: Professional manual.* Palo Alto, CA: Consulting Psychologists Press.

Constantinople, A. (1973). Masculinity-femininity: An exception to the famous dictum. *Psychological Bulletin, 80*, 389-407.

Crocker, L., & Algina, J. (1986). *Introduction to classical and modern test theory.* New York: Holt, Rinehart and Winston.

Dawis, R. V. (1987). Scale construction. *Journal of Counseling Psychology, 34*, 481-489.

Fleming, J. S., & Courtney, B. E. (1984). The dimensionality of self esteem II: Hierarchical facet model for revised measurement scales. *Journal of Personality and Social Psychology, 46*, 404-421.

Gronlund, N. E., & Linn, R. L. (1990). *Measurement and evaluation in teaching* (6th ed.). New York: Macmillan. [522]

Meier, S. T., & Davis, S. R. (1990). Trends in reporting psychometric properties of scales used in counseling psychology research. *Journal of Counseling Psychology, 37*, 113-115.

Mittag, K. C., & Thompson, B. (2000). A national survey of AERA members' perceptions of statistical significance tests and other statistical issues. *Educational Researcher, 29*(4), 21-27.

Pedhazur, E. J., & Schmelkin, L. P. (1991). *Measurement, design, and analysis: An integrated approach.* Hillsdale, NJ: Erlbaum.

Pedhazur, E. J., & Tetenbaum, T. J. (1979). *Bem Sex-Role Inventory:* A theoretical and methodological critique. *Journal of Personality and Social Psychology, 37*, 996-1016.

Rosenberg, M. (1965). *Society and the adolescent self-image.* Princeton, NJ: Princeton University Press.

Sawilowsky, S. S. (2000). Psychometrics vs. datametrics: Comment on Vacha-Haase's "Reliability Generalization" method and some *EPM* editorial policies. *Educational and Psychological Measurement, 60*, 157-173.

Silber, E., & Tippett, J. S. (1965). Self-esteem: Clinical assessment and measurement validation. *Psychological Reports, 16*, 1017-1071.

Simmelink, S., & Vacha-Haase, T. (1999, April). *Reliability generalization with the Rosenberg Self-Esteem Instrument.* Paper presented at the annual meeting of the Rocky Mountain Psychological Association, Fort Collins, CO.

Simons, R. G., Rosenberg, F., & Rosenberg, M. (1973). Disturbance in the self image at adolescence. *American Sociological Review, 38*, 553-568.

Thompson, B. (1989). Meta-analysis of factor structure studies: A case study example with Bem's androgyny measure. *Journal of Experimental Education, 57*, 187-197.

Thompson, B. (1990). ALPHAMAX: A program that maximizes coefficient alpha by selective item deletion. *Educational and Psychological Measurement, 50*, 585-589.

Thompson, B. (1992). Two and one-half decades of leadership in measurement and evaluation. *Journal of Counseling and Development, 70*, 434-438.

Thompson, B. (1994). Guidelines for authors. *Educational and Psychological Measurement, 54*, 837-847.

Thompson, B. (1999). Journal editorial policies regarding statistical significance tests: Heat is to fire as *p* is to importance. *Educational Psychology Review, 11*, 157-169.

Thompson, B., & Snyder, P. A. (1998). Statistical significance and reliability analyses in recent *JCD* research articles. *Journal of Counseling and Development, 76*, 436-441.

Thompson, B., & Vacha-Haase, T. (2000). Psychometrics *is* datametrics: The test is not reliable. *Educational and Psychological Measurement, 60,* 174-195.

Vacha-Haase, T. (1998). Reliability generalization: Exploring variance in measurement error affecting score reliability across studies. *Educational and Psychological Measurement, 58,* 6-20.

Vacha-Haase, T., Ness, C., Nilsson, J., & Reetz, D. (1999). Practices regarding reporting of reliability coefficients: A review of three journals. *Journal of Experimental Education, 67,* 335-341.

Vacha-Haase, T., Nilsson, J. E., Reetz, D. R., Lance, T. S. & Thompson, B. (2000). Reporting practices and APA editorial policies regarding statistical significance and effect size. *Theory & Psychology, 10,* 413-425.

Whittington, D. (1998). How well do researchers report their measures? An evaluation of measurement in published educational research. *Educational and Psychological Measurement, 58,* 21-37.

Wilkinson, L., & APA Task Force on Statistical Inference. (1999). Statistical methods in psychology journals: Guidelines and explanations. *American Psychologist, 54,* 594-604. [reprint available through the APA Home Page: http://www.apa.org/journals/amp/amp548594.html]

Willson, V. L. (1980). Research techniques in *AERJ* articles: 1969 to 1978. *Educational Researcher, 9*(6), 5-10.

11

How Well Do Researchers Report Their Measures?

An Evaluation of Measurement in Published Educational Research

Dale Whittington
John Carroll University

[21]

Abstract

The present study describes how much and in what ways the authors of articles fail to include adequate information about data collection. The instrumentation reported in 220 articles from 22 randomly selected journals was coded and tabulated using a scheme based on criteria from current research textbooks that are consistent with American Educational Research Association/American Psychological Association/National Council on Measurement in Education (AERA/APA/NCME) standards. Results suggest that the quality of measurement reporting continues to be a problem. Eight of the most

Whittington, D. (1998). How well do researchers report their measures?: An evaluation of measurement in published educational research. *Educational and Psychological Measurement*, *58*, 21-37.

common reporting failures are identified. It is recommended that journal editors and referees more thoughtfully consider the quality of measurement reporting when reviewing and editing submitted articles.

The 1980s witnessed a flurry of efforts to upgrade standards regarding the development and use of measurement instruments in a variety of contexts. In the last half of the decade, joint committees representing several organizations began issuing standards. The *Standards for Educational and Psychological Testing* (American Educational Research Association/ American Psychological Association/National Council on Measurement in Education [AERA/APA/NCME], 1985) addressed a broad audience of test users and developers. Other more specialized standards came forth for new circumstances—*Guidelines for Computer-Based Tests and Interpretations* (Drummond, 1996)—and for specific groups employing measurement instruments: *Standards for Teacher Competence in Educational Assessment of Students* (American Federation of Teachers, NCME, National Education [22] Association [AFT, NCME, NEA], 1990), *The Personnel Evaluation Standards* (Joint Committee on Standards for Educational Evaluation, 1988), *Responsibilities of Users of Standardized Tests* (American Association for Counseling and Development/Association for Measurement and Evaluation in Counseling and Development [AACD/AMECD], 1989), and *The Program Evaluation Standards* (Joint Committee on Standards for Educational Evaluation, 1994).

Teachers' assessment skills and attitudes were the subject of several studies (Frary, Cross, & Weber, 1993; Plake, Impara, & Fager, 1993; Stiggins, Conklin, & Bridgeford, 1986; Stiggins, Frisbie, & Griswold, 1989). How teachers are trained and what they should learn about measurement were also studied and discussed (Airasian, 1991; Frisbie & Friedman, 1987; Gullikson & Hopkins, 1987; O'Sullivan & Chalnick, 1991; Schafer, 1991; Stiggins, 1991). Clearly there is concern regarding what educators know about assessment, how they put it into practice, and how they are prepared to perform measurement tasks.

There is some evidence that similar concern also should exist with respect to those who conduct and publish research in education and related fields. As Pedhazur and Schmelkin (1991) noted, "Measurement is the Achilles' heel of sociobehavioral research" (p. 2). [. . .] For example, Ward, Hall, and Schram (1975) reported the results of an evaluation of educational research. Members of AERA's Division D judged the qualities of 114 previously published articles with respect to 33 characteristics; 42 of these articles came from journals classified as primarily research journals. Each judge recommended acceptance or rejection of the article and substantiated his or her decision. They recommended only 39% of the articles (and 40% of the primarily educational research articles) for acceptance. The third most common shortcoming was failing the criterion, "Validity and reliability of data-gathering procedures are established." Twenty-two percent of the articles failed this criterion and were therefore recommended for rejection or acceptance with major revision.

Hall, Ward, and Comer (1988) replicated this study using 128 articles published in 1983; 43 of these articles were classified as "educational journals, primarily research." Judges recommended 58% of the articles (51% of the articles from educational research journals) for publication. The standard regarding establishment of validity and reliability of data-gathering procedures became the most frequently cited shortcoming (43% of the rejected articles). [23]

Some problems in reporting measurement characteristics of scores can be traced to researchers' believing the myth that the reliability is a property of a test, as against a given set of scores (Thompson, 1994b). As Dawis (1987) observed, "Because reliability is a function of sample as well as of instrument, it should be evaluated on a sample from the intended target population—an obvious but sometimes overlooked point" (p. 486).

A major consequence of this regrettably persistent myth is that, as Meier and Davis (1990) pointed out, any "perusal of contemporary psychology journals demonstrated that quantitative reports of scale reliability and validity estimates are often missing or incomplete" (p. 113). Of course, the same phenomenon occurs in doctoral dissertations (Thompson, 1994a).

Based on one empirical study of the *American Educational Research Journal* (AERJ), Willson (1980) reported that, "Only 37% of the *AERJ* studies explicitly reported reliability coefficients for the data analyzed" (pp. 8-9). [. . .] More recently, Meier and Davis (1990) reported that "the majority [95%, 85%, and 60%] of the scales described in the [three *Journal of Counseling Psychology*] JCP volumes [1967, 1977, and 1987] were not accompanied by reports of psychometric properties" (p. 115).

Purpose

Studies suggest that many researchers who published in education and related journals in 1971 and 1983 failed to establish the reliability and validity of their data, and that improvement with respect to this practice was not apparent over time. However, previous studies did not clarify how this failure took place. We do not know if authors failed to articulate the relationship of their study measures to their study variables, if they justi-fied the use of a particular test merely because it was "widely used in the field," or if they employed scores that had been validated with a different testing situation or population.

The primary purpose of the present study, then, was to examine how well the instrumentation of research studies is reported in research journals to describe more specifically how articles fail to include adequate informa-tion about data collection procedures. In addition, the study determined the degree to which the failure to report adequate reliability and validity information continues. In effect, this was a survey of how educational researchers report the instrumentation for original research studies in published educational research journals. This study was confined to articles in journals that are selective (acceptance rate < 20%). [24]

Procedure

Sample Selection

Ward et al. (1975) and Hall et al. (1988) employed journals that were indexed in Education Index and were also cited 10 or more times over a specified number of years in chapter bibliographies of the *Review of Educational Research*. The resulting population of journals fell into three categories: education journals with primarily research articles, education journals with primarily nonresearch articles, and journals from related professionals. The sampling procedure for the present study differed from that employed by Ward et al. and Hall et al. for three reasons. First, the purpose of the present study was to examine articles from journals report-ing primary research. Second, the relative importance of Education Index as an index of education journals has declined (Gay, 1992) to the extent that some education libraries have discontinued use of the index. Finally, consistency with the previous studies was already precluded because the populations of journals reported by Ward et al. and Hall et al. differed from each other.

Selection of articles took place using a two-stage procedure. First, a sample of journals was selected. Second, articles were selected from the journals. The source for selecting journals was *Cabell's Directory of Publishing Opportunities in Education* (Cabell, 1992). Although not as comprehen-sive as Current Index to Journals in Education (Gay, 1992), this directory offers information about several journal qualities that could be used to select journals: journal selectivity, types of articles published (i.e., research vs. reviews of research or other types of essays), and readership. *Cabell's* lists information pertaining to 447 journals including an address for manuscript submission, circulation data, review information, manuscript topics, and manuscript guidelines. All journals that were selective (20% or less acceptance rate), that included "academic" as one type of reader of the journal, and that reported interest in publishing original research studies were identified. Of the 447 journals, 74 clearly met these criteria and another 18 were identified as potentially meeting these criteria, but the manuscript guidelines were unclear regarding the publication of research studies. Review of at least two issues of each of these journals revealed that 9 of the 18 journals published at least two research articles per issue. The resulting list consisted of 83 journals. From this list, 30 were randomly selected. Of this set of 30, 22 journals were in print in 1994 and published at least five empirical studies per year: *Adolescence, American Annals of the Deaf, American Journal of Orthopsychiatry, Child Welfare, Community College Review, Early Childhood Research Quarterly, Educational Research Quarterly, Educational Technology Research and Development, Journal of Academic Librarianship, Journal of Broadcasting and Electronic Media, Journal of Business Communication,* [25] *Journal of Career Development, Journal of Creative Behavior, Journal of Educational Psychology, Journal of Research in Science Teaching, Journal of Teacher Education, Language Learning, Merrill-Palmer Quarterly, Nurse Educator, Research in Higher Education, The Urban Review,* and *The Volta Review.*

From each journal, 10 articles were selected. The goal was to select the 10 most recent research articles published as of December 30, 1994. To qualify as a research article for the present study, the article had to report original empirical research. There were, however, some exclusion criteria:

1. The study was not based on a preexisting data set, such as "High School and Beyond."

2. The study could not be a meta-analysis.

3. The study could not be exclusively qualitative research.

Criteria 1 and 2 were established because of the tendency of such articles to refer readers to other sources for information about measurement and the data-gathering process. Criterion 3 was established because the measurement process related to this emerging form of research can substantially differ from that employed in quantitative studies (Krathwohl,

1993). The resulting sample consisted of 220 articles and contained a total of 749 measures (i.e., data collection procedures).

Measurement

A coding form for assessing the reporting of measurement of each article was developed. The content of the form was based on criteria reported in several commonly used textbooks in educational research: Borg, Gall, and Gall (1993); Fraenkel and Wallen (1993); Gay (1992); and Kerlinger (1986). All of these textbooks contain sections that describe what should be included in a research report. An additional source is the guidelines from standards A5-Validity Information and A6-Reliability Information from *The Program Evaluation Standards* (Joint Committee, 1994). The criteria from each text and the guidelines from the standards were listed and cross-checked. To be included, a criterion had to appear in at least two sources. The resulting list of criteria was cross-checked against the *Standards for Educational and Psychological Testing* (AERA/APA/NCME, 1985).

The draft coding form contained a section for recording the number and types of measures employed in each article and the number and sources of the measures (i.e., published, developed by an author, employed in another study but not published). The form included a general section pertaining to description of the measures, relating each to study variables, administration contexts, and so forth. This draft form was reviewed by a faculty member from another school of education who teaches research methods and whose [26] area of expertise includes measurement. It was also piloted with a sample of 10 articles. Based on this review and the pilot, the form was revised. A copy of the final coding form is available from the author.

Coding took place over 6 months. Therefore, to enhance consistency of decision making, I maintained a coding "diary" in which I recorded all decisions related to unanticipated situations and rationales for those decisions. I also discussed those decisions with the colleague who helped develop the coding form.

To determine whether the consistency of the coding remained stable, I employed a percentage agreement procedure. I randomly selected one article from each journal and recoded it. After all articles were coded, then for each section of the coding form that required judgment about the measures, I compared how many measures fell into each category for both codings and determined the percentage of agreement of the classifications. I computed a separate percentage agreement for each section of the form. The resulting percentages of agreement ranged from a low of 89% to a

Table 11.1   How Often Each Type of Measure Appeared

Type of Measure	Number of Article	Number of Measures	Median per Article	Range per Articles
Objective measure knowledge	47	104	1	1–11
Objective test: ability/aptitude	21	33	2	1–2
Objective assessment: interests	11	25	2	1–7
Measure of interpersonal relations	25	46	1	1–12
Scale: attitudes/opinions	51	132	1	1–4
Questionnaire: facts	40	58	1	1–6
Questionnaire: attitudes/opinions	17	19	1	1–2
Questionnaire: both	22	27	1	1–4
Observation coding	30	44	1	1–4
Personality measure	31	65	2	1–7
Open-ended measure: cognition	18	35	1	1–8
Open-ended questionnaire/interview	32	39	1	1–4
Questionnaire/interview: combined item types	38	61	1	1–13
Checklist	7	9	1	1–2
Other	38	53	1	1–6
Total	220	750[a]	—	—

NOTE: [a]One measure was double counted for this table because of dual modes of administration for the deaf.

high of 98%. The faculty member who reviewed the draft coding form assessed a smaller sample ($n = 11$) of articles drawn from the sample employed to assess consistency over time. The percentages of agreement ranged from a low of 90% to a high of 95%.

Analysis of the Data

Description of Measures

All measures were coded into 1 of 15 categories, which are presented in Table 11.1. Table 11.1 reports the breakdown based on the number of articles in which each type of measure appeared and the total number of measures reported in the sample articles. Authors generally reported employing more than one type of measure. The most common type of measures included attitude or opinion scales, objective measures of knowledge or skills, personality measures, and questionnaires (or interviews) that included a combination of open-ended and closed item types. Least common were checklists, open-ended measures of cognition or related skills, questionnaires about opinions or attitudes, and objective assessments of interests.

I also coded measures based on their source: published, developed elsewhere, developed for this study, preexisting data, or other. In distinguishing whether a measure was published, I relied on the reference list. If the citation was an article, a report, or a book that was not a test manual, I assumed the measure was not a published measure. If the citation indicated that the measure came from a publisher or if a test manual was cited, I treated it as published. Adapted measures included measures from other sources that were [27] reported to be modified in any way. Preexisting data included grades, test scores, or other information that came from records or other sources but were not gathered for the purposes of the study reported in the article. Authors of the articles included in the present study more often developed their own measures for research (79% of articles; 59% of measures) rather than employing published measures or measures developed elsewhere.

Measures were also coded according to the type of data-gathering procedure employed in the study. I used four coding categories: completed by respondent, interview (or individual administration) by researcher, observation, and other. Generally, completed by respondent meant a paper-and-pencil instrument completed by respondents, but in some cases it also meant completion of some kind of measure on the computer. The one exception to this was computerized administration in which the computer was functioning in an interactive capacity, rather like an interviewer. In that case, the code "other" was used. Observation included direct observation or observation of a recorded situation. The recording could include videotape or audiotape. The great majority of measures in the present study involved having the respondent provide answers (66% of measures).

Please note that for the purposes of some of the subsequent analysis in this study, I treated published measures and measures from other sources separately from measures that were adapted or developed for the reported [28] research study. Some "other" measures, such as grades or school records, were excluded for these subsequent analyses.

Findings

Attempts to Meet Reporting Criteria

A basic set of reporting criteria was developed to cover measurement features that should appear in any article using any kind of measurement:

1. The measure should be explicitly related to study variables (for example, "Achievement was measured by scores from the California Achievement Test").

Table 11.2   Attempts at Appropriate Reporting

Information Reported	Articles (%)	Measures (%)
Related to study variables	98	95
Type of measure made clear	96	93
Reliability reported in some way	54	41
Validity reported in some way	94	79
Source of measure clear	95	91
Total (N)	220	749

2. The type of measure should be clear.

3. Reliability should be reported.

4. Evidence of validity should be reported (other than evidence cited in 1 above).

5. The source of the measure (self-developed, other source) should be clear.

The description of each measure for each article was reviewed to determine whether the author attempted to report this information. If there was evidence of an attempt, regardless of its quality, credit was given. For example, if the author(s) of the article cited the source for a published measure, or listed the traits measured by each scale in a personality measure, this was treated as an attempt at reporting validity. Table 11.2 reports the results of this analysis. A review of Table 11.2 reveals that the authors of the articles consistently made an attempt to describe the measures they employed and explicitly related them to the study variables. However, they were less consistent in their attempts to report some kind of validity evidence beyond linking measures to variable names (79% of measures) and some kind of reliability evidence (41% of measures). I carried out a supplementary analysis of these data by type of measure. The analysis revealed a consistent pattern across all types of measures. The most common problem for all types of measures was *failure to attempt to report reliability evidence*. Despite this common failing, authors rarely or almost never failed to link the measures to the study variables, and they usually reported whether the measure was self-developed or obtained from another source.

Measures From Other Sources

Two hundred six measures from other sources (i.e., published measures or measures developed for another study) from 90 articles were reviewed to determine whether they conformed to eight criteria that appear in Table 11.3. As can be seen from the table, a majority of authors cited

Table 11.3   Reporting Information About Measures From Other Sources

Information Reported	Articles (%)	Measures (%)
1. Cite the source of the measure.	86	90
2. Report reliability based on the study sample or a similar sample from another source.	36	25
3. Report the measure to be reliable based on results of another study, but the sample characteristics are unclear. The citation is provided so that it is possible to check the source.	54	54
4. Report validity based on the study sample or a similar sample from another source.	18	14
5. Report the measure to be valid based on results of another study, but the sample characteristics are unclear. The citation is provided so that it is possible to check the source.	69	67
6. Report content validity.	48	45
7. Report that the measure is used in a way that is consistent with its use elsewhere in terms of setting and population.	29	20
8. Report that the measure is used in a way that is consistent with its use in other similar research.	33	25
Total measures from other sources (N)	90	206

the source(s) of the measures they employed. They also cited evidence of reliability and validity [29] from other sources. However, rarely did an author cite reliability or validity from another source and then go on to report such evidence from his or her study sample. Indeed, it appears that most authors failed to consider the issue of sample characteristics when discussing reliability or validity results. I conducted a supplementary analysis by type of measurement. This analysis permitted me to consider evidence in light of the type of measure and its use in the study. For most measurement types, failure to report reliability and/or validity based on the same or similar samples was the most common form of missing information. Additionally, for two measurement types—objective tests of knowledge and checklists—a frequent and important omission is [30] mention of content validity (mentioned less than 5% of the time for each type of measure).

Table 11.4   Reporting Information About Measures Developed for Reported Study

Information Reported	Articles (%)	Measures (%)
1. Explain why the measure was developed (or adapted from another source).	40	13
2. Describe how the measure was developed (or adapted).	29	17
3. Report whether the measure was piloted before its final use in the study.	21	15
4. Report appropriate evidence of reliability.	44	40
5. Report appropriate evidence of validity	78	61
6. Describe the measure.	81	78
7. Provide sample items.	49	29
Total measures developed (N)	191	507

Measures Developed or Adapted for the Reported Study

Five hundred seven measures developed or adapted for studies reported in 191 articles were analyzed to determine the degree to which they conformed to seven criteria that appear in the first column of Table 11.4. Although I did not expect all stages of the development process to be reported (Criterion 2), I looked for some discussion of the measure's development—the sources used to generate items, use of experts, review process, the procedures followed. Inclusion of any of these topics would give the measure credit for that criterion. Judgment about reliability and validity was based on the nature of the measure and its use. For example, internal reliability reported for an attitude measure for which individual items, not total scores, were used would have been less salient than assessment of test-retest reliability of the item scores. Content validity was less central to a personality measure than for a measure of knowledge or skill.

Table 11.4 reports the results of this analysis. Review of this table shows that a majority of authors provided appropriate information about validity and described the measures. However, in other respects, information about the measures was limited. Seldom did an author explain why he or she developed a measure rather than employing one already developed and validated elsewhere. Little evidence was present about the development process or that these self-developed measures were ever piloted. Although close to half of the authors provided sample items, they did so for only some of the measures in their studies. [31]

Administration Context

I reviewed the description of the administration of the measure in reference to questions of potential bias, particularly if the study involved special populations: people with exceptionalities, individuals whose language or dialect differed from that employed in the development and validation of scores on study measures, populations where questions of trust or rapport might be important (i.e., young children, emotionally disturbed subjects), and groups whose experience with testing or data collection might be minimal or unsuccessful. In such cases, I looked to see if sources of error or bias were acknowledged and addressed by the author(s).

In all cases, I looked for evidence regarding context, particularly what participants were told. For example, in cases of self-report measures, I looked to see if the study was explained and for evidence of whether confidentiality was assured and the right to refuse was clearly communicated.

Of the 220 articles in the present study, 43% reported the administration context in a way that addressed issues of potential bias or error. Of the 749 measures in the study, 37% were reported in this way. I also examined this concern for each type of measurement. Failure to adequately report administration conditions surfaced as a limitation for the majority (> 50%) of studies for each type of measurement with seven exceptions: personality measures (45%), factual questionnaires (43%), attitudinal questionnaires (41%), observation coding (40%), objective measures of interests (36%), open-ended measures of cognition (33%), and other (29%).

Use of Interviewers, Administrators, and Coders

Of the 220 articles, 116 included measures that required someone trained to interview, administer a measure, conduct observations, or code. Specially qualified or trained persons were required by 257 of the 749 measures. Of this reduced sample of 116 articles, only 57 (49%) reported qualifications or training of the individuals who interviewed subjects, observed, or coded data. Based on the number of measures rather than articles, 129 measures (50% of the measures requiring trained persons) were reported with reference to training or qualifications of the individuals gathering or coding data.

Coding was defined broadly to include not only formally developed coding schemes but also summaries of open-ended responses to interviews or questionnaires. Using this definition, 103 articles that included 180 measures required coding of some kind. Less than half of the articles (45%) and approximately one third of the measures (34%) reported any kind of interrater reliability. A slightly higher percentage of the time authors reported information [32] about the development or source of their coding scheme(s) (50% of the articles/41% of the measures).

General Evaluation of the Adequacy of Measurement Reporting

Based on this analysis, I rated the adequacy of the measures reported in each article using the following categories: (a) appeared appropriate for the study, (b) probably appropriate for the study, (c) appropriateness difficult to determine, (d) may be questionable, or (e) appeared to be inappropriate.

To be deemed appropriate, the measure needed to be described, scores reported needed to be reliable and valid with no evidence of problems associated with administration, and, when applicable, trained individuals needed to be employed and interrater reliability assessed. In sum, all criteria would need to be met. A measure that is probably appropriate would be thoroughly reported but with one or two omissions of information that might be deemed less central. Measures whose appropriateness was difficult to determine generally had little information reported about them. For a measure to have questionable appropriateness, some hint of a problem may be provided. For example, an administration of a measure to very young children with no evidence that the children were prepared would be questionable. The few measures that were classified as inappropriate generally presented problems associated with validity. For example, in one case, college students in China were administered a set of personality tests; the results were assessed using Western norms. Furthermore, the authors failed to indicate which language was used to administer the measures.

The results of this analysis appear in Table 11.5. As can be inferred from a comparison of the percentage of articles in each category with the percentage of measures, authors often were more thorough or careful in their reporting of some measures in their studies than they were for others. Consequently, articles have measures that fall into more than one category. Although "probably appropriate" is the modal category for articles, a large percentage of the articles included measures whose appropriateness was difficult to [33] determine. Indeed, close to half of the measures

Table 11.5   Overall Adequacy of Measures

Category	Articles (%)	Measures (%)
Appropriate	29	15
Probably appropriate	55	36
Too little information to judge	41	36
Possibly questionable	20	10
Inappropriate	2	1
Total (N)	220	749

reported in these articles from selective journals are reported in a way that leaves the reader *not knowing* the merits of the measures or questioning their appropriateness.

Conclusion

The results of the present study suggest that previously identified problems related to validity and reliability of data-gathering procedures continue to exist in the educational research literature, at least among the more selective research journals in the field of education. Many research articles provide too little information about measures for the reader to judge their adequacy, and in at least one fifth of the articles, questionable practices are evident. The most prevalent problems included the following:

1. Failure to report *any* reliability evidence (61% of measures/46% of articles).

2. Failure to consider sample/population characteristics when reporting reliability (75% of measures from other sources/64% of articles) or validity evidence (86% of measures from other sources/82% of articles).

3. Failure to report that potential problems of bias or error were addressed when administering a measure, particularly when the study sample consisted of people who are very young, emotionally disturbed, exceptional, or culturally or linguistically distinctive or disadvantaged (63% of measures/57% of articles).

4. Failure to report evidence of content validity for checklists or objective tests of knowledge (< 5 % of articles reporting such measures from other sources).

5. Failure to report any information about the development and/or piloting of new measures (85% of measures developed or adapted for study/79% of articles including such measures).

6. Failure to describe the qualifications or training of individuals who administered measures, interviewed, observed, or coded (51% of articles involving such individuals).

7. Failure to describe the source or development of coding schemes (59% of measures involving coding or summarizing of open-ended information/ 50% of articles).

8. Failure to report evidence of interrater reliability of scores for open-ended measures or observations (66% of relevant measures/45% of articles including such measurement).

Based on this analysis, the poor practice of measurement is less evident than the failure to report sufficient information for the reader to make a judgment. Therefore, it is unclear whether researchers have improperly conducted their studies or conducted their research properly and simply failed to report what they did.

The impact of failure to report adequate information about a study's measures limits readers' ability to make reasoned judgments about results. Sometimes this limitation may seem technical, of interest only to academics. [34] For example, failure to report reliability may seem to be less of a problem when samples are large (Thorndike & Hagen, 1977), but in any study in which correlation or regression is employed, reliability information gives the reader an idea of the upper limit to which a measure can correlate with any other measure. However, many of the failures identified in the present study are associated with the heart of any measure—its validity for measuring a particular characteristic of a particular population. When this information is missing, the meanings of a study's results are jeopardized, regardless of the importance of the research question, the quality of the research design, or the sophistication of the data analysis techniques. The reader cannot tell whether the study variables were measured with accuracy, or in some cases, whether they were measured at all!

The implications of this failure are serious. Researchers build on the work of others. To the extent that the foundation of a line of studies is soft, the meaning of the body of evidence is questionable. Reviews of literature abound with discussions of inconsistent results. Is it possible that many of these inconsistencies are simply due to poor measurement? Even more serious is the impact that research has had on the practices and decisions of teachers, parents, psychologists, and policy makers. The journals in the present study are among the elite of the educational research world. They report the results of research that guide developments in such areas as early childhood, mental health, education of people with exceptionalities, and urban education. Although there are differences in the kind and degree of measurement problems from one journal to the next, all of them have problems. Yet, the studies reported in these journals inform decisions about how teachers are trained to work with children, what parents are told to expect and demand for their children, and how mental health professionals should intervene on behalf of children who are at risk.

Whether the problem is one of research conduct or reporting, it is clear that improvement in the reporting of measurement is needed in published research. First, the quality of the reviewing process needs to be considered. Based on the articles in the present study, the reviewers either did not notice that important measurement information was missing or they did not insist that their concerns be addressed. For the validity of future educational research results to be ensured, journal editors need to insist on proper reviews that consider proper reporting of measurement. This could be accomplished by considering the expertise of reviewers with respect to measurement and/or developing journal guidelines that delineate what to include with respect to measurement. Just as the APA, NCME, and AERA have had a role in establishing guidelines for those who develop and make use of tests in schools, in the personnel office, and in mental health settings, they could guide journal editors in the development of such guidelines. [35]

Another focus of concern should be the competency of those who conduct and report research. Whether the failures of the articles in the present study are due to the process of conducting or reporting research, it appears that the authors of these studies "didn't know any better." Many authors seemed to not know enough to comment on the sample-specific nature of reliability or validity evidence, to report their analysis of open-ended data with care, or to comment on factors surrounding the data-gathering process that could introduce measurement bias or error. This calls into question the measurement knowledge of these authors, as well as the expertise of reviewers.

Just as earlier authors explored the job requirements, knowledge, and training of teachers (Airasian, 1991; Stiggins, 1991; Stiggins et al., 1986) and related standards of practice to teacher preparation (Frisbie & Friedman, 1987; O'Sullivan & Chalnick, 1991; Schafer, 1991), similar issues need to be explored in the realm of educational research training and practice. The present study expanded on earlier work and confirmed that contemporary practice continues to have major limitations. Further work is needed to explore how measurement is reported in other, less selective journals, in ERIC documents, and in other nonrefereed reports. The training of researchers, particularly those with academic goals, needs to be examined as well. As a follow-up of this study, therefore, I recommend further study of the kind and quality of measurement training graduate students receive in preparation for the doctorate, particularly the future "practitioners" of educational study, those doctoral students who have academic aspirations but plan to specialize in fields other than research, statistics, or measurement—the practitioners of educational study.

In some respects, the results of the present study should come as no surprise. Those of us who read large numbers of empirical studies from a methodological perspective have known for a long time that the quality of many studies is limited. However, these limitations need to be identified in a systematic fashion before journal editors can take steps to upgrade the quality of the studies they publish and those of us in the measurement profession can begin to promote changes in the training and practice of those who conduct and report research.

References

Airasian, P. (1991). Perspectives on measurement instruction. *Educational Measurement: Issues and Practice, 10*(1), 13-16.

American Association for Counseling and Development/Association for Measurement and Evaluation in Counseling and Development (AACD/AMECD). (1989, May). Responsibilities of users of standardized tests. *Guidepost,* pp. 12, 16, 18, 27, 28.

American Educational Research Association/American Psychological Association/National Council on Measurement in Education (AERA/APA/NCME). (1985). *Standards for educational and psychological testing.* Washington, DC: American Psychological Association. [36]

American Federation of Teachers, National Council on Measurement in Education, National Education Association (AFT, NCME, NEA). (1990). Standards for teacher competence in educational assessment of students. *Educational Measurement: Issues and Practice, 9*(4), 30-32.

Borg, W. R., Gall, J .P., & Gall, M. D. (1993). *Applying educational measurement: A practical guide* (3rd ed.). White Plains, NY: Longman.

Cabell, D. W. E. (1992). *Cabell's directory of publishing opportunities in education.* Beaumont, TX: Cabell.

Dawis, R. V. (1987). Scale construction. *Journal of Counseling Psychology, 34,* 481-489.

Drummond, R. J. (1996). *Appraisal procedures for counselors and helping professionals.* Columbus, OH: Merrill.

Fraenkel, J. R., & Wallen, N. E. (1993). *How to design and evaluate research in education* (2nd ed.). New York: McGraw-Hill.

Frary, R. B., Cross, L. M., & Weber, L. J. (1993). Testing and grading practices and opinions of secondary teachers of academic subjects: Implications for instruction in measurement. *Educational Measurement: Issues and Practice, 12*(3), 23-30.

Frisbie, D. A., & Friedman, S. J. (1987). Test standards—Some implications of the measurement curriculum. *Educational Measurement: Issues and Practice, 6*(3), 17-23.

Gay, L. R. (1992). *Educational research: Competencies for analysis and application* (4th ed.). New York: Macmillan.

Gullikson, A. R., & Hopkins, K. D. (1987). The context of educational measurement instruction for preservice teachers: Professor perspectives. *Educational Measurement: Issues and Practice, 6*(3), 12-16.

Hall, B. W., Ward, A. W., & Comer, C. B. (1988). Published education research: An empirical study of its quality. *Journal of Educational Research, 81,* 182-190.

Joint Committee on Standards for Educational Evaluation. (1988). *The personnel evaluation standards.* Newbury Park, CA: Sage.

Joint Committee on Standards for Educational Evaluation. (1994). *The program evaluation standards: How to assess evaluations of educational programs* (2nd ed.). Thousand Oaks, CA: Sage.

Kerlinger, F. N. (1986). *Foundations of behavioral research* (3rd ed.). New York: Holt, Rinehart & Winston.

Krathwohl, D. R. (1993). *Methods of educational and social science research: An integrated approach.* White Plains, NY: Longman.

Meier, S. T., & Davis, S. R. (1990). Trends in reporting psychometric properties of scales used in counseling psychology research. *Journal of Counseling Psychology, 37,* 113-115.

O'Sullivan, R. G., & Chalnick, M. K. (1991). Measurement-related course work requirements for teacher certification and recertification. *Educational Measurement: Issues and Practice, 10*(1), 17-19.

Pedhazur, E. J., & Schmelkin, L. P. (1991). *Measurement, design, and analysis: An integrated approach.* Hillsdale, NJ: Lawrence Erlbaum.

Plake, B. S., Impara, J. C., & Fager, J. J. (1993). Assessment competencies of teachers: A national survey. *Educational Measurement: Issues and Practice, 12*(4), 10-12.

Schafer, W. D. (1991). Essential assessment skills in professional education of teachers. *Educational Measurement: Issues and Practice, 10*(1), 3-6.

Stiggins, R. J. (1991). Relevant classroom assessment training for teachers. *Educational Measurement: Issues and Practice, 10*(1), 7-12.

Stiggins, R. J., Conklin, N. F., & Bridgeford, N. J. (1986). Classroom assessment: A key to effective education. *Educational Measurement: Issues and Practice, 5*(2), 5-17.

Stiggins, R. J., Frisbie, D. A., & Griswold, P. A. (1989). Inside high school grading practices: Building a research agenda. *Educational Measurement: Issues and Practice, 8*(2), 5-14. [37]

Thompson, B. (1994a, April). *Common methodology mistakes in dissertations, revisited.* Paper presented at the annual meeting of the American Educational Research Association, New Orleans. (ERIC Document Reproduction Service No. ED 368 771)

Thompson, B. (1994b). Guidelines for authors. *Educational and Psychological Measurement, 54,* 837-847.

Thorndike, R. L., & Hagen, E. (1977). *Measurement and evaluation in psychology and education* (4th ed.). New York: John Wiley.

Ward, A. W., Hall, B. W., & Schram, C. F. (1975). Evaluation of published educational research: A national survey. *American Educational Research Journal, 12,* 109-128.

Willson, V. L. (1980). Research techniques in *AERJ* articles: 1969 to 1978. *Educational Researcher, 9*(6), 5-10.

12

The Degree of Congruence Between Test Standards and Test Documentation Within Journal Publications

Audrey L. Qualls
University of Iowa

Angela D. Moss
National Board of Osteopathic
Medical Examiners

[209]

Abstract

The present study examined the extent to which testing practices comply with professional guidelines regarding examination of relevant reliability and validity evidence. The focus on testing use was limited to published research investigations appearing in 1992 American Psychological Association journals. Data regarding the use of paper

Qualls, A. L., & Moss, A. D. (1996). The degree of congruence between test standards and test documentation within journal publications. *Educational and Psychological Measurement*, 56, 209-214.

and pencil tests, type of instrument, and reliability and validity
information were abstracted from each article. Reliability and validity
evidence supporting the use of a particular test for a specific contextual application was often lacking. Documentation of both of these
key psychometric properties was reported for 20% of the 2,167
instruments used. About half (49%) of instrumentation was supported with evidence of one type or the other. When reported, test
use was generally supported by internal consistency reliability and
construct validity evidence.

The use of paper and pencil testing instruments within the psychological
community appears to be both widespread and reasonably accepted.
Tests are employed as informational tools in a variety of contexts such as
educational planning, career development, clinical treatment plans, counseling interventions, and a multitude of research investigations. The acceptance and continuing use of tests must rest, at least in part, on the belief
that the information yielded through such assessments is useful. Recognizing that the actual utility of test information is situationally specific, the
potential benefits that can be gained through tests are always dependent on
the psychometric qualities of the given scores in hand as well as the professional abilities of the user. Sound use begins with a careful examination
of the instrument and its supporting [210] documentation in light of
intended use and desired inferences. Psychologists, whether acting as test
developers or users, are charged with the responsibility of ensuring sound
psychological testing practices (American Psychological Association [APA],
1992). However, the extent to which actual use mirrors professional standards is unknown and was the major focus of this investigation.

The intent of the assessment standards included in the Ethical Principles
of Psychologists is further delimited in the *Standards for Educational and
Psychological Testing*:

The appropriateness of specific test uses cannot be evaluated in the abstract
but only in the context of the larger assessment process. The principal questions to be asked in evaluating test use are whether or not the test is appropriate (valid) for its specific role in the larger assessment process and whether
or not the test user has accurately described the extent to which the score
supports any decision made or administrative action taken.

Although it is not appropriate to tell a test user that particular levels of predictive validity and reliability need to be met, it is appropriate to ask the user to ascertain that procedures result in adequately valid predictions or reliable classifications for the purposes of the testing. (American Educational Research Association [AERA]/APA/National Council on Measurement in Education [NCME], 1985, p. 41)

If psychologists employ testing tools as an informational source, it is imperative that they first examine the appropriateness and quality of the instruments in light of their contextual purpose.

The actual use of psychological instruments in day-to-day practice is difficult to determine. However, the use of tests in published research investigations, a leading force in indicating actual applications, can provide some insight regarding the degree of congruence between actual and intended test use. The extent to which actual practice mirrors professional standards is of great interest to all parties involved in the testing process: developers, users, and examinees. It is only when the strengths and weaknesses of scores from an instrument are clearly understood by both test developers and users that useful information to guide inferences can occur.

The impact of testing on current practices, courses of interventions, theoretical modeling, and future directions for research cannot be overemphasized. Test development efforts lay the necessary foundation for test quality; however, the actual merit of the testing information must be judged within the context of a specific application.

The primary purpose of the present study was to determine the extent to which testing practices comply with professional AERA/APA/NCME (1985) guidelines regarding examination—or, in the case of new instruments, documentation—of relevant reliability and validity evidence. Of course, other standards (e.g., Joint Committee on Standards for Educational Evaluation, 1988, 1994) also emphasize the importance of reliability and validity evidence. [211]

Assuming an alignment exists between developmental purpose and the intended contextual application, validity evidence and reliability evidence are by far the two most crucial elements that underlie judgments regarding the quality of scores derived from instruments. The effect of these two psychometric properties on resulting inferential decisions must be understood.

Validity can be established only with reference to a specific application. As Messick (1989) stated, "What is to be validated is not the test or observation device as such but the inferences derived from test scores" (p. 13). It is only when the test user examines pertinent supporting evidence that any level of confidence can be attached to decisions resulting, at least in part, from test score interpretations.

Psychological measurement, like measurement in any other field, is imprecise. Scores will contain a certain amount of error from one or more sources. It is the presence of error, quantified by the reliability coefficient, that results in the inconsistency of test scores. The particular source of error that is of greatest concern is dependent on the intended use of the resulting test information. Per professional standards, some responsibility for establishing reliability evidence rests with the test developer; however, test users have the responsibility of determining the relevance of this information for their intended use of instrument scores (AERA/APA/NCME, 1985).

The present study considers the following questions:

1. What percentage of researchers report supporting reliability and validity evidence for scores used in their investigations?

2. Are reliability and validity considerations reported equally for both established and new types of instruments?

Method

All articles published in 22 of the 25 APA journals for the year 1992 were examined. The *Journal of Family Psychology* and the *Journal of Experimental and Applied Psychopharmacology* were not examined due to local unavailability. Given the focus on nonoriginal works, *The Clinician's Digest* was excluded. Data regarding the use of paper and pencil tests, type of instrument (established or new), and reliability and validity information were abstracted from each article. It should be noted that measures of socioeconomic status, interviews, and observational procedures were not considered. The resulting variables of interest in the present investigation were (a) type of instrument; reliability evidence: (b) internal consistency, (c) test-retest, and/or (d) parallel forms; validity evidence: (e) construct, (f) criterion related, and/or (g) content. No attempt was made to judge the quality or the appropriateness of cited psychometric evidence.

Of the 22 journals, 8 did not include articles employing the type of paper and pencil instruments of interest in the present investigation, and as such [212] they were excluded from further analysis. The excluded journals were *Contemporary Psychology*, *Journal of Comparative Psychology*, the four *Journals of Experimental Psychology*, *Psychological Abstracts*, and *Psychological Bulletin*.

The documentation of reliability and validity evidence was determined and summarized via frequencies and percentages for each instrument employed in each article. In addition to overall percentages, the specific type of evidence reported was also noted. These overall and specific level percentages were also computed separately for each journal and type of instrument.

Results and Discussion

The full sample of 1,265 articles yielded a subset of 622 studies (49%) in which testing information contributed to the overall study's conclusions. Within these articles, a total of 2,167 instruments, an average of 3.48 per study, were used. Score reliability information was reported for 888 (41%) of these instruments. For the majority of instruments, the reported reliability evidence tended to be established within the scope of the investigation, based on data collected in the study; however, in 172 cases, external references were relied on. Validity information was offered for only 687 instruments (31.7%). External references were again offered as a singular source of evidence for 251 instruments. Surprisingly, psychometric information of either type was *lacking for 1,029 of the 2,167 instruments*. Authors considering one source of evidence were most likely to consider both.

Table 12.1 provides a general summary of information reported across the journals. As is evident by this summary, the frequency of test use and the reporting of evidence supporting use both varied by journal. Within a journal, the proportion of articles using testing information ranged from 1.7% (*American Psychologist*) to 82.6% (*Journal of Abnormal Psychology*). Documentation of either source ranged from 0% (*American Psychologist*) to 100% (*Psychological Review*). A better perspective, however, would center on journals in which test use was a more common occurrence. Journals in which at least half the articles relied on testing tools were also the ones in which proportionally the greatest amount of psychometric information was provided. Articles in the *Journal of Counseling Psychology* tended to provide the most support for testing inferences. The majority of tests used in all journals were established instruments. In almost all cases, the new instruments were questionnaire surveys.

In general, the articles that did report psychometric information relied on internal consistency reliability (90.4%) and construct validity (79.4%) evidence. Multiple support for a test's score reliability was rare (8.8%) but tended to be more frequent than was multiple support regarding validity

Table 12.1   Score Reliability and Validity Evidence

Journal	Number of Articles Using Instruments	Instrument Type		Percentage Containing Evidence	
		Established	New	Reliability	Validity
American Psychologist	2 (1.7)	0	2	0.0	0.0
Behavioral Neuroscience	3 (3.0)	11	0	54.6	0.0
Developmental Psychology	33 (28.0)	80	20	21.0	22.2
Health Psychology	42 (77.8)	79	79	38.0	24.7
Abnormal Psychology	76 (82.6)	275	32	34.5	33.6
Applied Psychology	37 (38.1)	75	48	57.7	10.6
Consulting & Clinical Psychology	64 (50.8)	218	38	45.7	37.5
Counseling Psychology	49 (79.0)	156	47	67.5	48.8
Educational Psychology	28 (47.5)	70	40	41.8	29.1
Personality & Social Psychology	141 (83.4)	239	247	38.3	22.2
Psychology & Aging	56 (75.7)	142	44	30.1	30.0
Psychological Assessment	57 (77.0)	163	10	36.4	57.2
Professional Psychology	31 (37.8)	23	24	40.4	34.0
Psychological Review	3 (7.9)	0	5	0.0	100.0
Totals	622	1,531	636	41.0	31.7

NOTE: Percentages of total 1992 articles are in parentheses in the column for Number of Articles.

(5.1%). In some instances ($n = 50$), authors inappropriately relied on inter-rater reliability information to support test score interpretations. [213]

   In terms of documenting support for the use of a test, established instruments were obviously positioned advantageously. Publishers of these instruments have the resources of multiple stakeholders on which to draw: their developers and numerous users. Given the shared responsibility for deriving and documenting evidence supporting testing inferences, it was reasonable to assume that a relatively larger body of support would be garnered for established tests. Establishment of supporting evidence for the newer instruments, typically questionnaires developed specifically for the given study, resides with the researcher. Although it would be foolish to expect either the breadth or the depth of evidence for new instruments to equal that of established tests, it was reasonable to expect *some* support for the test's most basic but essential qualities: score reliability and validity. The proportions of instruments, established and new, that were supported with score reliability information were 33.8% and 31.3%, respectively. Validity evidence was supplied for 21.9% of the established instruments and 15.7% of the new instruments.

Summary

The importance of information about score integrity is emphasized in the editorial policies of this journal, as presented in the author guidelines in the [214] December 1994 issue. Unfortunately, reliability and validity evidence supporting the use of a particular test in a given contextual application is all too often lacking. In published research, documentation of both major test qualities was provided for 20.2% (437) of the 2,167 instruments used. Almost half (49%) of the instruments were accompanied with evidence for one or the other. More often than not, the score reliability was substantiated in the absence of validity evidence being presented. Unfortunately, reliability is a necessary but not sufficient condition for validity; a consistent set of measures does not guarantee the instrument is measuring what it purports to measure. The use of established instruments, as opposed to the use of new instruments constructed for the specific investigations abstracted, tended to be supported more often with accompanying technical information.

Perhaps reliability and validity issues were neglected based on a commonly held *misconception* that these are generic features of an instrument that are applicable for all conceivable purposes and populations, as against characteristics of scores. If this is the case, compliance with professional test standards and ethical guidelines cannot be expected to occur without provisions for additional resources to better educate test users.

The extent to which lack of documentation can be equated with lack of consideration is unclear. It is quite possible that many of the researchers did in fact critically examine the psychometric information for instruments but, for whatever reasons, failed to share this in their articles. At issue is whether reliability and validity information supporting the specific contextual use of an instrument should be reported when the testing tool is not the specific focus of investigation. In conjunction with similar previous studies (cf. Dawis, 1987; Willson, 1980), the results of the present study suggest that a disconcerting number of authors are not complying with various professional standards dealing with testing.

References

American Educational Research Association, American Psychological Association, National Council on Measurement in Education, (AERA, APA, NCME). (1985). *Standards for educational and psychological testing.* Washington, DC: American Psychological Association.

American Psychological Association. (1992). Ethical principles of psychologists and code of conduct. *American Psychologist, 47,* 1597-1611.

Dawis, R. V. (1987). Scale construction. *Journal of Counseling Psychology, 34,* 481-489.

Joint Committee on Standards for Educational Evaluation. (1988). *The personnel evaluation standards: How to assess systems for evaluating educators.* Newbury Park, CA: Sage.

Joint Committee on Standards for Educational Evaluation. (1994). *The program evaluation standards: How to assess evaluations of educational programs* (2nd ed.). Thousand Oaks, CA: Sage.

Messick, S. (1989). Validity. In R. Linn (Ed.), *Educational measurement* (3rd ed., pp. 13-103). Washington, DC: American Psychological Association.

Willson, V. L. (1980). Research techniques in *AERJ* articles: 1969 to 1978. *Educational Researcher, 9*(6), 5-10.

The previous three chapters document, from different but complimentary perspectives, that measurement practices within the contemporary research literature are strikingly problematic. These practices may arise, in part, because many researchers do not sufficiently understand score reliability.

It is striking that so few researchers even mention reliability within their substantive studies. It is also striking, as illustrated in Chapter 10, that many other researchers who at least mention reliability only "induct" the reliability from prior reports, and that they do so without explicitly comparing (a) the sample *compositions* in their studies with the sample composition in the inducted report or (b) the sample score *variabilities* in their samples with the sample score variance in the inducted report. How reasonable such inductions are should be a matter of evidence and direct argument, rather than being a matter of mere presumption. Of course, reporting the reliability of one's own scores is usually (or always) what is most relevant to the interpretation of one's own effect sizes and other results!

Your Own Investigation

Go to the library and find recent issues of a journal published by the American Psychological Association, the American Counseling Association, the Council for Exceptional Children, or the *American Educational Research Journal*. Randomly select an article to examine. Exclude essays or other nonempirical reports. Determine whether the article you have randomly selected (a) reports reliability for the data being analyzed, (b) makes no mention of reliability, or (c) makes a "reliability induction" from a prior report. If the previous three chapters are any guide, the ratios of these three occurrences will be roughly 1 : 6 : 3, respectively. Keep randomly selecting articles from the journal you have selected until you locate an article making a "reliability induction."

1. Did the author(s) *explicitly* compare (a) the sample *composition* in the study with the sample composition in the inducted report and (b) the sample score *variability* in the sample with the sample score variance in the inducted report?

2. If no explicit comparisons were made to justify the induction as being reasonable, locate the original inducted report (e.g., inducted test manual, inducted prior study). How comparable were the sample compositions and variabilities in the article you identified and in the inducted report? Does the induction seem reasonable to you?

PART IV

Reliability Generalization

"Reliability Generalization" is a meta-analysis of score reliability or standard-error-of-measurement (SEM) coefficients. This extension of "validity generalization" was first elaborated in detail by Vacha-Haase's (1998) *Educational and Psychological Measurement* article, reproduced here as Chapter 13.

Also included are several subsequent "RG" studies. [The August, 2002 issue of *EPM* is a theme RG issue consisting exclusively of RG studies.] These various chapters make clear that RG is not a single, monolithic method always using fixed analyses or graphs. Indeed, RG is a generic rubric of methods only limited by the creativity and thoughtfulness of the RG researcher.

13

Reliability Generalization

Exploring Variance in Measurement
Error Affecting Score Reliability Across Studies

Tammi Vacha-Haase
Western Michigan University

[6]   *Abstract*

Because tests are not reliable, it is important to explore score reliability in virtually all studies. The present chapter proposes and illustrates a new method, reliability generalization, which can be used in a meta-analysis application similar to validity generalization. Reliability generalization characterizes: (a) the typical reliability of scores for a given test across studies, (b) the amount of variability in reliability coefficients for given measures, and (c) the sources of variability in reliability coefficients across studies. The use of reliability generalization is illustrated here by analyzing 87 reliability coefficients reported for the two scales of the Bem Sex Role Inventory (BSRI).

Vacha-Haase, T. (1998). Reliability generalization: Exploring variance in measurement error affecting score reliability across studies. *Educational and Psychological Measurement, 58*, 6-20.

It is unfortunately all too common to find authors of education and psychology journal articles describing the "reliability of the test" or stating that "the test is reliable." Such statements contribute to the endemic confusion and misunderstanding of the concept and features of score reliability.

The purpose of the present chapter is to propose an innovative method for evaluating the sources of score measurement error variances as these occur across studies. The article proposes a new method, *reliability generalization*, which can be used to characterize the mean measurement error variance across studies, and also the sources of variability of these variances across studies. The proposed method, reliability generalization, is an extension of the notable method, validity generalization, described by Schmidt and Hunter (1977) and by Hunter and Schmidt (1990). However, prior to describing the proposed method, and then illustrating the method's application, the editorial [7] policies of this journal [*EPM*] are first reviewed, so as to establish a context for the presentation of reliability generalization.

EPM Editorial Policy: Tests Are Not Reliable

The editorial policies of *EPM*, articulated in December 1994 Author Guidelines (Thompson, 1994b), and in occasional "Guidelines Editorials" (Thompson, 1995; Thompson & Daniel, 1996), emphasize that scores, *not* tests, are reliable, and explicitly proscribe the description of tests as being reliable, because tests are simply not reliable. As Thompson (1992) noted,

> This is not just an issues of sloppy speaking—the problem is that sometimes we unconsciously come to think what we say or what we hear, so that sloppy speaking does sometimes lead to a more pernicious outcome, sloppy thinking and sloppy practice. (p. 436)

[. . .]

Because "reliability is a characteristic of data" (Eason, 1991, p. 84), researchers must attend to the influence that the participants themselves have on score quality. As Thompson (1994b) explained, because total score variance is an important aspect of reliability, the type of participants involved in the study will affect scores: "the same measure, when administered to more heterogenous or more homogenous sets of subjects, will yield scores with differing reliability" (p. 839). [8]

Given the diversity of participants across studies, simple logic would dictate that authors of *every* study should provide reliability coefficients of the scores for the data being analyzed, even in non-measurement substantive inquiries. However, reporting reliability coefficients for one's own data is the exception, rather than the norm, and too few reliability estimates are provided in both journals (Meier & Davis, 1990) and doctoral dissertations (Thompson, 1994a).

For example, Meier and Davis (1990) reported, "[T]he majority (95%, 85%, and 60%) of the scales described in the [three *Journal of Counseling Psychology*] *JCP* volumes [1967, 1977, and 1987] were not accompanied by reports of psychometric properties" (p. 115). In an examination of the *American Educational Research Journal (AERJ)*, Willson (1980) reported that only 37% of *AERJ* articles explicitly provided reliability coefficients for the data analyzed in the studies. [. . .] Fortunately, some journals have better records as regards these analytic and reporting practices (cf. Thompson & Snyder, 1998).

Pedhazur and Schmelkin (1991) commented on the cause of these practice oxymorons, and pointed a finger at doctoral programs that too often do not require the rigorous study of measurement. These authors concluded, "It is, therefore, not surprising that little or no attention is given to properties of measures used in many research studies" (p. 3).

Even in substantive studies, reliability is *not* an extraneous consideration! Because measurement error attenuates the effect sizes that can be detected in a given study, the reliability of the data in hand should be considered as part of the interpretation of effect sizes. Of course, more and more journals, including this journal, require effect sizes to be reported and interpreted (Thompson, 1994b).

Meta-Analysis of Psychometric Coefficients

Hunter and Schmidt (1990) reminded readers that meta-analysis of validity coefficients began in the late 1970s, with the testing of the hypothesis of "situation specific validity." These analyses were referred to as "validity generalization" studies and were conducted to test whether the validity of scores for a given measure or set of related measures was generalizable. As Hunter and Schmidt (1990) explained, "Formulas for full artifact distribution meta-analysis were first developed in the specialized area of personnel selection research under the rubric 'validity generalization'" (p. 173).

In validity generalization inquiries (Schmidt & Hunter, 1977), studies are used as the unit of analysis, and means, standard deviations and other descriptive statistics are computed for the validity coefficients across studies. The validity coefficients across studies may also be used as the dependent variables in regression or other analyses. In these analyses, the features of the [9] studies (e.g., sample sizes, types of samples, ages of participants) that best predict the variations in the obtained validity coefficients are investigated.

It is proposed here that the same premises and methods can be applied to study score reliability. The reliability generalization method will next be illustrated with a concrete example.

Reliability Generalization Example

The BSRI

The Bem Sex Role Inventory (BSRI; Bem, 1974; 1981), one of the most widely used instruments for research in the area of gender orientation, was chosen as the instrument to present an example application of reliability generalization. The Bem Sex-Role Inventory (BSRI), first published in 1974 (Bem, 1974), assesses masculine and feminine sex-role orientation or gender identity. This popular inventory has been translated into numerous languages and utilized with various populations. The measure has been the focus of numerous measurement studies, and has also been employed in a wide range of substantive studies.

The BSRI's development can be traced to Constantinople (1973), who argued that stereotypically masculine and stereotypically feminine psychological traits are distinct dimensions. Persons can possess varying amounts of the two traits in any combinations, regardless of physical gender. For example, persons who are *both* masculine and feminine in their psychological outlook are termed "androgynous." Prior to Constantinople's seminal work, most personality measures incorporated a gender scale, but these scales posited that masculinity and femininity were bi-polar opposites on a single dimension, rather than two separate dimensions.

Bem (1979) explained that the BSRI was "designed to assess the extent to which the culture's definitions of desirable female and male attributes are reflected in an individual's self-description" (p. 1048). The long version of this self-description instrument consists of 60 adjectives or short phrases, 20 items which are "Masculine," 20 considered "Feminine," and 20 items that are described as being "Neutral." A short form of the Bem Sex-Role Inventory (Bem, 1981) consists of only 10 items associated with each of the "Masculine," "Feminine," and "Neutral" traits. In conventional use, BSRI masculine (M) and feminine (F) scores often are used to create a four-fold contingency table with four cells: (a) masculine (high M, low F); (b) feminine (high F, low M); (c) androgynous (high M, high F); and (d) undifferentiated (low M, low F).

The BSRI is an intriguing example of the fact that scores, not tests, are reliable. Thompson (1990) noted, "Notwithstanding erroneous folk-wisdom to the contrary, sometimes scores from shorter tests are more reliable than scores from longer tests" (p. 586). In fact, the 20-item short-form of the Bem generally yields more reliable scores (r_{XX} for the feminine scale ranging from [10] .84 to .87) than does the 40-item long-form (r_{XX} for the feminine scale ranging from .75 to .78) (Bem, 1981).

The BSRI has been the focus of considerable debate. For example, Pedhazur and Tetenbaum (1979) presented a stinging critique of the measure and the methods used to develop the measure. Bem (1979) responded to the criticisms and the related empirical findings.

The BSRI continues to stimulate research interest in both substantive and psychometric studies. The structure underlying responses to the Bem Sex-Role Inventory has been investigated using various analytic methods across diverse samples. Many of these studies have used exploratory factor analysis (EFA) (cf. Thompson & Melancon, 1986). In fact, so many EFA studies have been conducted that Thompson (1989) developed, applied, and reported a method of EFA meta-analysis that was illustrated using using previous BSRI EFA studies.

Sample

A search of the data base PsycINFO was conducted for articles published from 1984 to July 1997. Using the key word, "bem," all articles from 1984 to the present were identified. Of the initial 798 articles, 75 were not included in the present example as they were either not written in English or were not able to be located. An additional 95 articles were deleted from the original pool as they were "false hits," either being theoretical in nature or having been identified only due to having "bem" as an author name. A total of 628 articles included an administration of the BSRI and were included for the present study.

These 628 articles were each read and then divided into three separate categories. The first category consisted of articles reporting the collection of BSRI data but in which no mention of reliability was made; authors of these 413 (413/628 = 65.76%) articles did not provide any information regarding score reliability for the data in hand, or score reliability from previous studies or from the manual. The second category included articles that presented specific reliability coefficients from either the manual

(Bem, 1974, 1981) or previous studies ($n = 92$; $92/628 = 14.65\%$) or at least referenced reliability as having been previously reported elsewhere, although specific coefficients were not cited ($n = 41$; $41/628 = 6.53\%$). The third category included articles ($n = 82$; $82/628 = 13.06\%$) that provided reliability coefficients from the data actually analyzed in the article.

Of these 82 articles in which authors provided reliability coefficients for their own data, 57 reported the reliability coefficients in a meaningful manner. However, nine of the articles stated only ranges for reliability coefficients and seven articles provided only one reliability coefficient involving combined M and F scales (e.g., Damji & Lee, 1985; Levit, 1991; Singh & Kaur, 1985). Nine additional articles were not included in the final analysis, as [11] three utilized a child/adolescent version of the BSRI with reworded items (e.g., Jones & Dembo, 1989; Wilson, McMaster, Greenspan, Mboyi, Ncube, & Sibanda, 1990) and six used factor scores from BSRI data rather than scores produced from conventional BSRI scoring keys (e.g., Feldman, Nash, & Aschenbrenner, 1983; Turner & Turner, 1991). However, because scales labeled Instrumentality/Expressiveness and Agency/Communion are reported to be similar to M/F scales, these articles were included in the analysis.

Of the 57 articles that reported reliability coefficients for the data analyzed, authors of some articles reported more than one set of reliability coefficients, as coefficients describing the different participants included in the study were provided. For example, several articles provided reliability coefficients separately for the two genders, various ethnic backgrounds, ages of participants, or population settings (e.g., clinical vs. non-institutionalized). Consequently, a total of 87 pairs of M and F reliability coefficients from 57 studies were analyzed in the present study; these 57 studies are presented in the references with asterisks.

Method

For the 87 pairs of M and F reliability coefficients that were available for analysis in the present study, a coding system was developed. The *sample sizes* for the pairs of reliability coefficients were recorded as a continuous variable.

Other features of the studies were dummy coded. The *types of reliability* coefficients computed were coded as 1 for coefficient alpha or a Kuder-Richardson formula, or 0 for test-retest. The *referents* used in the BSRI study were coded 1 for "me" as the referent, and 0 for other referents (e.g., ratings of an ideal person). The BSRI comes in long or short forms, as mentioned previously, and some have developed slight variations on scoring keys; these were coded as *form length* using a 1 to represent long form (40 or 38 items) and a 0 for a short form (usually 20 items).

Gender of study participants was dummy coded in two ways. First, studies with both male and female participants (coded 1) were contrasted with studies (coded 0) using either all males or all females. Second, studies with all female participants (coded 1) were contrasted with studies (coded 0) using either all males or both genders. Studies were coded as regards *article type* (1 = substantive study; 0 = measurement study). Studies were also coded regarding the *language* in which the BSRI was administered (1 = English; 0 = not English).

Sample type was coded in two ways. First, studies with student participants (coded 1) were contrasted with studies (coded 0) not involving student participants. Second, studies with all college student samples (coded 1) were contrasted with studies (coded 0) involving either other student samples or [12] non-student samples. Finally, *response format* was dummy coded. The BSRI conventionally employs a seven-point Likert-type response format (coded 1), so as to maximize score variance and thus hopefully score reliability, but some authors have taken the view that this response format is too unusual or too demanding for some participants, and have used fewer responses for Likert responses (usually five; coded 0).

Results

The first task in the reliability generalization meta-analysis was to characterize both typical reliability and the variability of M and F score reliability coefficients, each expressed in squared metrics. Figure 13.1 presents box-and-whisker plots for these results. Such graphics can be very useful, though certainly other mechanisms are available for conveying related results.

Regression analyses were conducted to explore how well the coded study features predicted variations in the 87 pairs of M and F reliability coefficients. These results are reported in Table 13.1. Because standardized coefficients can almost never be the sole basis for interpreting general linear model results, and structure coefficients are usually essential for these interpretations (Thompson, 1997; Thompson & Borrello, 1986), both beta weights and structure coefficients are reported for both analyses.

However, because the BSRI has two scales, which across the 87 pairs of coefficients were only partially correlated ($r^2 = 29.59\%$), a multivariate reliability generalization analysis was also of interest in this case. Table 13.2

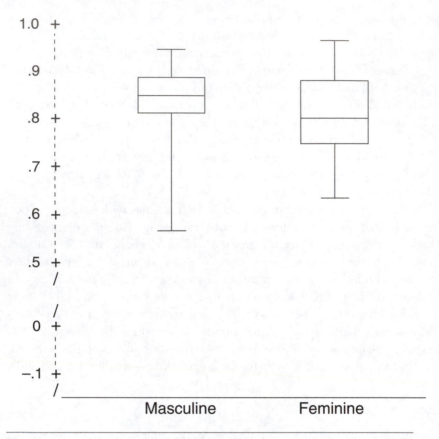

Figure 13.1   Box Plot of Reliability Coefficients Across Studies for Both the BSRI Masculine and Feminine Scales

NOTE: Although reliability coefficients are in a squared metric, and therefore theoretically should not be negative, coefficients such as alpha can indeed be negative, and even less than −1.0 (see Reinhardt [1996] for an extensive and understandable explanation).

presents results from a canonical correlation analyses (Thompson, 1984, 2000) of the data.

Discussion

Of the articles reviewed for the present study, 65.76% made *absolutely no reference* to reliability. At the other extreme, authors of only 13.06% of the articles accurately reported reliability coefficients for the data analyzed in the respective studies.

Table 13.1   Regression Coefficients for Predicting Reliability Coefficients for Both BSRI Scales

Predictor Variable	Masculine beta	r_s	Feminine beta	r_s	Mean r_s^2
Type reliability (1 = α or KR; 0 = not)	.623	.932	.335	.501	56.0%
Sample size	−.054	−.021	.317	.498	12.4%
Referent (1 = me; 0 = not me)	−.159	−.239	−.192	−.300	7.4%
BSRI form (1 = 38 − 40 items; 0 = < 38 items)	.046	.052	−.209	−.374	7.1%
Gender2 (1 = all female; 0 = not)	−.098	−.135	−.098	−.311	5.8%
Article type (1 = substantive; 0 = measurement)	.047	.310	−.150	.036	4.9%
Gender1 (1 = mixed; 0 = all males or females)	.028	.034	.055	.277	3.9%
Language (1 = English; 0 = not English)	.116	.011	.279	.260	3.4%
Sample1 (1 = student; 0 = not student)	−.100	−.084	−.245	−.211	2.6%
Response format (1 = 7 pt. Likert; 0 = not)	−.101	−.045	−.145	.119	.8%
Sample2 (1 = college student; 0 = other)	−.193	.011	−.244	.082	.3%
R^2	43.9%		34.6%		
Adjusted R^2	35.7%		25.0%		

NOTE: The bivariate r^2 between reliability coefficients for scores on the two scales across the 87 reports was 29.59%.

Good examples of reporting reliability coefficients for scores in hand included statements such as,

> During the present study, coefficient alpha was computed separately. . . . The results showed both scores to be reliable for both groups (masculinity = .8409 for Anglo-American and .7824 for African American subjects; femininity = .9239 for Anglo-American and .9343 for African American subjects). (Harris, 1996, p. 187)

Additional examples of meaningful reliability statements included, "Cronbach's α reliability score in the present study was .84 for masculinity and .78 [13] for femininity" (Erez, Borochove, & Mannheim, 1989, p. 355) and "Cronbach's alpha for masculine traits among subjects of the study was .78 for the men and .80 for the women, and for feminine traits was .73 for the women and .78 for the men" (Rubinstein, 1995, p. 577). Another author wrote, "For this sample of 44, Cronbach reliability coefficients were .80 for the feminine scale and .86 for the masculine scale" (Bledsoe, 1983, p. 712).

Table 13.2 Canonical Correlation Coefficients for Simultaneous Prediction of Both Sets of Reliability Coefficients

Variable/Statistic	Function I			Function II			
	Func.	r_s	r_s^2	Func.	r_s	r_s^2	h^2
Reliability for Masculine	1.096	.985	97.0%	−.469	.170	2.9%	100%
Reliability for Feminine	−.203	.393	15.4%	1.174	.919	84.5%	100%
Adequacy coefficient		56.2%		43.7%			
Redundancy coefficient		24.9%		14.3%			
Rc²		44.2%		32.8%			
Redundancy coefficient		4.3%		3.1%			
Adequacy coefficient		9.6%		9.5%			
Type reliability (1 = α or KR; 0 = not)	.924	.928	86.1%	.176	.099	1.0%	87%
Sample size	−.186	−.112	1.3%	.693	.611	37.3%	39%
BSRI form (1 = 38 – 40 items; 0 = <38 items)	.140	.123	1.5%	−.466	−.479	22.9%	24%
Article type (1 = substantive; 0 = measurement)	.123	.332	11.0%	−.346	−.124	1.5%	13%
Gender1 (1 = mixed; 0 = all males or females)	.029	−.013	.0%	.091	.316	10.0%	10%
Gender2 (1 = all female; 0 = not)	−.131	−.092	.8%	−.121	−.302	9.1%	10%
Referent (1 = me; 0 = not me)	−.203	−.207	4.3%	−.263	−.233	5.4%	10%
Language (1 = English; 0 = not English)	.106	−.035	.1%	.477	.308	9.5%	10%
Sample1 (1 = student; 0 = not student)	−.090	−.054	.3%	−.420	−.209	4.4%	5%
Response format (1 = 7 pt. Likert; 0 = not)	−.123	−.070	.5%	−.214	.168	2.8%	3%
Sample2 (1 = college student; 0 = other)	−.243	−.003	.0%	−.343	.093	.9%	1%

Unfortunately, reliability coefficients were also sometimes presented in a somewhat confusing manner. One confusing example presented the following representation:

> Coefficient alpha was computed separately for the masculinity and femininity scales with two normative samples of college students. Masculine scale alpha for one sample was .86 and femininity was .80. For the second sample, masculinity alpha = .86 and femininity alpha = .82. (Brouse, 1985, p. 38)

Although initially this statement appears to be [14] meaningful regarding the reliability coefficients, because no *explicit* reference was given as to from where these coefficients were derived, an assumption might be made that the author analyzed her own scores. However, when taking a closer look, it becomes clear that the study did not include college students, and the coefficients must have been derived for some other unnamed data.

To emphasize the editorial policies of this journal (Thompson, 1994b), authors are directed not to use phrases such as "the reliability of the test" or "the test is reliable." And authors should report reliability coefficients for the data being analyzed, even in substantive studies where measurement is not the primary focus. Even in these studies measurement impinges upon the substantive results, and must be considered.

Furthermore, if authors of empirical studies routinely report reliability coefficients, even in substantive studies, the field will cumulate more evidence regarding the psychometric integrity of scores. Such practices would provide more fodder for reliability generalization analyses focusing upon the differential influences of various sources of measurement error.

Figure 13.1 illustrates how important it may be to recognize that reliability does not inure to tests, but rather to scores. As the Figure indicates, reliability coefficients were fairly variable across the 87 pairs of reports. Furthermore, absent an expectation that authors will routinely report reliability coefficients for their data, one is left to wonder if a "file drawer" problem as regards such [15] [16] results might mean that reliability coefficients for the remaining 546 sets of BSRI scores were even more variable than Figure 13.1 suggests. And Figure 1 illustrates that the two scales have a differential tendency to yield reliable scores; the F scale tends to be more variable than the M scale as regards the reliability of scores.

The results illustrate that reliability generalization also sheds noteworthy light on sources of score reliability variability. For example, the results presented in Tables 13.1 and 13.2 indicate that internal consistency and test-retest coefficients seem to present considerably different pictures of score quality. Also, sample size appears to be a much better predictor of variability in score reliability for the F scale than for the M scale.

Furthermore, as both Tables 13.1 and 13.2 indicate, test form or length was more predictive of score reliability for the F scale than for the M scale (e.g., r_s for length predicting F score reliability in Table 13.1 was $-.300$). As noted previously, this reliability generalization result is consistent with the finding reported in the manual (Bem, 1981) that the *long* form of the F scale tends to yield scores with *lower* reliability than the short form of the scale.

The tabled results also indicate which study features do *not* predict variations in score reliability. Such features in the present study included the origins of the sample (e.g., students or not) and variations in the Likert-type response format.

In summary, reliability generalization may provide an important tool for characterizing score quality. Score integrity varies across administrations, and reliability generalization provides a useful tool for characterizing the variabilities in score quality, and the study features that may best predict these variations.

Of course, different analytic tools than those illustrated here might be used in reliability generalization studies. For example, reliability coefficient means across partitions of study features might be reported, along with relevant effect size indices.

Reliability generalization is a potentially powerful method with which to characterize and explore variance in score reliability. The potentials of the method are honored in the editorial policies of this journal, which now encourage the submission of manuscripts employing reliability generalization.

References

*References marked with an asterisk indicate studies included in the meta-analysis.

*Abdalla, I. A. (1995). Sex, sex-role self-concepts and career decision-making self-efficacy among Arab students. *Social Behavior & Personality, 23,* 389-401.

*Alain, M. (1987). A French version of the Bem Sex-Role Inventory. *Psychological Reports, 61,* 673-674.

*Antill, J. K. (1983). Sex role complementarity versus similarity in married couples. *Journal of Personality & Social Psychology, 45,* 145-155.

*Ballard, R. D., & Elton, M. (1992). Gender orientation and the Bem Sex Role Inventory: A psychological construct revisited, *Sex Roles, 27,* 291-306. [17]

Bem, S. L. (1974). The measurement of psychological androgyny. *Journal of Consulting and Clinical psychology, 42,* 155-162.

Bem, S. L. (1979). Theory and measurement of androgyny: A reply to the Pedhazur-Tetenbaum and Locksley-Colten critiques. *Journal of Personality and Social Psychology, 37,* 1047-1054.

Bem, S. L. (1981). *Bem Sex-Role Inventory: Professional manual.* Palo Alto, CA: Consulting Psychologists Press.

*Bledsoe, J. C. (1983). Sex differences in female teachers' approval and disapproval behaviors as related to their self-definition of sex-role type. *Psychological Reports, 53*, 711-714.

Brouse, S. H. (1985). Effect of gender role identity on patterns of feminine and self-concept scores from late pregnancy to early postpartum. *Advances in Nursing Science, 7*(3), 32-48.

*Burke, R. J. (1994). Canadian business students' attitudes towards women as managers. *Psychological Reports, 75*, 1123-1129.

*Butcher, J. E. (1989). Adolescent girls' sex role development: Relationship with sports participation, self-esteem, and age at menarche. *Sex Roles, 20*, 575-593.

*Chusmir, L. H., & Koberg, C. S. (1989). Gender identity and sex role conflict among working women and men. *Journal of Psychology, 122*, 567-575.

*Chusmir, L. H., & Koberg, C. S. (1990). Dual sex role identity and its relationship to sex role conflict. *Journal of Psychology, 124*, 545-555.

Constantinople, A. (1973). Masculinity-femininity: An exception to the famous dictum. *Psychological Bulletin, 80*, 389-407.

*Costos, D. (1986). Sex role identity in young adults: Its parental antecedents and relation to ego development. *Journal of Personality & Social Psychology, 50*, 602-611.

*Costos, D. (1990). Gender role identity from an ego developmental perspective. *Sex Roles, 22*, 723-741.

Damji, T., & Lee, C. M. (1985). Gender role identity and perceptions of Ismaili Muslim men and women. *Journal of Social Psychology, 135*, 215-223.

*Dean-Church, L. (1993). Relation of sex-role orientation to life satisfaction in a healthy elderly sample. *Journal of Social Behavior and Personality, 8*, 133-140.

Eason, S. (1991). Why generalizability theory yields better results than classical test theory: A primer with concrete examples. In B. Thompson (Ed.), *Advances in educational research: Substantive findings, methodological developments* (Vol. 1, pp. 83-98). Greenwich, CT: JAI Press.

*Erez, M., Borochov, O., & Mannheim, B. (1989). Work values of youth: Effects of sex or sex role typing? *Journal of Vocational Behavior, 34*, 350-366.

*Farmer, H. S. (1985). Model of career and achievement motivation for women and men. *Journal of Counseling Psychology, 32*, 363-390.

*Faulkender, P. J. (1987). Validity of using Bem Sex-Role Inventory norms on other samples: Analysis of a Southern sample. *Psychological Reports, 60*, 399-406.

Feldman, S. S., Nash, S. C., & Aschenbrenner, B. G. (1983). Antecedents of fathering. *Child Development, 54*, 1628-1636.

*Fischer, J. L., & Narus, L. R. (1981). Sex-role development in late adolescence and adulthood. *Sex Roles, 7*, 97-106.

*Francis, L. J., & Wilcox, C. (1996). Religion and gender orientation. *Personality & Individual Differences, 20*, 119-121.

*Gijsbers van Wijk, C. M., & Kolk, A. M. (1996). Psychometric evaluation of symptom perception related measures. *Personality and Individual Differences, 20*, 55-70.

*Goldsmith, W. M., & Ekhardt, B. N. (1984). Personality factors of men and women pastoral candidates: II. Sex-role preferences. *Journal of Psychology & Theology, 12*, 211-221. [18]

*Harris, A. C. (1996). African American and Anglo-American gender identities: An empirical study. *Journal of Black Psychology, 22*, 182-194.

Hunter, J. E., & Schmidt, F. L. (1990). *Methods of meta-analysis: Correcting error and bias in research findings.* Newbury Park, CA: Sage.

*Jones, D. C., & Costin, S. E. (1995). Friendship quality during preadolescence and adolescence: The contributions of relationship orientations, instrumentality, and expressivity. *Merrill-Palmer Quarterly, 41*, 517-535.

Jones, G. P., & Dembo, M. H. (1989). Age and sex role differences in intimate friendships during childhood and adolescence. *Merrill-Palmer Quarterly, 35*, 445-462.

*Juni, S., & Grimm, D. W. (1994). Sex roles as factors in defense mechanisms and object relations. *Journal of Genetic Psychology, 155*, 99-106.

*Kirchmeyer, C. (1993). Multicultural task groups: An account of the low contribution level of minorities. *Small Group Research, 24,* 127-148.

*Knight, K. H., Elfenbein, M. H., & Messina, J. A. (1995). A preliminary scale to measure connected and separate knowing: The Knowing Styles Inventory. *Sex Roles, 33,* 499-513.

*Kolbe, R. H., & Langefeld, C. D. (1993). Appraising gender role portrayals in TV commercials. *Sex Roles, 28,* 393-417.

*Krampen, G., Effertz, B., Jostock, U., & Muller, B. (1990). Gender differences in personality: Biological and/or psychological? *European Journal of Personality, 4,* 303-317.

*Krampen, G., Galli, I., & Nigro, G. (1992). Sex-role orientations and control orientations of Southern Italian and West German university students. *Journal of Cross-Cultural Psychology, 23,* 240-250.

*Kurdek, L. A., & Schmitt, J. P. (1986). Interaction of sex role self-concept with relationship quality and relationship beliefs in married, heterosexual cohabiting, gay, and lesbian couples. *Journal of Personality & Social Psychology, 51,* 365-370.

*Langis, J., Sabourin, S., Lussier, Y., Mathieu, M. (1994). Masculinity, femininity, and marital satisfaction: An examination of theoretical models. *Journal of Personality, 62,* 393-414.

*Lau, S. (1989). Sex role orientation and domains of self-esteem. *Sex Roles, 21,* 415-422.

*Leary, M. R., & Snell, W. E. (1988). The relationship of instrumentality and expressiveness to sexual behavior in males and females. *Sex Roles, 18,* 509-522.

Levit, D. B. (1991). Gender differences in ego defenses in adolescence: Sex roles as one way to understand the differences. *Journal of Personality and Social Psychology, -3 61,* 992-999.

*Lippa, R. (1991). Some psychometric characteristics of gender diagnosticity measures: Reliability, validity, consistency across domains, and relationship to the Big Five. *Journal of Personality & Social Psychology, 61,* 1000-1011.

*Lippa, R., & Connelly, S. (1990). Gender diagnosticity: A new Bayesian approach to gender-related individual differences. *Journal of Personality & Social Psychology, 59,* 1051-1065.

*Lobel, T. E., Gur, S., & Yerushalmi, H. (1989). Cheating behavior of sex-type and androgynous children in sex-stereotyped and non-sex-stereotyped tasks. *Journal of Research in Personality, 23,* 302-312.

*McCall, M. E., & Struthers, N. J. (1994). Sex, sex-role orientation and self-esteem as predictors of coping style. *Journal of Social Behavior and Personality, 9,* 801-810.

*McChrystal, J., & Dolan, B. (1994). Sex-role identity and separation-individuation pathology. *Counselling Psychology Quarterly, 7,* 25-34. [19]

*McCreary, D. R., & Korabik, K. (1994). Examining the relationships between the socially desirable and undesirable aspects of agency and communion. *Sex Roles, 31,* 637-651.

*Martin, H. J., & Ramanaiah, N. V. (1988). Confirmatory factor analysis of the Bem Sex-Role Inventory. *Psychological Reports, 62,* 343-350.

*Matsui, T. (1994). Mechanisms underlying sex differences in career self-efficacy expectations of university students. *Journal of Vocational Behavior, 45,* 177-184.

*Maznah, I., & Choo, P. F. (1986). The factor structure of the Bem Sex-Role Inventory (BSRI). *International Journal of Psychology, 21,* 31-41.

Meier, S. T., & Davis, S. R. (1990). Trends in reporting psychometric properties of scales used in counseling psychology research. *Journal of Counseling Psychology, 37,* 113-115.

*Nagoshi, C. T., Pitts, S. C., & Nakata, T. (1993). Intercorrelations of attitudes, personality, and sex role orientation in a college sample. *Personality & Individual Differences, 14,* 603-604.

Pedhazur, E. J., & Schmelkin, L. P. (1991). *Measurement, design, and analysis: An integrated approach.* Hillsdale, NJ: Erlbaum.

Pedhazur, E. J., & Tetenbaum, T. J. (1979). *Bem Sex-Role Inventory:* A theoretical and methodological critique. *Journal of Personality and Social Psychology, 37,* 996-1016.

*Portello, J. Y., & Long, B. C. (1994). Gender role orientation, ethical and interpersonal conflicts, and conflict handling styles of female managers. *Sex Roles, 31,* 683-701.

*Ramanaiah, N. V., & Martin, H. J. (1984). Convergent and discriminant validity of selected masculinity and femininity scales. *Sex Roles, 10,* 493-504.

Reinhardt, B. (1996). In B. Thompson (Ed.), *Advances in social science methodology* (Vol. 4, pp. 3-20). Greenwich, CT: JAI Press.

Rowley, G. L. (1976). The reliability of observational measures. *American Educational Research Journal, 13*, 51-59.

*Rubinstein, G. (1995). Right-wing authoritarianism, political affiliation, religiosity, and their relation to psychological androgyny. *Sex Roles, 33*, 569-586.

*Salminen, S. (1990). Sex role and participation in traditionally inappropriate sports. *Perceptual & Motor Skills, 71*, 1216-1218.

*Salminen, S. (1994). Sex roles and values of school children using self-esteem as a moderating factor. *Adolescence, 29*, 875-884.

Schmidt, F. L., & Hunter, J. E. (1977). Development of a general solution to the problem of validity generalization. *Journal of Applied Psychology, 62*, 529-540.

Singh, S., & Kaur, J. (1985). Motive to avoid and approach success: Two dimensions of the same motive. *Indian Journal of Clinical Psychology, 123*, 5-11.

*Smoreda, Z. (1995). Power, gender stereotypes and perceptions of heterosexual couples. *British Journal of Social Psychology, 34*, 421-435.

*Stericker, A. B., & Kurdek, L. A. (1982). Dimensions and correlates of third through eighth graders' sex-role self-concepts. *Sex Roles, 8*, 915-929.

Thompson, B. (1984). *Canonical correlation analysis: Uses and interpretation.* Thousand Oaks, CA: Sage.

Thompson, B. (1989). Meta-analysis of factor structure studies: A case study example with Bem's androgyny measure. *Journal of Experimental Education, 57*, 187-197.

Thompson, B. (1990). ALPHAMAX: A program that maximizes coefficient alpha by selective item deletion. *Educational and Psychological Measurement, 50*, 585-589.

Thompson, B. (1992). Two and one-half decades of leadership in measurement and evaluation. *Journal of Counseling and Development, 70*, 434-438.

Thompson, B. (1994a, April). *Common methodology mistakes in dissertations, revisited.* Paper presented at the annual meeting of the American Educational Research Association, New Orleans. (ERIC Document Reproduction Service No. ED 368 771)

Thompson, B. (1994b). Guidelines for authors. *Educational and Psychological Measurement, 54*, 837-847.

Thompson, B. (1995). Stepwise regression and stepwise discriminant analysis need not apply here: A guidelines editorial. *Educational and Psychological Measurement, 55*, 525-534.

Thompson, B. (1997). The importance of structure coefficients in structural equation modeling confirmatory factor analysis. *Educational and Psychological Measurement, 57*, 5-19.

Thompson, B. (2000). Canonical correlation analysis. In L. Grimm & P. Yarnold (Eds.), *Reading and understanding more multivariate statistics* (pp. 285-316). Washington, DC: American Psychological Association.

Thompson, B., & Borrello, G. M. (1985). The importance of structure coefficients in regression research. *Educational and Psychological Measurement, 45*, 203-209. [20]

Thompson, B., & Daniel, L. G. (1996). Factor analytic evidence for the construct validity of scores: An historical overview and some guidelines. *Educational and Psychological Measurement, 56*, 197-208.

Thompson, B., & Melancon, J. G. (1986). Factor structure of the Bem Sex-Role Inventory. *Measurement and Evaluation in Counseling and Development, 19*, 77-83.

Thompson, B., & Snyder, P. A. (1998). Statistical significance and reliability analyses in recent *JCD* research articles. *Journal of Counseling and Development, 76*, 436-441.

*Thompson, E. H. (1991). The maleness of violence in dating relationships: An appraisal of stereotypes. *Sex Roles, 24*, 261-278.

Turner, B. F., & Turner, C. B. (1991). Bem Sex-Role Inventory stereotypes for man and women varying in age and race among National Register psychologists. *Psychological Reports, 69*, 931-944.

*Uleman, J. S., & Weston, M. (1986). Does the BSRI inventory sex roles? *Sex Roles, 15*, 43-62.

*Walsh, A. (1993). Love styles, masculinity/femininity, physical attractiveness, and sexual behavior: A test of evolutionary theory. *Ethology & Sociobiology, 14*, 25-38.

*Weider, H.D. (1987). Differences in self-reported leadership behavior as a function of biological sex and psychological gender. *Women's Studies in Communication, 10,* 1-14.

*Williams, D. E., & D'Alessandro, J. D. (1994). A comparison of three measures of androgyny and their relationship to psychological adjustment. *Journal of Social Behavior and Personality, 9,* 469-480.

Willson, V. L. (1980). Research techniques in *AERJ* articles: 1969 to 1978. *Educational Researcher, 9*(6), 5-10.

Wilson, D., McMaster, J., Greenspan, R., Mboyi, L., Ncube, T., & Sibanda, B. (1990). Cross-cultural validation of the BEM Sex Role Inventory in Zimbabwe. *Personality Individual Differences, 11,* 651-656.

*Wilson, F. R., & Cook, E. P. (1984). Concurrent validity of four androgyny instruments. *Sex Roles, 11,* 813-837.

*Wong, F. Y., McCreary, D. R., & Duffy, K. G. (1990). A further validation of the Bem Sex Role Inventory: A multitrait-multimethod study. *Sex Roles, 22,* 249-259.

*Yanico, B. J. (1985). BSRI scores: Stability over four years for college women. *Psychology of Women Quarterly, 9,* 277-283.

*Yarnold, P. R., Bryant, F. B., & Litsas, F. (1989). Type A behaviour and psychological androgyny among Greek college students. *European Journal of Personality, 3,* 249-268.

14

Assessing the Reliability of Beck Depression Inventory Scores

Reliability Generalization Across Studies

Ping Yin
University of Iowa

Xitao Fan
Utah State University

[201]   *Abstract*

The reliability estimates for the Beck Depression Inventory (BDI) scores across studies were accumulated and summarized in a meta-analysis. Only 7.5% of the articles reviewed reported meaningful reliability estimates, indicating that the logic of "test score reliability" generally has not prevailed in clinical psychology regarding application of BDI. Analyses revealed that for BDI, the measurement error due to time sampling as captured by test-retest reliability estimate is considerably larger than the measurement error due to item heterogeneity and content sampling as captured by internal consistency

Yin, P., & Fan, X. (2000). Assessing the reliability of Beck Depression Inventory scores: Reliability Generalization across studies. *Educational and Psychological Measurement, 60*, 201-223.

reliability estimate. Also, reliability estimates involving substance addicts were consistently lower than reliability estimates involving normal subjects, possibly due to restriction of range problems. Correlation analyses revealed that standard errors of measurement (SEMs) were not correlated with reliability estimates but were substantially related to standard deviations of BDI scores, suggesting that SEMs should be considered in addition to reliability estimates when interpreting individual BDI scores.

S ince its debut more than 20 years ago (Glass, 1976, 1977), meta-analysis has experienced an exponential growth in its application in disciplines across a wide spectrum of social and behavioral sciences (Hunter & Schmidt, 1990). Although it is probably less well known, the development and application of meta-analytic approaches in psychometrics has almost paralleled that of meta-analysis itself (Schmidt & Hunter, 1977). More recently, Vacha-Haase (1998) proposed the extension of the meta-analytic validity generalization approach (Hunter & Schmidt, 1990; Schmidt & Hunter, 1977) to measurement reliability generalization for the purpose of gaining better understanding [202] about (a) what the typical score reliability is for an instrument, (b) what the salient factors are that contribute to the variability of reliability estimates across studies, and (c) what the typical measurement conditions are under which the application of an instrument tends to exhibit higher (or lower) score reliability. Because it is often unclear why considerable variability exists among the reliability estimates across studies, and because meta-analysis has often led to better understanding about a body of seemingly inconsistent literature, a meta-analytic approach appears natural for summarizing score reliability of a measurement instrument across studies with different study characteristics.

The Beck Depression Inventory (BDI) is probably the most popular measurement instrument in clinical psychology for measuring depression symptoms. Like any other measurement situation, the score reliability from a BDI application always should be a legitimate psychometric concern. Because BDI has been applied in such a variety of research and clinical situations, the reported score reliability of BDI has, not surprisingly, varied across studies. Without the meta-analytic approach for reliability generalization as proposed by Vacha-Haase (1998), it is difficult to understand how, and/or why, the score reliability of BDI varies across studies. The major objective of the present study was to use the meta-analytic reliability generalization procedure as proposed by Vacha-Haase to explore how the score reliability of BDI varies and what, if any, the identifiable factors are that contribute to the variation of score reliability of BDI. Before we proceed to describe the details of our study and the findings, we briefly review some relevant issues related to (a) the meta-analytic approach for generalization of score reliability and (b) BDI and its application in practice.

Meta-Analytic Approach to Reliability Generalization

Meta-Analysis

Meta-analysis and related techniques were borne out of a dire need to make some quantitative sense out the explosive growth in the literature of educational/psychological research in particular and of social science in general (Glass, 1977). The explosive growth in research literature makes it very difficult for a narrative literature review to adequately distill and verbally summarize what often appear to be conflicting and contradictory findings from many studies. The difficulty of relying on narrative review was illustrated by Hunter and Schmidt (1990) when they cited then-Senator Mondale's assertion that "for every study, statistical or theoretical, that contains a proposed solution or recommendation, there is always another, equally well documented, challenging the assumptions or conclusions of the first" (p. 35). [203]

More specifically, the traditional literature review for social and behavioral sciences has been described as narrative, unsystematic, and unscientific (Shaver, 1991; Wolf, 1986). This type of review has been criticized for several major potential problems: (a) selective inclusion of the studies based mainly on the reviewer's perspectives; (b) overly subjective methodologies, which often solely rely on whether the results were statistically significant; (c) failure to provide enough information about the magnitude of the statistical findings, which could lead to misleading interpretation of the findings; and (d) failure to consider study characteristics as potential factors contributing to the variability or even contradiction of study findings across different studies (Jackson, 1980; Shaver, 1991; Wolf, 1986).

Meta-analysis, as defined by Glass (1976), is "the analysis of analyses . . . , statistical studies of a large collection of analysis results from individual studies for the purpose of integrating the findings" (p. 3). Meta-analysis allows a researcher to use a systematic approach to make sense out of a large amount of seemingly inconsistent findings from many primary research studies. The application of meta-analysis usually involves the accumulation of measures of effect size, which is generally defined as "a metric of the magnitude of a result that is independent of scale of measurement and sample size" (Shaver, 1991, p. 87). Since the introduction of meta-analysis (Glass, 1976, 1977), more and more researchers have used this approach for synthesizing research literature (Jackson, 1980; Shaver, 1991; Wolf, 1986). Over the years, different variations of meta-analysis (e.g., Schmidt-Hunter meta-analysis, study effect meta-analysis, psychometric meta-analysis) and different statistical approaches and statistical models underlying meta-analysis (e.g., Hedges & Olkin, 1985; Hunter & Schmidt, 1990) have been proposed.

Measurement Reliability as a Characteristic of Measurement Outcomes

For any psychological educational measurement to have value, there must be reasonable degree of measurement reliability; otherwise, the measurement outcomes may only represent random measurement error. Conceptually, measurement reliability is the degree to which individuals' scores remain relatively consistent over repeated administrations of the same test or alternate forms of the same test. Although in true score theory, reliability coefficient is mathematically defined as the ratio of true score variance to observed score variance (Crocker & Algina, 1986), examinees' true scores, however, can never be obtained. Consequently, reliability for a set of scores can never be determined exactly; instead, it can only be estimated.

It is important to emphasize that reliability is a characteristic related to "a set of scores," not an inherent characteristic of a test or an instrument. Despite the popular and yet misleading use of "test reliability" both in the measurement [204] literature and in some less formal settings, as if reliability were an inherent characteristic of an instrument itself, many authors and researchers (e.g., Crocker & Algina, 1986, p. 144; Linn & Gronlund, 1995, p. 82; Pedhazur & Schmelkin, 1991, p. 82; Traub, 1994) have emphatically pointed out that it is the scores from a test administration, not the test itself, that we are concerned about when we discuss measurement reliability. As discussed by Worthen, White, Fan, and Sudweeks (1999), "reliability refers to the consistency of the results obtained, not to the instrument itself. It is the reliability of the test scores obtained by using a test that is the criterion for evaluating the test use" (p. 95). This point also has been articulated in the editorial policies of *Educational and Psychological Measurement* (Thompson, 1994), in which it is emphasized that the scores, not tests, are reliable. Of course, similar views have been expressed by the APA Task Force on Statistical Inference (Wilkinson & APA Task Force on Statistical Inference, 1999).

The distinction between *test reliability* and *test score reliability* should not be judged to be superficial or semantic only. If it were a test that is reliable, logically, it would be expected that the issue of reliability could be resolved once and for all at the time of test development, and there would be no need to worry about situation-specific reliability when the test is used in different situations. On the other hand, the logic of test score reliability dictates that, because total score variance is an important aspect of reliability, the characteristics of the participants involved in a measurement situation will affect the score variability and, subsequently, the measurement reliability in the situation. Furthermore, the logic of test score reliability also dictates that, because a reliability estimate describes the data collected, an estimate should *always* be reported to provide adequate description for the data used in a study. Unfortunately, some reviews of research practice have shown that this desirable practice has not generally prevailed among the reported studies (Meier & Davis, 1990; Willson, 1980), although some recent review appears to be more encouraging (Thompson & Snyder, 1998).

Reliability Estimates

To estimate test score reliability, methods that require two test administrations (alternate form and test-retest) and those that only require one test administration (split-half and internal consistency) have been developed and widely used in practice (Crocker & Algina, 1986). These different classical measurement theory approaches are designed not only for different measurement situations but also, more important, to capture different measurement error sources. Because the interval length between two test administrations contributes to measurement error, and consequently the reliability estimate, the actual interval used in test-retest reliability study is a relevant piece of information to report. [205]

Of course, a modern measurement theory, such as generalizability ("g") theory (see Shavelson & Webb, 1991; Webb, Rowley, & Shavelson, 1989), also may be employed to estimate score reliability. Estimates from this theoretical perspective have several advantages (cf. Thompson, 1991):

- Influences of several measurement error sources may be *simultaneously* estimated, which best honors a reality in which several error sources exist and jointly affect score integrity;

– the *interactions* of several measurement error influences, which are independent of the main effects of the error sources, can be estimated, again analytically honoring a reality in which multiple measurement error influences may interact; and
– the differential affects of score quality on different score applications (i.e., *relative* versus *absolute*) can be estimated.

Because a theory reliability estimates usually simultaneously consider multiple sources of error variance, unlike their true score theory counterparts that only consider a single measurement error source, a theory score reliability estimates may tend systematically to be lower than their true score theory counterparts.

Factors Affecting Reliability Estimates

Group homogeneity and test length are generally considered important factors that will affect reliability of measurement outcomes in a specific situation, even if only a single error influence is considered. Although test length is a characteristic of the instrument itself, group homogeneity with regard to the trait being measured is related to a particular participant sample in a study. The fact that group homogeneity is an important factor affecting the reliability of measurement underscores the logic discussed earlier that "reliability is a property of the scores on a test for a particular group of examinees" (Crocker & Algina, 1986, p. 144). Generally speaking, other things being equal, measurement reliability would be higher for a group that is heterogeneous with regard to the trait being measured than for another group that is more homogeneous.

Standard Error of Measurement (SEM)

A reliability estimate is a group statistic and, as already noted, is strongly influenced by the degree of heterogeneity of the group of examinees involved in a study. If we are interested in the interpretation of *3 individual* scores, then reliability coefficients are less directly useful than SEM. SEM relates both the group variability and measurement reliability to the accuracy of the individuals' scores and quantifies the amount of measurement error surrounding [206] an observed individual score. A larger SEM indicates that there is more measurement error around an observed individual score. SEM is defined as $SEM = SD_X \sqrt{1 - r_{tt}}$, and it can be interpreted as "the standard deviation of the discrepancies between a typical examinee's true score and the observed scores" over repeated testings (Crocker & Algina, 1986, p. 150). Because SEM is related to *both* the

Table 14.1   Reliability Coefficients and Standard Errors of Measurement (SEMs) for Two Pairs of Hypothetical Studies

	Studies in Pair 1		Studies in Pair 2	
Variance	A	B	A	B
True score	10	30	18	30
Error score	5	5	3	5
Observed score	15	35	21	35
Reliability	.667	.857	.857	.857
SEM	2.23	2.23	1.73	2.24

NOTE: The table is modeled on portions of a table presented by Crocker and Algina (1986, p. 144).

group variability and the reliability estimate, a lower reliability estimate does not necessarily mean the corresponding SEM will be larger, as shown in a hypothetical example in Table 14.1.

The hypothetical example in Table 14.1 shows that although Group 2 scores had a higher reliability coefficient than Group 1, its corresponding SEM is *not* smaller than that of Group 1 because of its large group variability. For this reason, the *Standards for Educational and Psychological Testing* (American Educational Research Association, American Psychological Association, and National Council on Measurement in Education [AERA/APA/NCME], 1985) emphasizes that SEM should be reported to accompany reliability estimates when appropriate.

Meta-Analytic Approach for Reliability Generalization

The development of *validity generalization* almost paralleled that of meta-analysis itself (Schmidt & Hunter, 1977). In validity generalization, the variance of the observed validity coefficients is tested against the hypothesis that they are due to different statistical artifacts, such as sampling error, differences in reliability of measurements for dependent and independent variables, range restriction, and other random errors (Hunter & Schmidt, 1990). As proposed by Hunter and Schmidt (1990), in a typical validity generalization study, validity coefficients across studies are used as the dependent variable, the characteristics of the studies are used as independent variables in an analysis within the framework of general linear model, and the variance that each factor accounts for the dependent variable is obtained and investigated (Schmidt & Hunter, 1977).

Vacha-Haase (1998) proposed the meta-analytic *reliability generalization* approach. This approach states that measurement reliability of scores on an instrument is at least partially sample dependent, potentially affected by a host of sample characteristics. To have a better understanding of the measurement reliability of an instrument's scores across various applications, a meta-analytic approach similar to validity generalization is needed. In a typical reliability generalization study, the reliability estimates across different studies for an instrument (e.g., the Bem Sex Role Inventory) are used as the dependent variable, the study characteristics (e.g., sample sizes, types of samples, ages of samples, response format, long versus short form) are used as independent variables within the framework of general linear model, and [207] the sources and amount of variation in the reliability coefficients associated with by those factors are assessed (Vacha-Haase, 1998).

The BDI

The BDI is one of the most widely used measures for depression. The BDI was selected for this reliability generalization study because it has been applied in such a variety of research or clinical situations, and not surprisingly, the reported score reliability for the BDI has consequently varied considerably. Without the benefits of the meta-analytic reliability generalization approach, it would be difficult to understand how and/or why the score reability of BDI varies across studies.

The BDI was first published in 1961 (Beck, Ward, Mendelson, Mock, & Erbaugh, 1961) to assess cognitive, behavioral, affective, and somatic components of depression. For each of the 21 items on BDI, a respondent selects from among four alternative responses that reflect increasing levels of severity of depressive symptomatology. Responses on each item ranges from (e.g., *I do not feel like a failure*) to 3 (e.g., *feel I am a complete failure as a person*). Possible scores range from O to 63, and the total score represents the severity of the depression symptoms. However, there is some ambiguity the literature about the cut-score ranges used in clinical categorization of normal, mildly depressed, moderately depressed, and severely depressed (e.g., Bumberry, Oliver, & McClure, 1978; Gallagher, 1986).

Forms

For the original BDI, administration involved a trained interviewer clinical psychologist who read each statement in the inventory and asked the respondent to select the statement that best fit "the way you feel today, that is, right now!" (Beck, 1967). However, the 1978 version of the BDI was [208] modified to be a self-administered questionnaire, and each respondent is asked to describe "how you have been feeling for the past week including today." The 1978 version of the BDI is used mostly in applied clinical situations, and the BDI is generally considered to be an adequate measure of depression that often does not require a clinical psychiatric interview (Beck & Steer, 1984; Watkins & Kligman, 1989; Zimmerman, 1986).

There are some derivatives from the 21-item BDI. Beck and Beck (1972) presented a 13-item short form of the BDI (BDI-SF) for screening medical patients for depression. This short form also has been used extensively (Beck & Beck, 1972; Foelker, Shewchuk, & Niederehe, 1987; Gould, 1982; Leahy, 1992; Reynolds & Gould, 1981; Scogin, Beutler, Corbishley, & Hamblin, 1988; Vredenburg, Krames, & Flett, 1985). Another form of the BDI is the Beck Depression Inventory for Primary Care (BDI-PC), a 7-item self-report instrument. This form was designed to differentiate medical inpatients with or without major depression disorders (Beck, Guth, Steer, & Ball, 1997).

Language

The BDI (both the 21-item standard form and the 13-item short form) has been translated into many other languages. For instance, there have been research studies that reported the use of the Dutch version of the BDI (Bosscher, Koning, & Van Meurs, 1986; Schotte, Maes, Cluydts, De Doncker, & Cosyns, 1997), the Chinese version of the BDI (Chan, 1991; Lee, 1996; Shek, 1990), the French version of the BDI (Baron & Joly, 1988; Baron & Perron, 1986; Byrne, Baron, & Campbell, 1992), and the Persian version of the BDI (Hajat & Shapurian, 1986).

Samples With Different Characteristics

Although the BDI was originally designed for clinical use, in practice, the BDI and its derivatives have been used widely in a variety of different populations over the years (Barrera & Garrison-Jones, 1988; Hatzenbuehler, Parpal, & Mattews, 1983). A quick glimpse of the literature indicates that the populations for which BDI has been used have been diverse, including, but not limited to, the general adult population (Baumgart & Oliver, 1981; Beck, 1967), the older adult population (Foelker et al., 1987; Gallagher, Nies, & Thompson, 1982), the adolescent population (Hankin, Roberts, & Gotlib, 1997), patients with cardiac diseases (Campbell, Burgess, & Finch, 1984), the deaf population (Leigh, Robins, & Welkowitz, 1988), patients with idiopathic Parkinson's disease (Elevin, Llabre, & Weiner, 1988), unselected college students (Catanzaro, 1993; Dobson & Breiter, 1983; Gould, 1982), the mildly depressed population (Golin & Hartz, 1979), and patients with clinically diagnosed psychological disorders (Cox, Swinson, Kuch, & Reichman, [209] 1993; Johnson, Crofton, & Feinstein, 1996; Steer, Beck, Brown, & Beck, 1993).

As discussed previously, the dependence of reliability on the observed score variance and sample characteristics may cause the reliability of scores in an application to deviate considerably from those reported in the original validation studies (e.g., those reported in the manual). It is important that the reliability estimate in an application be reported in *both* methodological and substantive studies (Vacha-Haase, 1998). But for studies involving BDI, authors have very commonly simply mentioned that the BDI was a well-known scale and that both reliability and validity had been established in previous studies or elsewhere (e.g., Blackbum & Tsiantis, 1979; Hartley & Kolenc, 1988; Hock & DeMeis, 1990; Joseph & Kuylden, 1993; Whittemore, 1986). Even worse, a larger number of studies involving BDI did not even bother to mention the reliability issue at all (e.g., Carter & Dacey, 1996; Kauth & Zettle, 1990; Love, 1987; Nelson-Gray, Herbert, Herbert, Sigmon, & Brannon, 1989; Smith, Christensen, Peck, & Ward, 1994; Stein, Gordon, Hibbard, & Sliwinski, 1992).

To gain a better understanding of the measurement reliability of BDI scores, and the relationship between study characteristics and the BDI score reliability, a meta-analytic reliability generalization study was carried out to explore the potential factors that contribute to the variability of BDI score reliability across studies.

Method

Data Source

A search in the database PSYCLIT was conducted for articles published from 1967 to 1998. Using the key words *Beck Depression Inventory*, 3,461 articles were identified. Of the initial 3,461 articles, 1,499 were not included in the present study because they were either not written in English or were impossible to locate. In addition, 762 articles were not included because they did not actually use the BDI in the study. A total of 1,200 articles that reported the use of BDI were included for the present study.

The 1,200 articles were each read and then divided into four categories. The first category consisted of articles that used BDI but failed to mention the issue of reliability ($n = 961$; $961/1,200 = 80.1$ %). The second category consisted of articles that mentioned the issue of reliability but did not cite any reliability estimate either from other sources nor from their own data ($n = 67$; $67/1,200 = 5.6\%$). The third category consisted of articles that used BDI but only cited reliability estimates from other (e.g., the manual) sources ($n = 82$; $82/1,200 = 6.8\%$). The fourth category included articles that used the BDI and reported reliability coefficients for the data collected ($n = 90$; 7.5%). For [210] the purpose of the present study, only these 90 articles in the last category were usable. These 90 articles are listed with asterisks in the References section of this chapter.

Because multiple reliability coefficients were reported in many studies, a total of 164 reliability coefficients were collected from these 90 articles. The types of reliability coefficients collected include Cronbach's alpha, split-half reliability estimates, and test-retest reliability coefficients. Because there was only a very limited number of split-half coefficients, and conceptually, split-half coefficients are in the same category as Cronbach's coefficient alpha (internal consistency), they were grouped together with Cronbach's coefficients of alpha and called "internal consistency" in later analyses. In addition to BDI reliability coefficients, the majority of the 90 articles also provided the standard deviation of the observed scores for constructing SEMs, and a total of 121 SEMs were collected. The fact that only 7.5% of studies that used BDI for data collection actually reported reliability estimates for their data shows that the concept of test score reliability has not generally prevailed in research involving BDI, and research practice in this area still leaves much to be desired (Wilkinson & APA Task Force on Statistical Inference, 1999).

Coding Method

A coding system was developed for summarizing the characteristics of the studies used in the present reliability generalization study:

1. Form of BDI: 0 for 21-item long form BDI, 1 for 13-item short form BDI, 2 for other forms of BDI;

2. Language of BDI: 0 for the English BDI version, 1 for any non-English versions;

3. Age range of study participants: 0 for adolescents (10 to 17.99) (adolescent), 1 for adults (18 to 49.99), 2 for senior adults (50 to 100);

4. Gender of study participants: 0 for studies with both male and female participants, 1 for studies with male participants only, 2 for studies with female subjects only;

5. Race of study participants: 0 for general population (e.g., any combinations of Caucasian, African American, Hispanic, Asian), 1 for any single race;

6. Type of study participants coded in four contrasts: (a) student participants (high school, college, and graduate students) versus nonstudent participants, (b) clinical psychiatric patients versus nonclinical respondents, (c) participants with any physical (other than mental) diseases versus physically normal participants, (d) participants who were addicts of some substance (e.g., alcohol, drugs) versus those who were not;

7. Type of reliability coefficient: internal consistency coefficient (Cronbach's alpha, Kuder-Richardson coefficient, or split-half reliability coefficient) and test-retest reliability coefficient (for test-retest reliability coefficient, if the interval between two test administrations was provided, this was coded as a separate variable on a continuous scale with week as the unit); [211]

8. Reliability coefficient: coded as continuous variable;

9. Sample size: coded as a continuous variable; and

10. Standard deviation for the BDI scores: a continuous variable if available. For some articles that involved two groups of subjects (e.g., male and female), and in which the composite reliability coefficients and separate group's standard deviations were reported, pooled weighted standard deviations were calculated.

Weighting

Sample size typically plays an important role for the stability of a statistical estimate: The larger the sample size, the more stable a statistical estimate tends to be. For this reason, sample size is usually considered as being relevant in meta-analysis in general. Typically, in a meta-analysis, sample size is used to construct a weighting variable that is applied to an effect size measure from each study so that the accumulated effect size measure across studies is a weighted effect size measure. This approach gives more weight to an effect size measure from a large sample and less weight to an effect size measure derived from a small sample.

Statistically, the weighting procedure based on sample size tends to reduce the potential bias introduced by unstable estimates derived from small samples. In the validity generalization approach as proposed by Schmidt and Hunter (1977), this weighting procedure is used. Although Vacha-Haase (1998) did not discuss the sample-size weighting approach in a reliability generalization study, in our opinion, such a weighting procedure is statistically sound and should be applied when possible. Of course, Vacha-Haase proposed the idea of reliability generalization and did not advocate the use of a monolithic series of analysis choice as part of her method. In the present study, this weighted approach was adopted, and in all the analyses, the reliability estimate and the corresponding SEM from a study is weighted by the following weight variable w_i (Hunter & Schmidt, 1990, chap. 3):

$$w_i = n_i / \sum n_i,$$

where n_i is the sample size on which a reliability coefficient is based, and $\sum n_i - 3$ is the sum of sample sizes across the studies used in the reliability generalization. This weighting procedure gives more weight to a reliability estimate derived from a large sample than that from a small sample.

Results and Discussions

Partitioning the Variances Across Studies

The general linear model was used to investigate the relationship between study characteristics and the variability of the BDI reliability estimates and [212] that between study characteristics and the variability of the SEMs. In these analyses, either the reliability estimate or SEM was used as the dependent variable, and the study characteristics described previously in the Method section were used as independent variables. The independent variables include the following: BDI form; BDI language; age range, gender, and race of participants; types of participants (four contrasts); and type of reliability coefficients.

Eta squared (η^2) is used as the effect size measure representing the percentage of variation associated with each independent variable. The η^2 for each independent variable is obtained through

$$\eta^2 = [SS_{a\ source} / SS_{total}] \times 100,$$

where SS represents the sum of squares. For $SS_{a\ source}$, because the independent variables were correlated, the unique (Type III) sum of squares due to a source was used for the calculation of η^2. As a result, the individual η^2s do not add up to the total R^2 of the model. Such variance partitioning within the framework of a general linear model allows systematic examination of the influence of a study characteristic on the dependent variable (reliability coefficient or SEM). Table 14.2 presents

Table 14.2   Eta Squares Due to Different Sources of Variation for Reliability Coefficients and Standard Errors of Measurement (SEMs)

	Reliability Coefficient[a]			SEM[b]		
Source	Overall (153)[c]	Alpha (131)	T-R (22)	Overall (113)	Alpha (100)	T-R (13)
BDI form	1.90	1.01	8.42*	4.47	6.33*	—
BDI language	0.01	0.18	—	0.00	0.02	—
Age range	0.74	5.41*	3.70	1.79	1.44	9.19
Gender	0.44	0.75	0.94	1.02	1.06	0.69
Race	0.11	0.12	0.02	0.05	—	—
Student versus non-student subject	2.72*	4.49*	0.59	0.82	1.10	37.61*
Psychiatric patient versus nonpsychiatric patient	0.42	0.73	0.01	0.15	0.00	2.17
Physically ill versus physically normal subject	1.57*	1.45	7.65*	0.02	0.00	—
Substance addicts versus normal subjects	9.72*	6.63*	26.15*	0.28	0.94	45.15*
Type of reliability coefficient	27.18*	N/A	N/A	0.57	N/A	N/A
R² (%)	55.18	28.77	83.16	19.33	18.69	88.50

NOTES: [a]Overall = all reliability coefficients, including both internal consistency and test-retest reliability coefficients; Alpha = internal consistency reliability coefficients only; T-R = test-retest reliability coefficients only.

[b]There are SEMs corresponding to the different reliability coefficients explained in note a above.

[c]Number of reliability coefficients used in the model.

*$p < .05$

the results of variance partitioning for both the reliability estimates and the corresponding SEMs.

In Table 14.2, when no distinction was made between internal consistency and test-retest reliability coefficients, the general linear model with study characteristics as the predictors was able to account for about 55% of the total variability in the reliability coefficients. Among the predictors in the model, type of reliability coefficients (i.e., internal consistency versus test-retest reliability coefficients) stands out to be the most meaningful predictor in terms of both statistical significance and practical significance. In addition, among the four contrasts related to participants, the contrast for substance addicts versus normal subjects appears to affect reliability coefficients.

The relatively large n^2 (27%) associated with the variable of type of reliability estimates indicates that the two types of reliability coefficients may differ substantially in their values. For this reason, separate analyses were conducted for the two types of reliability coefficients, and the results are presented in the same table (alpha for internal consistency reliability estimates; T-R for test-retest reliability estimates). For the separate analyses, the general linear model was able to account for substantially more variation for the test-retest reliability coefficients and the corresponding SEMs (approximately 83% and 89%) than for the internal consistency reliability coefficients and the corresponding SEMs (approximately 29% and 19%). Because the number of test-retest reliability coefficients used in the models was quite small relative to the number of predictors in the model ($n = 22$ for reliability coefficients, and $n = 13$ for SEMs), the modeling results related to test-retest [213] reliability coefficients are probably less trustworthy than those related to the internal consistency coefficients ($n = 131$ for reliability coefficients, and $n = 100$ for SEMs).

Mean Reliability Coefficients and Corresponding SEMs

Table 14.3 presents the average reliability coefficients and the corresponding SEMs. Because internal consistency reliability coefficients are not numerically comparable to test-retest reliability coefficients, as shown by the large η^2 (27%) associated with the predictor of type of reliability coefficients, the descriptive analyses were conducted separately for internal consistency reliability estimates and for test-retest reliability estimates. For each type of reliability coefficient, the mean reliability estimates were broken down for the predictor variables that accounted for a relatively larger proportion of variability of the reliability estimates. For internal consistency reliability coefficients, the descriptive analyses were broken down by (a) age range ($\eta^2 = 5.41\%$), (b) student versus nonstudent subjects ($\eta^2 = 4.49\%$), and (c) substance addicts versus normal subjects ($\eta^2 = 6.63\%$). For test-retest reliability [214] estimates, the descriptive analyses were broken by (a) BDI form ($\eta^2 = 8.42\%$), (b) age range ($\eta^2 = 3.70\%$), (c) physically ill versus physically normal subjects ($\eta^2 = 7.65\%$), and (d) substance addicts versus normal subjects ($\eta^2 = 26.15\%$).

It is seen that the (weighted) average internal consistency reliability coefficient of BDI scores is about 0.84, whereas the (weighted) average test-retest reliability coefficient is only about 0.69. This indicates that, in BDI applications, the measurement error associated with time (test-retest) is substantially larger than the measurement error associated with item heterogeneity and item sampling (internal consistency). This strongly suggests that, for the BDI, not only internal consistency and test-retest reliability coefficients are conceptually different in terms of the measurement

Table 14.3   Mean Reliability Coefficients and Corresponding Standard Errors of Measurement (SEMs)

Coefficients/Study Characteristics	Reliability			SEM		
	n	M	(SD)	n	M	(SD)
Type of reliability coefficient						
Overall	165	.824	(.008)	122	2.739	(.122)
Internal consistency	142	.837	(.007)	108	2.768	(.127)
Test-retest	23	.690	(.009)	14	2.456	(.057)
Internal consistency reliability coefficients						
Age range						
Adolescent	9	.828	(.008)	4	3.052	(.033)
Adult	106	.848	(.006)	83	2.878	(.140)
Senior adult	27	.796	(.006)	21	2.339	(.058)
Study participants						
Student participants	71	.835	(.007)	58	2.804	(.154)
Nonstudent participants	69	.841	(.007)	49	2.760	(.089)
Substance addicts	5	.769	(.008)	3	2.296	(.088)
Nonsubstance addicts	137	.843	(.006)	105	2.835	(.127)
Test-retest reliability coefficients						
Beck Depression Inventory (BDI) form						
21-item BDI	20	.720	(.008)	11	2.691	(.057)
13-item BDI	3	.583	(.006)	3	2.023	(.063)
Age range						
Adult	19	.670	(.009)	11	2.368	(.059)
Senior adult	3	.862	(.004)	3	2.927	(.004)
Study participants						
Physically ill	2	.630	(.003)	0		
Normal	21	.693	(.010)	14	2.456	(.057)
Substance addicts	4	.586	(.005)	1	3.720	(.000)
Nonsubstance addicts	19	.713	(.009)	13	2.362	(.051)

error each reliability estimate assesses, but also they tend to be numerically different because of the amount of measurement error associated with different error sources. It is [215] thus important to report not only the reliability estimate in a particular BDI application but also be specific about the *type* of reliability estimate, exactly as suggested in test standards (e.g., AERA/APA/NCME, 1985).

For both internal consistency and test-retest reliability estimates, the difference between the average reliability coefficients from studies with substance addicts as participants and those with "normal" participants turns out to be quite conspicuous (0.77 versus 0.84 for internal consistency reliability coefficients, and 0.59 versus 0.71 for test-retest reliability coefficients). Although it is not clear why the reliability estimates from studies involving substance addicts are lower than those from studies involving normal participants, one possible reason for the discrepancy may be statistical range restriction. Most substance addicts might have some degree of depression, and this group might represent a restricted range of sample on the trait of depression. It is well known that statistical range restriction tends to reduce the total variance and, subsequently, the reliability coefficient (Anastasi & Urbina, 1997; Worthen et al., 1999). It should be noted, however, that the number of studies involving substance addicts as participants is small for both internal consistency ($n = 5$) and test-retest reliability estimates ($n = 4$). Some caution is thus warranted in interpreting these results. The same caution is also warranted because of small numbers of studies for several comparisons under test-retest reliability coefficients that appear to show obvious differences, for example, 21-item BDI versus 13-item BDI forms (.72 and .58, respectively) and adults versus senior adults (.67 and .86, respectively).

Correlation Analyses

Several correlation analyses were conducted. The first correlation analysis examined the relationship of SEM with (a) the reliability coefficient and (b) the standard deviation of the scores. The correlation between SEM and its corresponding reliability coefficient was 0.097 (statistically nonsignificant at $\alpha = .05$ level), an extremely small coefficient that indicates little relationship between SEM and the associated reliability coefficient for BDI. On the other hand, the correlation coefficient between SEM and the standard deviation of BDI scores was 0.857 (statistically significant at $\alpha = .05$ level), indicating a strong positive relationship between SEM and the standard deviation of BDI scores. These observations show that, for BDI, its SEM is more dependent on the standard deviation of the scores than on the reliability coefficient. As a result, a lower reliability coefficient does not necessarily mean that the interpretation for an *individual* BDI score will necessarily contain more error around the true score.

The second correlation analysis examined the relationship between test-retest reliability coefficients and the length of interval between test and retest (measured in weeks). The correlation obtained was -0.586 (statistically [216] significant at $\alpha = .05$ level), indicating a moderately strong negative relationship between the length of the retesting interval and the test-retest reliability coefficient. The finding was expected, because the longer the interval, the more measurement error is expected between the two testing administrations.

Summary and Conclusions

The reliability estimates for the BDI scores across different studies were accumulated and summarized in a meta-analysis. Reliability generalization (Vacha-Haase, 1998) was used to explore the sources for the variability of reliability estimates and the amount of measurement error in the BDI scores. Of the articles reviewed for the present study, only 7.5% of the articles reported meaningful reliability coefficients for the data used in the studies. The overwhelming majority of the articles (80.1%) reviewed in this study did not even mention the reliability issue in their reports, let alone provide reliability estimates for their data. The BDI has been used primarily in clinical psychology. Our present review indicates that the logic of test score reliability has not generally prevailed in clinical psychology with regard to the application of BDI, and consequently, the overwhelming majority of articles involving the use of BDI either were not concerned about measurement reliability at all or simply assumed that reliability was an issue for instrument development but not for the application of the instrument. No study reported the SEM for the BDI scores.

The results from partitioning the variances in the BDI score reliability estimates indicated that type of reliability coefficients (internal consistency vs. test-retest reliability coefficients) and type of study participants (primarily substance addicts versus normal subjects) were statistically significant and practically meaningful predictors in the general linear model with reliability estimates as the dependent variable. Subsequent analyses revealed that for BDI, the measurement error due to time sampling as captured by test-retest reliability estimate was considerably larger than the measurement error due to item heterogeneity and content sampling as captured by the internal consistency reliability estimate. As a result, test-retest reliability estimates of BDI are obviously lower than internal consistency reliability estimates in general. It also was noted that reliability estimates from studies involving substance addicts were consistently lower than reliability estimates from studies involving normal subjects as participants. It was tentatively suggested that restriction of range on the trait measured by BDI might have contributed to the lower reliability estimates from studies involving substance addicts. Of course, the value of reliability generalization here is demonstrated in the realization that persons using the BDI with substance abusers for either clinical or research purposes must recognize that BDI score reliabilities in these applications tend to be smaller. [217]

Correlation analyses revealed that SEMs were not correlated with reliability estimates, but SEMs were substantially related to the standard deviations of the BDI scores in different studies. This suggests that SEM should be considered in addition to the reliability estimate when interpreting *individual* BDI scores, because a lower reliability estimate does not necessarily mean that the corresponding score band based on SEM would be wider around the hypothetical true score. As expected, test-retest reliability estimates are negatively correlated with the interval length between two test administrations.

It is noticed that for internal consistency reliability estimates, a substantially large proportion of variation is due to random error, unaccounted for by the predictors we considered in the model. For test-retest reliability estimates, the predictors used in the model were much better in accounting for the variation in the reliability estimates. But because of the small number of studies that provided test-retest reliability estimates, caution is warranted in interpreting the modeling results related to test-retest reliability coefficients.

Finally, it must be noted with some shock that *only 7.5%* of the BDI articles reported meaningful reliability estimates. To quote Willson's (1980) view of this matter two decades ago, such a pattern is "inexcusable at this late date" (p. 9). The finding here is even worse than the related results reported in recent reviews (cf. Thompson & Snyder, 1998), including the review of three journals conducted by Vacha-Hasse, Ness, Nilsson, and Reetz (1999). These patterns may occur as people misperceive reliability as a property of tests (rather than of scores)—a property they incorrectly misperceive as if what has been revealed a single time in test manuals remains fixed across all samples (a) of different compositions and/or (b) of different variabilities. Misconceptions such as these may flourish in an era in which measurement training receives less and less emphasis throughout various doctoral programs (Aiken, West, Sechrest, & Reno, with Roediger, Scarr, Kazdin, & Sherman 1990).

References

*References marked with an asterisk indicate articles that used the Beck Depression Inventory and reported reliability coefficients for the data collected.

Aiken, L. S., West, S. G., Sechrest, L., & Reno, R. R. (with Roediger, H. L., Scarr, S., Kazdin, A. E., & Sherman, S. J.). (1990). The training in statistics, methodology, and measurement in psychology. *American Psychologist, 45,* 721-734.

American Educational Research Association, American Psychological Association, & National Council on Measurement in Education (AERA, APA, NCME). (1985). *Standards for educational and psychological testing* (3rd ed.). Washington, DC: American Psychological Association.

Anastasi, A., & Urbina, S. (1997). *Psychological testing* (4th ed.). Upper Saddle River, NJ: Prentice Hall.

*Andersen, S. M., & Schwartz, A. H. (1992). Intolerance of ambiguity and depression: A cognitive vulnerability factor linked to hopelessness. *Social Cognition, 10,* 271-298.

*Anderson, G., Melin, L., Lindberg, P., & Scott, B. (1995). Dispositional optimism, dysphoria, health, and coping with hearing impairment in elderly adults. *Audiology, 34*(2), 76-84. [218]

Baron, P., & Joly, E. (1988). Sex differences in the expression of depression in Adolescents. *Sex Roles, 18,* 1-7.

Baron, P., & Perron, L. M. (1986). Sex differences in the Beck Depression Inventory scores of adolescents. *Journal of Youth and Adolescence, 15,* 165-171.

*Barrera, M., Jr., & Garrison-Jones, C. V. (1988). Properties of the Beck Depression Inventory as a screening instrument for adolescent depression. *Journal of Abnormal Child Psychology, 16,* 263-273.

*Baumgart, E. P., & Oliver, J. M. (1981). Sex-ratio and gender differences in depression in an unelected adult population. *Journal of Clinical Psychology, 37,* 570-574.

*Beck, A. T. (1967). *Depression: Causes and treatment.* Philadelphia: University of Pennsylvania Press.

Beck, A. T., & Beck, R. W. (1972). Screening depressed patients in family practice: A rapid technique. *Postgraduate Medicine, 52,* 81-85.

*Beck, A. T., Guth, D., Steer, R. A., & Ball, R. (1997). Screening for major depression disorders in medical inpatients with the Beck Depression Inventory for primary care. *Behaviour Research and Therapy, 35,* 785-791.

*Beck, A. T., & Steer, R. A. (1984). Internal consistencies of the original and revised Beck Depression Inventory. *Journal of Clinical Psychology, 40,* 1365-1367.

*Beck, A. T., Steer, R. A., & Brown, G. K. (1996). *Manual for Beck Depression Inventory-II.* San Antonio, TX: Psychological Corporation.

Beck, A. T., Ward, C. H., Mendelson, M., Mock, J., & Erbaugh, J. (1961). An inventory for measuring depression. *Archives of General Psychiatry, 4,* 53-63.

*Beck, T., & Strong, S. R. (1982). Stimulating therapeutic change with interpretations: A comparison of positive and negative connotations. *Journal of Counseling Psychology, 29,* 551-559.

Blackburn, I. M., & Tsiantis, J. (1979). The temporal relationship between hostility and depressed mood. *British Journal of Social and Clinical Psychology, 18,* 227-235.

*Bosscher, R. J., Koning, H., & Van Meurs, R. (1986). Reliability and validity of the Beck Depression Inventory in a Dutch college population. *Psychological Reports, 58,* 696-798.

*Bryson, S. E., & Pilon, D. J. (1984). Sex differences in depression and the method of administering the Beck Depression Inventory. *Journal of Clinical Psychology, 40,* 529-534.

Bumberry, W., Oliver, J. M., & McClure, J. N. (1978). Validation of the Beck Depression Inventory in a university population using psychiatric estimates as the criterion. *Journal of Consulting and Clinical Psychology, 46,* 150-155.

*Byerly, F. G., & Calson, W. A. (1982). Comparison among inpatients, outpatients, and normals on three self-report depression inventories. *Journal of Clinical Psychology, 30,* 797-804.

Byrne, B. M., Baron, P., & Campbell, T. L. (1992, July). *Gender differences in adolescent depression: Testing for invariant measurement and structure for the BDI (French version).* Paper presented at the International Congress of Psychology, Brussels, Belgium.

*Campbell, I. M., Burgess, P. M., & Finch, S. J. (1984). A factorial analysis of BDI scores. *Journal of Clinical Psychology, 40,* 992-996.

*Carr, J. G., Gilroy, F. D., & Sherman, M. F. (1996). Silencing the self and depression among women. *Psychology of Women Quarterly, 20,* 375-392.

Carter, C. L., & Dacey, C. M. (1996). Validity of the Beck Depression Inventory, MMPI, and Rorschach in assessing adolescent depression. *Journal of Adolescence, 9,* 223-231.

*Cascardi, M., & O'Leary, L. D. (1992). Depressive symptomatology, self-esteem, and self-blame in battered women. *Journal of Family Violence, 7,* 249-259.

*Catanzaro, S. J. (1993). Mood regulation expectancies, anxiety sensitivity, and emotional distress. *Journal of Abnormal Psychology, 102,* 327-330.

*Chan, D. W. (1991). The Beck Depression Inventory: What difference does the Chinese version make? *Psychological Assessment, 3,* 616-622. [219]

*Cook, M. L., & Peterson, C. (1986). Depressive irrationality. *Cognitive Therapy and Research, 10,* 293-298.

*Cox, B. J., Swinson, R. P., Kuch, K., & Reichman, J. T. (1993). Self-reported differentiation of anxiety and depression in an anxiety disorders sample. *Psychological Assessment, 5,* 484-486.

Crocker, L., & Algina, J. (1986). *Introduction to classical and modern test theory.* Orlando, FL: Harcourt Brace Jovanovich.

*Dobson, K. S., & Breiter, H. J. (1983). Cognitive assessment of depression: Reliability and validity of three measures. *Journal of Abnormal Psychology, 92,* 107-109.

*Elevin, B. E., Llabre, M. M., & Weiner, W. J. (1988). Parkinson's disease and depression: Psychometric properties of the Beck Depression Inventory. *Journal of Neurology, Neurosurgery, and Psychiatry, 51,* 1401-1404.

*Ellis, T., Rudd, M. D., Rajab, M. H., & Wehrly, T. (1996). Cluster analysis of MCMT scores of suicidal psychiatric patients: Four personality profiles. *Journal of Clinical Psychology, 52,* 411-422.

*Feather, N. T. (1983). Some correlates of attributional style: Depressive symptoms, self-esteem, and protestant ethic values. *Personality and Social Psychology Bulletin, 9,* 125-135.

*Feather, N. T. (1987). The rosy glow of self-esteem: Depression, masculinity, and causal attributions. *Australian Journal of Psychology, 39,* 25-41.

*Feather, N. T., & Bond, M. J. (1983). Time structure and purposeful activity among employed and unemployed university graduates. *Journal of Occupational Psychology, 56,* 241-254.

*Foelker, G. A., Jr., Shewchuk, R. M., & Niederehe, G. (1987). Confirmatory factor analysis of the short form Beck Depression Inventory in elderly community samples. *Journal of Clinical Psychology 43,* 111-118.

Gallagher, D. (1986). The Beck Depression Inventory and older adults: Review of its development and utility. *Clinical Gerontology, 5,* 149-163.

*Gallagher, D., Nies, G., & Thompson, L. W. (1982). Reliability of the Beck Depression Inventory with older adults. *Journal of Consulting and Clinical Psychology, 50,* 152-153.

*Gatewood-Colwell, G., Kaczlliarek, M., & Allies, M. H. (1989). Reliability and validity of the Beck Depression Inventory for a White and Mexican-American gerontic population. *Psychological Reports, 65,* 1163-1166.

*Giallibra, L. M. (1977). Independent dimensions of depression: A factor analysis of three self-report depression measures. *Journal of Clinical Psychology, 33,* 928-935.

Glass, G. V (1976). Primary, secondary, and meta-analysis of research. *Educational Researcher, 5*(10), 3-8.

Glass, G. V (1977). Integrating findings: The meta-analysis of research. *Review of Research in Education, 5,* 351-379.

*Golin, S., & Hartz, M. A. (1979). A factor analysis of the Beck Depression Inventory in a mildly depressed population. *Journal of Clinical Psychology, 35,* 322-325.

*Gorenstein, C., & Pompeia, S. (1995). Scores of Brazilian University students on the Beck Depression and the State-Trait Anxiety Inventories. *Psychological Reports, 77,* 635-641.

*Gotlib, I. H. (1984). Depression and general psychopathology in university students. *Journal of Abnormal Psychology, 93,* 19-30.

*Gould, J. (1982). A psychometric investigation of the standard and short form Beck Depression Inventory. *Psychological Reports, 51,* 1167-1170.

Hajat, M., & Shapurian, R. (1986). Psychometric properties of a Persian version of the short form of the Beck Depression Inventory for Iranian college students. *Psychological Reports, 59,* 331-338.

*Hankin, B. L., Roberts, J., & Gotlib, I. H. (1997). Elevated self-standards and emotional distress during adolescence: Emotional specificity and gender differences. *Cognitive Therapy and Research 21,* 663-679. [220]

Hartley, D. L., & Kolenc, K. (1988, August). *Mild depression: Its relation to stress, coping and gender.* Paper presented at the annual meeting of the American Psychological Association, Atlanta, GA.

*Hatzenbuehler, L. C., Parpal, M., & Mattews, L. (1983). Classifying college students as depressed or nondepressed using the Beck Depression Inventory: An empirical analysis. *Journal of Consulting and Clinical Psychology, 51*, 360-366.

Hedges, L. V., & Olkin, I. (1985). *Statistical methods for meta-analysis.* Orlando, FL: Academic Press.

*Hjelle, L. A., & Bernard, M. (1994). Private self-consciousness and the retest reliability of self-reports. *Journal of Research in Personality, 28*, 52-67.

Hock, E., & DeMeis, D. K. (1990). Depression in mothers of infants: The role of maternal employment. *Developmental Psychology, 26*, 285-291.

*Hojat, M., & Schapurian, R. (1986). Psychometric properties of a Persian version of the short form of the Beck Depression Inventory for Iranian college students. *Psychological Reports, 59*, 331-338.

Hunter, J. E., & Schmidt, F. L. (1990). *Methods of meta-analysis.* Newbury Park, CA: Sage.

Jackson, G. B. (1980). Methods for integrative reviews. *Review of Educational Research, 50*, 438-460.

*Joe, G. W., Knezek, L., Watson, D., & Simpson, D. D. (1991). Depression and decision making among intravenous drug users. *Psychological Reports, 68*, 339-347.

*Johnson, J. G., Crofton, A. & Feinstein, S. B. (1996). Enhancing attributional style and positive life events predict increased hopefulness among depressed psychiatric inpatients. *Motivation and Emotion, 20*, 285-297.

Joseph, S., & Kuylden, W. (1993). Linking causal attributions and inhibitory processes. *Social Behavior and Personality, 21*, 1-6.

Kauth, M. R., & Zettle, R. (1990). Validation of depression measures in adolescent population. *Journal of Clinical Psychology, 46*, 291-295.

*Kirkham, M. A., Schinke, S. P., Schilling, R. F., II, Meltzer, N. J., & Norelius, K. L. (1986). Cognitive, behavioral skills, social supports, and child abuse potential among mothers of handicapped children. *Journal of Family Violence, 1*, 235-245.

*Knight, R. G. (1984). Some general population norms for the short form Beck Depression Inventory. *Journal of Clinical Psychology, 40*, 751-753.

*Kwon, S. M., & Dei, T.P.S. (1992). Differential causal roles of dysfunctional attitudes and automatic thoughts in depression. *Cognitive Therapy and Research, 16*, 309-328.

*Leahy, J. M. (1992). Validity and reliability of the Beck Depression Inventory-Short Form in a group of adult bereaved females. *Journal of Clinical Psychology, 48*, 64-68.

*Leahy, J. M. (1993). A comparison of depression in women bereaved of a spouse, child or a parent. *Omega, 26*, 207-217.

*Lee, A. M. (1996). Disordered eating and its psychosocial correlates among Chinese adolescent females in Hong Kong. *International Journal of Eating Disorders, 20*, 177-183.

*Leigh, I. W., Robins, C. J ., & Welkowitz, J. (1988). Modification of the Beck Depression Inventory for use with a deaf population. *Journal of Clinical Psychology, 44*, 728-732.

Linn, R. L., & Gronlund, N. E. (1995). *Measurement and assessment in teaching* (7th ed.). Saddle River, NJ: Merrill.

Love, A. W. (1987). Depression in chronic low back pain patients: Diagnostic efficiency of three self-report questionnaires. *Journal of Clinical Psychology, 43*, 84-89.

*Marcovitz, R. J., & Smith, J. E. (1983). Patients' perceptions of curative factors in short-term group psychotherapy. *International Journal of Group Psychotherapy, 33*, 21-39.

*McCabe, K. M. (1997). Sex differences in the long term effects of divorce on children: Depression and heterosexual relationship difficulties in the young adult years. *Journal of Divorce and Remarriage, 27*, 123-135. [221]

Meier, S. T., & Davis, S. R. (1990). Trends in reporting psychometric properties of scales used in counseling psychology research. *Journal of Counseling Psychology, 37*, 113-115.

*Michelson, L., & Mavissakalian, M. (1983). Temporal stability of self-report measures in agoraphobia research. *Behavior Research and Therapy, 21*, 695-698.

*Moilanen, D. L. (1995). Validity of Beck's cognitive theory of depression with nonreferred adolescents. *Journal of Counseling and Development, 73*, 438-442.

Moore, D. S., &McCabe, G. P. (1993). *Introduction to the practice of statistics.* New York: W. H. Freeman.

Nelson-Gray, R. 0., Herbert, J. D., Herbert, D. L., Sigmon, S. T., & Brannon, S. (1989). Effectiveness of matched, mismatched, and package treatments of depression. *Journal of Behavior Therapy and Experimental Psychiatry, 20,* 295-302.

*Oliver, J. M., & Baumgart, E. P. (1985). The dysfunctional attitude scale: Psychometric properties and relations to depression in an unselected adult population. *Cognitive Therapy and Research, 9,* 161-167.

*Oliver, J. M., & Burkham, R. (1979). Depression in university students: Duration, relation to calendar time, prevalence, and demographic correlates. *Journal of Abnormal Psychology, 88,* 667-670.

*Oliver, J. M., & Simmons, M. E. (1985). Affective disorders and depression as measures by the diagnostic interview schedule and the Beck Depression Inventory in an unselected adult population. *Journal of Clinical Psychology, 41,* 469-477.

*Palinkas, L. A., Wingard, P. L., & Barrett-Connor, E. (1996). Depressive symptoms in over-weight and obese older adults: A test of the "jolly fat" hypothesis. *Journal of Psychosomatic Research, 40,* 59-66.

Pedhazur, E. J., & Schmelkin, L. P. (1991). *Measurement, design, and analysis; An integrated approach.* Hillsdale, NJ: Lawrence Erlbaum.

*Peterson, C. (1979). Uncontrollability and self-blame in depression: Investigation of the paradox in a college population. *Journal of Abnormal Psychology, 88,* 620-624.

*Peterson, C., & Avila, M.E.D. (1995). Optimistic explanation style and the perception of health problems. *Journal of Clinical Psychology, 51,* 128-132.

*Peterson, C., & Barrett, L. (1987). Explanatory style and academic performance among university freshman. *Journal of Personality and Social Psychology, 53,* 603-607.

*Peterson, C., Rosenbaum, A. C., & Conn, M. K. (1985). Depression mood reactions to breaking up: Testing the learned helplessness model of depression. *Journal of Social and Clinical Psychology, 3,* 161-169.

*Pulos, S. (1996). Validity of the Beck Depression Inventory with eating disorder patients. *Educational and Psychological Measurement, 56,* 139-141.

*Radnitz, C. L., McGrath, R. E., Tirch, D. D., Willard, J., Perez-Strumolo, L., Festa, J., Binks, M., Broderick, C. P., Schlein, I. S., Walczak, S., & Lillian, L. (1997). Use of the Beck Depression Inventory in veterans with spinal cord injury. *Rehabilitation Psychology, 42,* 93-101.

*Rapp, S. R., Walsh, D. A., Parisi, S., & Wallace, C. (1988). Detecting depression in elderly medical inpatients. *Journal of Consulting and Clinical Psychology, 56,* 509-513.

*Rees, A., Hardy, G. E., & Barkham, M. (1997). Covariance in the measurement of depression/anxiety and three cluster C personality disorders (avoidant, dependent, obsessive-compulsive). *Journal of Affective Disorders, 45,* 143-153.

*Reynolds, W. M., & Gould, J. W. (1981). A psychometric investigation of the standard and short form Beck Depression Inventory. *Journal of Consulting and Clinical Psychology, 49,* 306-307.

*Schaefer, A., Brown, J., Watson, C. G., Plemel, D., DeMotts, J., Howard, M. T., Petrik, N., & Balleway, B. J. (1985). Comparison of the validities of the Beck, Zung, and MMPI Depression Scales. *Journal of Consulting and Clinical Psychology, 53,* 415-418.

Schmidt, F. L., & Hunter, J. E. (1977). Development of a general solution to the problem of validity generation. *Journal of Applied Psychology, 62,* 529-540. [222]

*Schotte, C. K. W., Maes, M., Cluydts, R., De Doncker, D., & Cosyns, P. (1997). Construct validity of the Beck Depression Inventory in a depressive population. *Journal of Affective Disorders, 46,* 115-125.

*Scogin, F., Beutler, L., Corbishley, A., & Hamblin, D. (1988). Reliability and validity of the short form Beck Depression Inventory with older adults. *Journal of Clinical Psychology, 44,* 853-857.

Shavelson, R. J., & Webb, N. M. (1991). *Generalizability theory: A primer.* Newbury Park, CA: Sage.

Shaver, J. P. (1991). Quantitative reviewing of research. In J. P. Shaver (Eds.), *Handbook of research on social studies teaching and learning* (pp. 83-97). New York: Macmillan.

*Shek, D.T.L. (1990). Reliability and factorial structure of the Chinese version of the Beck Depression Inventory. *Journal of Clinical Psychology, 46,* 35-43.

Smith, T. W., Christensen, A. J., Peck, J. R., & Ward, J. R. (1994). Cognitive distortion, helplessness, and depressed mood in rheumatoid arthritis: A four-year longitudinal analysis. *Health Psychology*, *13*, 213-217.

*Somoza, E., Steer, R. A., Beck, A. T., & Clark, D. A. (1994). Differentiating major depression and panic disorders by self-report and clinical rating scales: ROC analysis and information theory. *Behavior Research and Therapy*, *32*, 771-782.

*Steer, R. A., Beck, A. T., Brown, G. K., & Beck, J. S. (1993). Classification of suicidal and non-suicidal outpatients: A cluster-analytic approach. *Journal of Clinical Psychology*, *49*, 603-614.

*Steer, R. A., Beck, A. T., Riskind, J. H., & Brown, G. (1987). Relationships between the Beck Depression Inventory and the Hamilton Psychiatric Rating Scale for depression in depressed outpatients. *Journal of Psychopathology and Behavioral Assessment*, *9*, 327-339.

*Steer, R. A., & Clark, D. A. (1997). Psychometric characteristics of the Beck Depression Inventory-II with college students. *Measurement and Evaluation in Counseling and Development*, *30*, 128-136.

*Steer, R. A., Mcelroy, M. G., & Beck, A. T. (1982). Structure of depression in alcoholic men: A partial replication. *Psychological Reports*, *50*, 723-728.

*Steer, R. A., Shaw, B. F., Beck, A. T., & Fine, E. W. (1977). Structure of depression in Black alcoholic men. *Psychological Reports*, *41*, 1235-1241.

Stein, P. N., Gordon, W. A., Hibbard, M. R., & Sliwinski, M. (1992). An examination of depression in the spouse of stroke patients. *Rehabilitation Psychology*, *37*, 121-130.

*Strober, M., Green, I., & Carlson, G. (1981). Utility of the Beck Depression Inventory with psychiatrically hospitalized adolescents. *Journal of Consulting and Clinical Psychology*, *49*, 482-483.

*Subkoviak, M., Enright, R. D., Wu, C-R., Gassin, E. A., Freedman, S., Olson, L. M., & Sarinopolos, I. (1995). Measuring interpersonal forgiveness in late adolescence and middle adulthood. *Journal of Adolescence*, *18*, 641-655.

*Tanaka, J. S., & Huba, G. J. (1987). Assessing the stability of depression in college students. *Multivariate Behavioral Research*, *22*, 5-19.

*Tangney, J. P., Wagner, P., & Granizow, R. (1992). Proneness to shame, proneness to guilt, and psychopathology. *Journal of Abnormal Psychology*, *101*, 469-478.

*Tanka-Matsumi, J., & Kameoka, V. A. (1986). Reliabilities and concurrent validities of popular self-report measures of depression, anxiety, and social desirability. *Journal of Consulting and Clinical Psychology*, *54*, 328-333.

*Tashakkori, A., Barefoot, J., & Mehryar, A. H. (1989). What does the Beck Depression Inventory measure in college students? Evidence from a non-western culture. *Journal of Clinical Psychology*, *45*, 595-602.

*Teri, L. (1982). The use of the Beck Depression Inventory with adolescents. *Journal of Abnormal Child Psychology*, *10*, 277-284.

Thompson, B. (1991). Review of Generalizability theory: A primer by R. J. Shavelson & N. W. Webb. *Educational and Psychological Measurement*, *51*, 1069-1075. [223]

Thompson, B. (1994). Guidelines for authors. *Educational and Psychological Measurement*, *54*, 837-347.

Thompson, B., & Snyder, P. A. (1998). Statistical significance and reliability analyses in recent *JCD* research articles. *Journal of Counseling and Development*, *76*, 436-441.

Traub, R. E. (1994). *Reliability for the social sciences: Theory and applications*. Thousand Oaks, CA: Sage.

Vacha-Hasse, T. (1998). Reliability generation: Exploding variance in measurement error affecting score reliability across studies. *Educational and Psychological Measurement*, *58*, 6-20.

Vacha-Hasse, T., Ness, C., Nilsson, J., & Reetz, D. (1999). Practices regarding reporting of reliability coefficients: A review of three journals. *Journal of Experimental Education*, *67*, 335-341.

*Vredenburg, K., Krames, L., & Flett, G. L. (1985). Reexamining the Beck Depression Inventory: The long and short form of it. *Psychological Reports*, *56*, 767-778.

*Watkins, A. J., & Kligman, E. (1989, November). *Psychometric properties of the Beck Depression Inventories when used with an elderly population*. Paper presented at the annual meeting of the Gerontological Society of America, Minneapolis, MN. (ERIC Document Reproduction No. ED 313 626)

Webb, N. M., Rowley, G. L., & Shavelson, R. J. (1989). Using generalizability theory in counseling and development. *Measurement and Evaluation in Counseling and Development*, *21*, 81-90.

*Webster-Stratton, C. (1985). Predictors of treatment outcome in parent training for conduct disordered children. *Behavior Therapy, 16,* 223-243.

*Welch, G., Hall, A., & Walkey, F. (1990). The replicable dimensions of the Beck Depression Inventory. *Journal of Clinical Psychology, 46,* 817-827.

*Westaway, M., & Wolmarans, L. (1992). Depression and self-esteem: Rapid screening for depression in Black, low literacy, hospitalized tuberculosis patients. *Social Science and Medicine, 35,* 1311-1315.

*Whisman, M. A., & Kwon, P. (1992). Parental representations, cognitive distortions, and mild depression. *Cognitive Therapy and Research, 16,* 552-568.

Whittemore, P. B. (1986). Phenylthiocarbamide (PTC) tasting and reported depression. *Journal of Clinical Psychology, 42,* 260-263.

Wilkinson, L., & APA Task Force on Statistical Inference. (1999). Statistical methods in psychology journals: Guidelines and explanations. *American Psychologists, 54,* 594-604.

Willson, V. L. (1980). Research techniques in *AERJ* articles: 1969 to 1978. *Educational Researcher, 9*(6), 5-10.

Wolf, F. M. (1986). *Meta-analysis: Quantitative methods for research synthesis.* Beverly Hills, CA: Sage.

Worthen, R. B., White, R. K., Fan, X., & Sudweeks, R. R. (1999). *Measurement and assessment in schools.* New York: Addison Wesley Longman.

*Zea, M. C., Belgrave, F. Z., Townsend, T. G., Jararna, S. L., & Banks, S. R. (1996). The influence of social support and active coping on depression among African Americans and Latinos with disabilities. *Rehabilitation Psychology, 41,* 225-242.

*Zemore, R. (1983). Development of a self-report measure of depression-proneness. *Psychological Reports, 52,* 211-216.

*Zemore, R., & Bretell, D. (1983). Depression-proneness, low self-esteem, unhappy outlook, and narcissistic vulnerability. *Psychological Reports, 52,* 223-230.

*Zimmerman, M. (1986). The stability of the revised Beck Depression Inventory in college students: Relationship with life events. *Cognitive Therapy and Research, 10,* 37-43.

15

Measurement Error in "Big Five Factors" Personality Assessment

Reliability Generalization Across Studies and Measures

Chockalingam Viswesvaran
Florida International University

Deniz S. Ones
University of Minnesota

[224]

Abstract

Meta-analysis was used to cumulate reliabilities of personality scale scores. A total of 848 coefficients of stability and 1,359 internal consistency reliabilities across the Big Five factors of personality were examined. The frequency-weighted mean coefficients of stability were .75 ($SD = .10$, $K = 221$). .76 ($SD = .12$, $K = 176$), .71 ($SD = .13$, $K = 139$), .69 ($SD = .14$, $K = 119$), and .72 ($SD = .13$, $K = 193$) for Emotional Stability, Extraversion, Openness to Experience, Agreeableness, and Conscientiousness, respectively. The corresponding

Viswesvaran, C., & Ones, D. (2000). Measurement error in "Big Five Factors" personality assessment: Reliability Generalization across studies and measures. *Educational and Psychological Measurement*, 60, 224-235.

internal consistency reliabilities were .78 (SD = .11, K = 370), .78 (SD = .09, K = 307), .73 (SD = .12, K = 251), .75 (SD = .11, K = 123), and .78 (SD = .10, K = 307). Sample-size-weighted means also were computed. The dimension of personality being rated does not appear to strongly moderate either the internal consistency or the test-retest reliabilities. Implications for personality assessment are discussed.

Recent meta-analytic reviews (e.g., Barrick & Mount, 1991; Hough, Eaton, Dunnette, Kamp, & McCloy, 1990; Ones, 1993) of personality have suggested that in contrast to earlier qualitative reviews (e.g., Guion & Gottier, 1965), personality traits are useful for prediction of behaviors in the work-place. The positive evaluation of the utility of personality variables in [225] predicting workplace behaviors has spurred research attempts to explain the causal mechanisms by which personality variables attain their predictive powers (e.g., Barrick, Mount, & Strauss, 1993). Attempts at explaining observed relationships between personality variables and work-place outcomes reflect efforts at theory building (Campbell, 1990). Theory building should focus more on correlations corrected for unreliability in the observed scores than on observed uncorrected correlations (Schmidt, 1992) so as to mitigate the downward bias caused by unreliability in the observed scores.

Recently, a cumulation of reliabilities was reported for the Bem Sex Role Inventory (Vacha-Haase, 1998). Vacha-Haase (1998) outlined the general principles for evaluating the magnitude of error variances as they occur across samples. This cumulation of error variances across studies was referred to as "reliability generalization" in line with previous work on "validity generalization" (e.g., Schmidt & Hunter, 1977), which focused on cumulating validity correlations across samples. In fact, industrial-organizational psychologists have concentrated for a long time on assessing the reliability of workplace outcomes such as job performance. A meta-analytic cumulation of the reliability of assessing workplace outcomes (cf. Viswesvaran, Ones, & Schmidt, 1996) exists. However, the literature on the reliability of personality assessment, although voluminous, is scattered in many different journals and test manuals. The objective in the present research is to cumulate the extant literature that reports the reliability of personality assessment as done in the workplace.

In cumulating the literature, an organizing framework is essential because individual studies have used a bewildering array of personality variables. Even though there is no complete consensus, the Big Five factors of personality seem to have been accepted by most meta-analysts who have reviewed the personality literature as it pertains to the workplace (e.g., Barrick & Mount, 1991; Ones, 1993; Ones, Schmidt, & Viswesvaran, 1994). As such, we employed the Big Five framework to cumulate the reliabilities across the individual personality studies.

The Big Five dimensions of personality have been labeled as Emotional Stability (or neuroticism, if measured from its negative pole), Extraversion, Openness to Experience (also termed intellect and culture), Agreeableness, and Conscientiousness. Emotional Stability refers to the anxiety, anger-hostility, self-consciousness, impulsiveness, vulnerability, and depression experienced by an individual. Extraversion refers to the extent to which a person is gregarious, assertive, excitement seeking, warm, and active. Positive emotions (enthusiastic, humorous, optimistic, jolly) are also part of Extraversion (Costa & McCrae, 1992). Openness to Experience has been interpreted as both intellect and culture. Traits commonly associated with this dimension include imagination, curiosity, originality, broad-mindedness, and artistic sensitivity. Traits associated with Agreeableness (likability) include [226] courteousness, flexibility, trust, good naturedness, cooperativeness, forgiveness, empathy, soft-heartedness, and tolerance. The Conscientiousness dimension has been called dependability, prudence, or conformity. Because of its relationship to a variety of educational achievement measures and its association with volition, the dimension also has been called "will to achieve." Traits associated with this dimension reflect both dependability (i.e., carefulness, thoroughness, responsibility, organization, efficiency, planfulness) and volition (i.e., hard work, achievement orientation, perseverance). Each of the Big Five dimensions is regarded as a continuum.

In addition to classifying the personality scales used in the individual studies to the Big Five factors, the different types of reliability coefficients need to be distinguished (Schmidt & Hunter, 1996; Viswesvaran et al., 1996). Reliability in classical theory has been defined as the ratio of true to observed variance. However, different reliability estimates construe different sources of variance as error variance. For example, the coefficient of stability, usually referred to as the test-retest reliability (when the same individual provides the measurements at the two points in time), construes variance specific to time (i.e., transient error) as error variance. An assumption is made that the true score does not change in the time interval between the two measurements, which is probably true in the case of stable traits such as the Big Five factors of personality. Of course, the coefficient of stability can be computed based on measurements obtained from different individuals (self-ratings at Time 1, a friend at Time 2 who evaluates that focal individual) at the two points in time, but such estimates are rare in the personality literature and will not be considered any further in the present article. The coefficient of stability is an important estimate in personality assessment because high estimates of stability are necessary to support the contention that what gets assessed are stable dispositions.

In addition to the coefficient of stability, most studies report internal consistency reliabilities (e.g., coefficient alpha). Coefficient alpha indicates the extent to which the items "hang together"—the extent to which the items in the scale are measuring the same construct. Variance that is specific to an item (i.e., variance that is not shared with all or most other items) is construed as error variance in estimating coefficient alpha. High values of coefficient alphas for the Big Five dimensions compared to the correlation between the Big Five dimensions (Ones, 1993) could be construed as evidence supporting the categorization of personality into five factors.

A hypothesis has been advanced in the personality literature that some dimensions are more easily assessed than other dimensions (e.g., Christensen, 1974). Specifically, this hypothesis translates to a statement that the "typical" reliability will be higher for some dimensions than others. A similar argument made with reference to ratings of different dimensions of job performance (cf. Borman, 1979; Wohlers & London, 1989) was only partially [227] supported in a meta-analytic cumulation of the job performance ratings literature (Viswesvaran et al., 1996). A comparison of the reliability estimates across the five factors will empirically evaluate this hypothesis of a gradient in reliability across the five dimensions.

The stability of personality traits as well as the low correlations among different measures of the same traits have been a major source of consternation for personality psychology. Researchers have decried the fact that inventories designed to assess the same construct have low intercorrelations—whether it be for the assessment of integrity or conscientiousness or customer service orientation. For example, some researchers (cf. Guion, 1994) have construed the low correlations among measures of conscientiousness as proof of an ill-defined construct, whereas others (cf. Sackett, 1996) point to the low correlation in customer service scales between the Hogan Personality Inventory and the London House Personnel Selection Inventory as evidence of construct deficiency in one or both the measures. The essential point to note here is that large specific variance associated with each scale or inventory does not invalidate scale use. As long as the items in each scale are homogeneous (high coefficient alphas), relate to external behaviors of interest, and have high coefficients of stability, other concerns are not serious. Comparing the different types of reliability estimates for each of the five factors will shed more light on these issues.

Thus, the primary objective in the present study was to use the principles of psychometric meta-analysis (Hunter & Schmidt, 1990) to cumulate the literature on the reliability of personality assessment. The personality scales used in the extant literature were grouped into one of the Big Five factors (Barrick & Mount, 1991; Ones, 1993). The mean observed correlations for each of the Big Five factors were estimated for the two types of reliability coefficients reported: stability and internal consistency reliabilities. Thus, 10 "bare-bones" meta-analyses (cf. Hunter & Schmidt, 1990) were undertaken.

For each meta-analysis, the observed means and standard deviations of the reliabilities were computed. We also cumulated and characterized the square root of the reliability estimates. The mean of the square root of the reliabilities is slightly different from the square root of the mean of the reliabilities; in artifact-distribution-based meta-analytic cumulation (Hunter & Schmidt, 1990, p. 185), the artifact distribution used for unreliability correction is composed of the square root of the reliability estimates. The results reported in the present article facilitate obtaining more precise estimates of the reliability corrections in future meta-analyses involving personality assessment. This is especially true because we have disaggregated the different types of reliability estimates, as did Vacha-Haase (1998); previous meta-analytic cumulations (cf. Barrick & Mount, 1991) involving personality assessment have combined test-retest and alpha reliability estimates together in one artifact distribution. By compiling separate distributions for each type of [228] reliability, the results reported here enable more precise estimates of the relationships (Schmidt & Hunter, 1996; Viswesvaran & Ones, 1995).

Because frequency-weighted means are used in artifact distributions, we computed the frequency or unit-weighted means and standard deviations. However, in addition to compiling artifact distributions, there is value in assessing the mean levels of reliabilities. Therefore, we also computed and report the sample-size-weighted means and standard deviations of the reliabilities for each of the five dimensions. The means and standard deviations of the number of items, item intercorrelations, as well as the time interval between stability estimates also are presented.

Method

Database

The objective was to include all personality inventories currently in use for personnel selection. The following inventories contributed data to the analyses: Adjective Checklist, Army Background and Life Experiences, California Psychological Inventory, Basic Personality Inventory, Comrey Personality Scales, Eysenck Personality Inventory, Global Personality Inventory, Goldberg Five Factor Markers, Goldberg's International Personality Item Pool, Guilford-Zimmerman Temperament Survey, Hogan Personality Inventory, Interpersonal Style Inventory, Jackson Personality Inventory, MMPI, Myers-Briggs Type Indicator, Multidimensional Personality Questionnaire, NEO-Personality Inventory, Occupational Personality Questionnaire, PDI Personality Inventory, Personal Characteristics Inventory, Personality Research Form, Singer Loomis Personality Inventory, 16 Personality Factors, and Wonderlic's Comprehensive Personality Profile. We included only studies that employed normal adults as samples. Studies using children were excluded. We also excluded those inventories that assessed compound personality traits (e.g., integrity). The technical manuals reporting score reliabilities for the normative samples were included. A total of $k = 2,207$ reliability estimates were reported in the manuals, of which 848 were coefficient of stability and 1,359 were internal consistency reliabilities. These $k = 2,207$ coefficients were derived from 28 technical manuals.

Analyses

The personality scales used in the individual studies (and for which a reliability estimate was reported) were grouped into one of the five observed distributions, each corresponding to one of the Big Five dimensions. If a study reported the reliability estimates on two scales that both [229] assessed the same dimension of the Big Five, we computed the reliability of the composite formed of the two scales (cf. Bommer, Johnson, Rich, Podsakoff, & MacKenzie, 1995; Viswesvaran, Schmidt, & Ones, 1994). However, when the study did not report the necessary intercorrelations, we entered the individual scale reliability estimates as independent estimates into our observed distribution.

To determine which scales assessed which one of the Big Five factors, we followed the guidelines provided in Ones (1993). Ones reported that she classified the various personality scales into one of the Big Five dimensions after integrating the classification of both Barrick and Mount (1991) as well as Hough et al. (1990). Whenever there were discrepancies between the classification of Barrick and Mount (1991) and Hough et al. (1990), Ones (1993) referred to the intercorrelation among the scales as reported in the extant literature in classifying the scales into one of the Big Five dimensions.

Two distributions were constructed for each of the Big Five factors. One distribution contained coefficients of stability (test-retest), and the second included internal consistency reliabilities. Note that the coefficients of stability for a given study all involved the same test taker completing the same measure at two points in time.

In cumulating coefficient alphas across individual studies, we encountered the issue of different estimates being based on a different number of items. However, because the number of items in the individual studies varied in a range in which the application of Spearman-Brown formula would not have made an appreciable difference, no corrections were made for differences in the number of items across the different estimates. The average number of items across the estimates as well as the standard deviations associated with the means are presented. In cumulating the coefficients of stability, the time interval varied across studies. The average time intervals and the associated standard deviations were computed. These delays ranged from 7 to 9,125 days.

For each of the 10 distributions (i.e., 5 factors × 2 types of reliability coefficients), we computed the mean and standard deviation. Furthermore, to facilitate meta-analytic cumulations that involve any of the Big Five dimensions, we also examined the square root of the reliability estimates. That is, we computed the means and standard deviations of the square root of the reliabilities for the 10 distributions.

The sampling error associated with the mean reliability estimate was computed as the standard deviation divided by the square root of the number of estimates. The sampling error of the mean may be used to estimate various confidence intervals around the mean estimates in the 10 distributions. Of course, it should be noted that this computation presumed a normal distribution of population values. [230]

Finally, in addition to the frequency- or unit-weighted means, we also computed sample-size-weighted means and standard deviations. Specifically, we checked whether there was a correlation between sample size and reliability estimate reported. For example, do large sample studies report higher reliability estimates (due to better measurement control)? We examined the

Table 15.1 Reliability Distributions: Coefficients of Stability and Internal Consistency Reliabilities

Coefficients of stability

Personality Dimension	Unit-Weighted Reliability Distribution			Square Root of Reliabilities			Sample-Size			Sample-Size-Weighted Reliability Distribution		Time Interval in Days Between Test Administration		
	K_r	M	SD	SE of Mean	M	SD	K_n	M	SD	M	SD	K_t	M	SD
Emotional Stability	221	.75	.10	.0068	.87	.06	158	259.96	1,150.51	.73	.10	154	440.78	1,623.31
Extraversion	176	.76	.12	.0087	.87	.07	153	219.41	955.79	.78	.11	158	615.06	1,997.54
Openness to Experience	139	.71	.13	.0107	.84	.08	119	177.86	767.58	.73	.13	123	657.80	1,969.43
Agreeableness	119	.69	.14	.0124	.83	.08	77	241.78	955.02	.75	.11	78	331.79	1,095.16
Conscientiousness	193	.72	.13	.0091	.84	.07	133	299.82	1,250.78	.76	.13	139	785.38	2,232.50

Internal consistency reliabilities

	Unit-Weighted Reliability Distribution			Square Root of Reliabilities			Sample-Size			Sample-Size-Weighted Reliability Distribution		Number of Scale Items			Item Intercorrelations	
	K_r	M	SD	SE of Mean	M	SD	K_n	M	SD	M	SD	K_{iw-2}	M	SD	M	SD
Emotional Stability	370	.78	.11	.0057	.88	.07	268	2,101.50	5,247.96	.82	.12	253	31.71	16.24	.15	.09
Extraversion	307	.78	.09	.0049	.88	.05	273	2,065.74	5,204.19	.81	.09	269	29.43	15.77	.16	.10
Openness to Experience	251	.73	.12	.0078	.85	.09	247	2,268.21	5,478.27	.80	.14	241	30.76	13.09	.12	.09
Agreeableness	123	.75	.11	.0098	.86	.07	97	981.38	1,227.18	.74	.11	91	20.34	14.32	.18	.10
Conscientiousness	307	.78	.10	.0057	.88	.06	260	2,075.60	5,311.02	.83	.12	248	31.08	13.67	.14	.08

NOTE: K_r = total number of reliabilities; SE of mean = standard error of the mean; K_n = number of studies reporting sample sizes associated with reliabilities; K_t = number of studies reporting time intervals for coefficients of stability; K_i = number of studies reporting number of scale items.

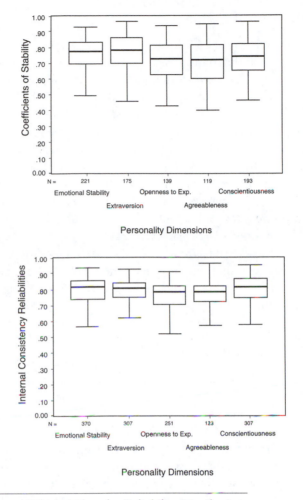

Figure 15.1   Box-and-Whisker Plots for Reliability Distributions

relationship between sample size and reliability magnitudes for stability and internal consistency estimates separately.

Results

Table 15.1 summarizes the results of the meta-analyses. Stability coefficients are presented first, followed by internal consistency estimates. Box-and-whisker plots are used to depict the results in Figure 15.1.

Coefficient of Stability

As seen in Table 15.1, the frequency-weighted mean coefficients of stability are in the .69 to. 76 range. The highest mean coefficient of stability was found for Extraversion (.76, $SD = .12$, $K = 176$), whereas the lowest coefficient of stability was found for Agreeableness (.69, $SD = .14$, $K = 119$). The mean test-retest reliabilities were .72 ($SD = .13$) for Conscientiousness, .71 ($SD = .13$) for Openness to Experience, and .75 ($SD = .10$) for Emotional Stability. The sample-size-weighted means also were comparable to the frequency-weighted means. Furthermore, the correlation between sample sizes and reliability values was .03 across the 640 estimates that reported sample sizes associated with reliabilities, suggesting that the stability estimates and sample sizes are probably not confounded. Note that the number of estimates averaged is higher for frequency-weighted estimates (in all five factors) because some estimates were reported without the associated sample size on which the estimates were based. Finally, also reported in the table is the mean (and SD) time interval between the stability estimates.

Internal Consistency Reliabilities

The mean internal consistency reliabilities ranged from .73 to .78. Emotional Stability, Extraversion, and Conscientiousness had an internal consistency reliability of .78 ($SD = .11$, .09, .10, respectively; $K = 370$, 307, 307, respectively), whereas the lowest coefficient of internal consistency was found for Openness to Experience (.73, $SD = .12$, $K = 251$). The mean internal consistency reliability was .75 ($SD = .11$) for Agreeableness. The sample-size-weighted mean reliability estimates (based on a fewer number of studies reporting sample size) were comparable. The correlation between sample size and reliability estimates was .17 (across 1,145 estimates). [231] [232]

Comparing Relative Magnitude of the Different Sources of Error

For Emotional Stability, the mean observed test-retest correlation was .75 ($SD = .10$), whereas the mean internal consistency reliability was .78 ($SD = .11$). For Extraversion, the mean observed coefficient of stability was .76 ($SD = .12$), whereas the mean internal consistency reliability was .78 ($SD = .09$). [233] For Openness to Experience, the mean observed test-retest reliability was .71 ($SD = .13$), whereas the mean internal consistency reliability was .73 ($SD = .12$). For Agreeableness, the mean observed coefficient of stability was .69 (*SD* = .14), whereas the mean internal consistency reliability was .75 (*SD* = .11). Finally, for Conscientiousness, the mean coefficient of stability was .72 (*SD* = .13), whereas the mean internal consistency reliability was .78 (*SD* = .10). The 95% confidence interval overlap suggests that all potential moderator effects are weak.

Discussion

In the present study, the reliability of personality assessment that is "typical" across the samples cumulated was summarized. It is important to stress that although the results of our reliability generalization can be used to investigate some hypotheses, it is inappropriate to use the results reported here to conclude that personality inventories are reliable. As noted by others (cf. Thompson, 1992; Vacha-Haase, 1998), reliability refers to the scores obtained, not the instrument itself. Individual researchers must continue to report the reliability coefficients estimated from their samples. The results reported here, however, can be used to test hypotheses such as the one that some dimensions of personality are more reliably assessed than others are (across samples). Our results lend only weak support for this hypothesis when the cumulation is at the level of the Big Five factors of personality.

Although the results reported here do not strongly support the hypothesis that some dimensions were more reliably rated than others were, it is possible that the specificity of the Big Five factors was not sufficient to reflect the gradient in reliability assessments. If so, given that the Big Five has shown promise as basic traits (Costa & McCrae, 1992), a question remains as to where the gradient hypothesis will be meaningful. Researchers who argue for more specificity in personality assessment should be more specific about where their specific measures will be more useful than the Big Five factors and should provide the necessary empirical and theoretical justification.

It is interesting to note that the typical coefficient of stability is consistently lower than the typical internal consistency coefficients for all the five dimensions. However, both types of reliabilities were found to be reasonably high, at least on the average, for all the dimensions of personality examined here. Of course, what is an acceptable degree of score reliability is largely a function of the context in which the scores will be used. Certainly, negative alphas, and especially negative alphas less than −1, are always troubling (cf. Reinhardt, 1996).

But establishing a floor of minimally acceptable coefficients may be a fool's errand. For example, Nunnally (1967) suggested that, for early-stage research with new measures, "reliabilities of .60 or .50 will suffice" (p. 226). However, in the second edition of his book, Nunnally (1978) argued that [234] "reliabilities of. 7 or higher will suffice" (p. 245). Thus, Pedhazur and Schmelkin (1991) noted that

> when approached by colleagues or students with a request for a reference in which they may find justification for the use of their reliability estimates, we suggest facetiously that, if their estimates are about .7, they use Nunnally (1978) but that, if they are about .5, they use Nunnally (1967). (p. 109)

The pattern of findings reported in this article indicates that the five factors are stable traits. That the internal consistency coefficients were higher than .70 (e.g., Nunnally, 1978) is somewhat gratifying; however, it should be remembered that personality scales have more items than most traditional scales used, and as such, the average item intercorrelation might therefore be lower. As reported in Table 15.1, the average interitem correlation is only in the .12 to .18 range. It appears that personality items have large amounts of specific variance, which is offset by the high number of items and high stability exhibited by these measures.

An important aspect of reliability generalization studies is an examination of whether there are systematic factors that affect the magnitude of error variance across studies. The standard deviations associated with our mean reliability estimates are low compared to other meta-analyses (cf. Vacha-Haase, 1998), which suggests that moderator effects, if any, will not be strong. One moderator that was investigated in the present article—dimension of personality assessed—was not found to be a moderator. Further research is needed to examine other potential moderators. Assessing and reporting reliability estimates is important, because the effect sizes on which the substantive conclusions of a study depend are affected by unreliability in the scores. Given the increasing use of personality assessment in the workplace, the reliability generalization results reported here would hopefully be of use to researchers and practitioners alike.

References

Barrick, M. R., & Mount, M. K. (1991). The Big Five personality dimensions and job performance. *Personnel Psychology, 44,* 1-26.

Barrick, M. R., Mount, M. K., & Strauss, J. P. (1993). Conscientiousness and performance of sales representatives: Test of the mediating effects of goal setting. *Journal of Applied Psychology, 78,* 715-722.

Bommer, W. H., Johnson, J. L., Rich, G. A., Podsakoff, P. M., & MacKenzie, S. B. (1995). On the interchangeability of objective and subjective measures of employee performance: A meta-analysis. *Personnel Psychology, 48,* 587-605.

Borman, W. C. (1979). Format and training effects on rating accuracy and rater errors. *Journal of Applied Psychology, 64,* 410-412.

Campbell, J. P. (1990). Modeling the performance prediction problem in industrial and organizational psychology. In M. Dunnette & L. M. Hough (Eds.), *Handbook of industrial organizational psychology* (Vol. 1, 2nd ed., pp. 687-732). Palo Alto, CA: Consulting Psychologists Press. [235]

Costa, P. T., Jr., & McCrae, R. R. (1992). Four ways five factors are basic. *Personality and Individual Differences, 13,* 653-665.

Christensen, L. (1974). The influence of trait, sex, and information accuracy of personality assessment. *Journal of Personality Assessment, 38,* 130-135.

Guion, R. M. (1994, August). *Thinking carefully about conscientiousness.* Paper presented at the symposium titled Relevance of Conscientiousness to Occupational Criteria held at the 102nd annual convention of the American Psychological Association, Los Angeles.

Guion, R. M., & Gottier, R. F. (1965). Validity of personality measures in personnel selection. *Personnel Psychology, 18,* 135-164.

Hough, L. H., Eaton, N. K., Dunnette, M. D., Kamp, J. D., & McCloy, R. A. (1990). Criterion-related validities of personality constructs and the effects of response distortion on those validities. *Journal of Applied Psychology, 75,* 581-595.

Hunter, J. E., & Schmidt, F. L. (1990). *Methods of meta-analysis: Correcting for error and bias in research findings.* Newbury Park, CA: Sage.

Nunnally, J. C. (1967). *Psychometric theory.* New York: McGraw-Hill.

Nunnally, J. C. (1978). *Psychometric theory* (2nd ed.). New York: McGraw Hill.

Ones, D. S. (1993). The construct validity of integrity tests. *Dissertation Abstracts International, 54*(09A), 3515.

Ones, D. S., Schmidt, F. L., & Viswesvaran, C. (1994, April). *Do broader personality variables predict job performance with higher validity?* Paper presented at the symposium titled Personality and Job Performance: Big Five Versus Specific Traits held at the ninth annual conference of the Society of Industrial and Organizational Psychologists, Nashville, TN.

Pedhazur, E. J., & Schmelkin, L. P. (1991). *Measurement, design, and analysis: An integrated approach.* Hillsdale, NJ: Lawrence Erlbaum.

Reinhardt, B. (1996). Factors affecting coefficient alpha: A mini Monte Carlo study. In B. Thompson (Ed.), *Advances in social science methodology* (Vol. 4, pp. 3-20). Greenwich, CT: JAI Press.

Sackett, P. R. (1996, April). *Discussant's comments.* Presented at the symposium titled Integrity Testing: Recent Controversies and New Empirical Findings held at the annual meeting of the Society for Industrial and Organizational Psychology, San Diego, CA.

Schmidt, F. L. (1992). What do data really mean? Research findings, meta-analysis, and cumulative knowledge in psychology. *American Psychologist, 47,* 1173-1181.

Schmidt, F. L., & Hunter, J. E. (1977). Development of a general solution to the problem of validity generalization. *Journal of Applied Psychology, 62,* 529-540.

Schmidt, F. L., & Hunter, J. E. (1996). Measurement error in psychological research: Lessons from 26 research scenarios. *Psychological Methods, 1-3 ,* 199-223.

Thompson, B. (1992). Two and one-half decades of leadership in measurement and evaluation. *Journal of Counseling and Development, 70,* 434-438.

Vacha-Haase, T. (1998). Reliability generalization: Exploring variance in measurement error affecting score reliability across studies. *Educational and Psychological Measurement, 58,* 6-20.

Viswesvaran, C., & Ones, D. S. (1995). Theory testing: Combining psychometric meta-analysis and structural equations modeling. *Personnel Psychology, 48,* 865-887.

Viswesvaran, C., Ones, D. S., & Schmidt, F. L. (1996). Comparative analysis of the reliability of performance ratings. *Journal of Applied Psychology, 81,* 557-574.

Viswesvaran, C., Schmidt, F. L., & Ones, D. S. (1994, April). *Examining the validity of supervisory ratings of job performance using linear composites.* Paper presented at the ninth annual conference of the Society for Industrial and Organizational Psychology, Nashville, TN.

Wohlers, A. J., & London, M. (1989). Ratings of managerial characteristics: Evaluation difficulty, co-worker agreement, and self-awareness. *Personnel Psychology, 42,* 235-261.

16

Reliability Generalization of the NEO Personality Scales

John C. Caruso
University of Montana

[236]

Abstract

A reliability generalization of 51 samples employing one of the NEO personality scales was conducted. Reliability generalization is a meta-analytic method for examining the variability in the reliability of scores by determining which sample characteristics are related to differences in score reliability. It was found that there was a large amount of variability in the reliability of NEO scores, both between and within personality domains. The sample characteristics that are related to score reliability were dependent on NEO domain. Agreeableness scores appear to be the weakest of the domains assessed by the NEO scales in terms of reliability, particularly in clinical samples, for male-only samples, and when temporal consistency was the criterion for reliability. The reliability of Openness to Experience scores was low when the NEO-Five Factor Inventory was used. The advantages of conceptualizing reliability as a property of scores, and not tests, are discussed.

Caruso, J. C. (2000). Reliability Generalization of the NEO personality scales. *Educational and Psychological Measurement*, 60, 236-254.

One of the lesser followed guidelines offered by measurement specialists is the fact that scores, and not tests, may or may not be reliable. Strictly speaking, it is inaccurate and misleading to refer to a test or measure as reliable or not reliable; it is the scores that have these properties (Joint Committee on Standards for Educational Evaluation, 1994, p. 155; Wilkinson & APA Task Force on Statistical Inference, 1999).

Scores may not show the same level of reliability in different samples for a variety of reasons, some obvious and some not. Pedhazur and Schmelkin (1991) remarked that "Statements about the reliability of a measure are inappropriate and potentially misleading" (p. 82). Based on this observation, a new type of meta-analysis recently has been introduced termed *reliability* [237] *generalization* (Vacha-Haase, 1998). Reliability generalization studies are conducted to examine the factors that influence score reliability for a particular test across diverse samples. The present study examines the reliability of scores on the NEO personality scales (Costa & McCrae, 1985, 1992a) by means of a reliability generalization analysis.

Importance of Reliability

Reliability is important for many reasons. A lack of reliability in measurement tends to obscure whatever lawfulness exists in nature. Ghiselli (1964) stated that

> unreliable scores are of little value when we wish to compare two or more individuals on the same test, to assign individuals to groups or classes, to predict other types of behavior, to compare different traits of an individual, or to assess the effects of various systematic factors upon an individual's performance. (p. 208)

It is hard to imagine a research situation or clinical application in which none of these operations is taking place.

A direct consequence of a lack of reliability is termed attenuation, the decrease in the observed correlation between two variables due to the fact that each is imperfectly measured. If two latent constructs have a true correlation of, say, .80 (and therefore share 64% of their variance), but assessment devices designed to measure them are less than perfectly reliable, then the value of the correlation between the observed scores will be less than .80. The lower the reliabilities, the lower this observed correlation will be. For example, if, in a particular sample, the two measures each had a reliability of .75, then the observed correlation between the two measures would be only .60, indicating that they share only 36% of their variance.

In psychological research, it is ultimately the latent constructs that we are interested in, with the actual measures or tests simply being the best available operationalizations of those constructs. Failing to consider reliability tends to result in underestimates of the true relationships between variables. Although typically presented in terms of correlations, attenuation affects other measures of effect size in the same way.

Reliability Is a Property of Scores, Not Tests

Many authors have discussed the importance of refraining from referring to the "reliability of the test" or the "reliability of the inventory" including Thompson (1994), Pedhazur and Schmelkin (1991), Gronlund and Linn (1990), and Dawis (1987). Although this may seem to be a technicality, this mode of thinking has several advantages. For example, being mindful of the [238] fact that it is a particular set of scores that has the property of reliability (or unreliability) may lead researchers to correct their effect size estimates for attenuation in the appropriate way. This typically results in more accurate estimates of the "true" relationship between constructs. Thompson (1994) remarked that

> the failure to consider score reliability in substantive research may exact a toll on the interpretations within research studies. For example, we may conduct studies that could not possibly yield noteworthy effect sizes, given that score [un]reliability inherently attenuates effect sizes. Or we may not accurately interpret the effect sizes in our studies if we do not consider the reliability of the scores we are actually analyzing. (p. 840)

Researchers who assume that a particular measure has the reliability stated in the manual, or in previous research, may not be reminded to correct effect size estimates for attenuation. Even if corrections are made, it is likely that the adjustment will be done incorrectly if the researcher presumes that tests per se are reliable (i.e., by using the reliabilities provided in the manual).

Another example involves restriction of range. When the sample used to estimate reliability in a test's manual is more diverse than subsequent samples employing the test to address substantive questions (as is often the case), the manual's reliability estimate will tend to overestimate the reliability of scores from the more homogenous samples. Conversely, when the data collected to validate a test by the authors or publishers comes from a less diverse group than subsequent substantive studies that use the test, the test often appears to offer less reliable scores than it actually does. As

Dawis (1987) stated, "because reliability is a function of sample as well as of instrument, it should be evaluated on a sample from the intended target population—an obvious but sometimes overlooked point" (p. 486). Again, thinking in terms of score reliability instead of test reliability may lead a researcher to note that the standard deviation of scores in his or her sample is greater than or less than in the data used to validate a test, resulting in appropriate corrections for restriction of range, if necessary.

Reliability Generalization

Reliability generalization studies attempt first to determine if a particular test tends to offer scores with adequate reliability and second to determine if there are particular circumstances in which score reliability is unacceptable. This information can then be used by researchers working on substantive issues: Use of a particular test in situations in which score reliability tends to be low can be avoided, or, if it is necessary to use the test in those situations, corrections can be made for unreliability. Another characteristic of reliability generalization studies is that they have the potential to provide empirical [239] support for the notion that reliability is a property of scores and not tests. If a test tends to give scores with highly variable reliabilities in different circumstances (e.g., different subject groups, different versions of a test) and this is found in a reliability generalization study, it can hardly be concluded that there is no harm in considering reliability to be a property of the test.

The NEO Personality Scales

Costa and McCrae (1985, 1992a) have introduced three versions of their personality scale, all of which measure the domains of the five-factor personality model (FFM). The domains of the FFM are Neuroticism, Extraversion, Openness to Experience, Agreeableness, and Conscientiousness. The first test introduced by Costa and McCrae (1985) was the NEO Personality Inventory (NEO-PI). In addition to giving scores on the domains of the FFM, the NEO-PI offered facet scale scores (six per domain) for Neuroticism, Extraversion, and Openness to Experience. A revision was published in 1992 and termed the NEO Personality Inventory-Revised (NEO-PI-R). The revision incorporated six facet scales for Agreeableness and Conscientiousness. Finally, a short form has been introduced, termed the NEO Five-Factor Inventory (NEO-FFI) (Costa & McCrae, 1992a), consisting of one quarter of the items from the NEO-PI-R but offering only domain scores.

The NEO is often referred to as "a reliable test." For example, Webster (1994) stated that "[The NEO] has a high degree of validity and reliability" (p. 71). Costa and McCrae (1992a) go further, stating that "The NEO-PI is one of the few instruments that has demonstrated that it does, in fact, measure enduring dispositions" (p. 45). This statement is written in absolute terms when in fact it must be qualified: In most of the samples in which score reliability has been computed, reliability has been adequate. This does not guarantee that the next sample in which one of the NEO scales is administered also will have high score reliability, particularly if the researcher fails *directly* to compare the specific *composition* and *variability* of the new sample with the composition and variability of the sample used in prior research to estimate reliability. That would only be true if reliability were a property of tests. It would be pointless to argue that the NEO has not undergone extensive psychometric evaluation, both by the test's authors and independent researchers: It has. In fact, this is what makes a reliability generalization study possible. But this is irrelevant to the fact that it is not the NEO scales themselves that are reliable.

Purpose

The present study had two primary purposes. First, the typical reliability of scores on the NEO personality scales was characterized with respect to [240] central tendency and variability. Second, the sample characteristics that are related to more or less reliable scores were investigated.

Method

Data

The data for the present study are the reliability coefficients (dependent variables) from 37 studies that administered one of the NEO versions, along with various sample characteristics (independent variables).

Procedure

The American Psychological Association's PsycINFO database was used to generate a list of articles relating to the NEO scales. The citation of any article containing either "NEO," "five-factor model," "FFI," or "five factor inventory" was saved. This resulted in a total of 352 articles. Of these, 46 were "false hits" having nothing to do with any of the NEO scales (most were psychopharmacological studies). Of the remaining 306 articles, 16 were published in a language other than English, and 28 were not located. Eighteen of the remaining 262 articles were either theoretical in nature or meta-analytic, and these were also discarded, leaving 244 empirical studies to be included in the present investigation.

Of these 244, 6 (2.5%) consisted of the administration of only certain facet or domain scales of the NEO, and 108 (44.3%) made *no mention* of NEO reliability whatsoever. Thirty (12.3%) simply stated that the reliability was acceptable. Forty-seven (19.3%) reported reliabilities from either the NEO manuals or from some data set other than the one collected for that article. An additional 16 (6.6%) provided reliability estimates from the data at hand but in a less than optimum form, either as a range of values or as the average reliability across the five domains. This left 37 articles that presented reliability in a form acceptable for their inclusion in the present investigation. These 37 articles are marked with asterisks in the reference section.

Many of these 37 articles provided reliability estimates for more than one set of scores. For example, in some studies the reliability of the scores was provided separately for males and females or for different ethnic groups. The total number of samples included in the results that follow is 51.

Several study characteristics were recorded for each group of subjects for which reliability data were presented. First, it was noted whether the referent for the NEO administration was the participant (self) or someone else (peer). Second, which of the three NEO versions was administered (NEO-PI, NEO-PI-R, or NEO-FFI) was recorded. Third, the language in which the NEO scale was administered was determined and recorded as either English [241] or not English. Fourth, samples were assigned to one of four types: student (groups involving only student subjects), general (groups involving nonstudent general population volunteers), clinical (groups of inpatients, outpatients, and other formally diagnosed individuals), and other (typically some combination of the above categories). Fifth, samples were grouped with respect to gender. All groups were defined as containing both genders, males only, or females only. Sixth, the type of reliability coefficient that was employed was recorded. In all cases, this was either Cronbach's α (internal consistency) or test retest. In addition to these nominal variables, sample size and mean age of the respondents was recorded for each group.

Data Analysis

Many options are available for analyzing reliability generalization data. In the present study, bivariate correlations were used between continuous sample characteristics and score reliability. For discrete (nominal) sample characteristics, the main method of analysis was ANOVA, including the calculation of η^2 effect size measures. All statistical tests were performed on Fisher's Z transforms of the original reliabilities, and all reliabilities presented in the Results section were back-transformed to the original metric.

Reliability coefficients, like any correlation coefficient, are dependent on dispersion (Nunnally, 1970, p. 129). That is, the reliability depends on the standard deviation of scores in a sample. If the standard deviation is low, the reliability will tend to be low and vice versa. This makes comparison across studies for which the standard deviation of scores is different a somewhat complex task. In the present study, this was addressed by using the correction for restriction of range formula on all reliability estimates prior to analysis using the appropriate standardization sample (Costa & McCrae, 1985, for the NEO-PI; or Costa & McCrae, 1992a, for the NEO-FFI and NEO-PI-R) as a reference. The samples have, therefore, been equalized with respect to their variability where possible, and the substantive conclusions about reliability can thus be interpreted without noting the differing variability across studies. This procedure should be followed in all reliability generalization studies (cf. Vacha-Haase, 1998).

Results

The first step in a study of this type is to characterize the reliability of each scale in terms of central tendency and variability. Table 16.1 presents the mean and median score reliability for the five NEO scales as well as the standard deviation and range of the reliabilities across all 51 groups. A set of paired t tests was then conducted to determine which of the five domains differed from each other in terms of score reliability. The score reliability from each [242] pair of domains was significantly different at the $\alpha = .01$ level with two exceptions. The reliabilities of Extraversion and Conscientiousness scores were not significantly different, and the reliabilities of Openness and Agreeableness scores were significantly different at only the $\alpha = .05$ level.

As can be seen in Table 16.1, the Neuroticism scale offers the most reliable scores, with both the highest mean (.88) and highest median (.88). Also, the reliability of Neuroticism scores appears to be less variable than the other domains, with the lowest standard deviation, .07, and the smallest range, .32. Openness to Experience and Agreeableness offer the least reliable scores, with means of .77 and .73, respectively. Additionally, an examination of the standard deviations and ranges of reliabilities indicates that they are the domains with the most variability in score reliability.

Table 16.1   Descriptive Statistics for the Reliability of Scores From Each NEO Domain

	NEO Scale				
Statistic	N	E	O	A	C
Mean	.88	.83	.79	.75	.83
Median	.88	.83	.79	.77	.84
Standard deviation	.07	.09	.13	.10	.08
Range	.32	.41	.65	.52	.47

NOTE: N = Neuroticism; E = Extraversion; O = Openness to Experience; A = Agreeableness; C = Conscientiousness. Mean reliabilities were computed using Fisher's Z transformation of r.

Table 16.2   Mean Reliability as a Function of Rating Target

	NEO Scale				
Statistic	N	E	O	A	C
Self (n = 45)					
M (SD)	.87 (.07)	.83 (.09)	.79 (.13)	.74 (.09)	.83 (.06)
Peer (n = 6)					
M (SD)	.89 (.06)	.85 (.12)	.78 (.11)	.82 (.12)	.86 (.17)
$F(1,49)$	.22	.29	.03	3.36	.96
η^2	.00	.01	.00	.06	.02

NOTE: N = Neuroticism; E = Extraversion; O = Openness to Experience; A = Agreeableness; C = Conscientiousness.

The next set of analyses consisted of computing the correlations between sample size and the five reliabilities from each study and between mean age of respondent and the five reliabilities from each study. None of these 10 correlations were statistically significant at the $\alpha = .05$ significance level. Sample size and age of respondent appear to have little effect on the reliability of scores attained from the NEO scales. The r values from these analyses ranged from .00 to .06.

The next step was to examine group differences for the nominal predictor variables in a series of ANOVAs. Table 16.2 presents the means and standard deviations along with η^2 estimates of effect size and the results of statistical significance tests for rating target (self or peer). None of the F ratios are statistically significant, and the largest η^2 is .02. The referent of the ratings from the NEO scales appears to have no effect on the reliability of those ratings: Ratings of another person are as reliable as ratings of one's self on each domain.

Table 16.3   Mean Reliability as a Function of Language of Administration

| Statistic | NEO Scale | | | | |
	N	E	O	A	C
English (*n* = 41)					
M (SD)	.86 (.07)	.81 (.09)	.77 (.13)	.73 (.10)	.83 (.08)
Not English (*n* = 10)					
M (SD)	.91 (.02)	.90 (.04)	.86 (.08)	.81 (.08)	.83 (.09)
F(1,49)	9.09**	14.09***	7.71**	3.36	.02
η^2	.16	.22	.14	.06	.00

NOTE: N = Neuroticism; E = Extraversion; O = Openness to Experience; A = Agreeableness; C = Conscientiousness.

*p < .01. ***p < .001.

Table 16.4   Mean Reliabilities as a Function of Sample Type

| Statistic | NEO Scale | | | | |
	N	E	O	A	C
Student (*n* = 17)					
M (SD)	.86 (.09)	.81 (.11)	.77 (.15)	.74 (.08)	.85 (.05)
General (*n* = 21)					
M (SD)	.89 (.04)	.85 (.06)	.81 (.10)	.79 (.08)	.84 (.07)
Clinical (*n* = 7)					
M (SD)	.85 (.06)	.82 (.11)	.79 (.12)	.62 (.11)	.78 (.13)
Other(*n* = 6)					
M (SD)	.87 (.07)	.79 (.07)	.74 (.16)	.75 (.09)	.81 (.10)
F(3,47)	1.59	1.18	.88	2.88*	1.28
η^2	.09	.07	.05	.16	.08

NOTE: N = Neuroticism; E = Extraversion; O = Openness to Experience; A = Agreeableness; C = Conscientiousness.

*p < .05.

Table 16.3 presents the analysis of NEO score reliability by language of administration. Neuroticism, Extraversion, and Openness score reliabilities are all related to this sample characteristic. Perhaps surprisingly, however, [243] because the NEO scales were originally designed in English, it is scores on the non-English versions of the NEO scales that have higher reliability. This relationship is most salient for Extraversion scores, where the η^2 indicates that about 22% of the variance in score reliability is attributable to language of administration.

Table 16.4 presents the ANOVAs for sample type. Overall, this appears to be unrelated to NEO score reliability. The one exception to this is for Agreeableness scores, for which sample type accounted for a statistically

Table 16.5   Mean Reliabilities as a Function of Gender of Participant

	NEO Scale				
Statistic	N	E	O	A	C
Both (n = 38)					
M (SD)	.87 (.07)	.82 (.09)	.77 (.13)	.75 (.11)	.85 (.07)
Males only (n = 7)					
M (SD)	.88 (.06)	.82 (.09)	.80 (.15)	.72 (.06)	.75 (.10)
Females only (n = 6)					
M (SD)	.90 (.04)	.88 (.06)	.85 (.09)	.77 (.07)	.80 .05)
F(2,48)	.92	1.27	1.58	.29	5.02**
η^2	.04	.05	.06	.01	.17

NOTE: N = Neuroticism; E = Extraversion; O = Openness to Experience; A = Agreeableness; C = Conscientiousness.

**p < .01.

significant 16% of the variance in score reliability. Post hoc multiple comparisons (Tukey's HSD; $\alpha = .05$) indicated that the clinical sample type's score reliability was significantly different from each of the three other types, whereas [244] student, general, and other sample types were not different from one another. The average reliability for scores on this domain for clinical samples was only .62.

Gender of respondent had very little effect on the reliability of scores, as can be seen in Table 16.5. Only Conscientiousness scores showed a reliability difference, with male-only samples having the poorest reliability, .75, and samples involving both male and female subjects having the highest, .85. Tukey's HSD tests ($\alpha = .05$) indicated that male-only samples differed from samples involving both male and female subjects. Roughly 17% of the variance in Conscientiousness score reliability was explained by the gender of the respondents.

Table 16.6 shows the effect of type of reliability coefficient on score reliability. Somewhat surprisingly, this variable accounted for statistically significant variance in reliability for only the Agreeableness ($\eta^2 = .10$) scores. As might be generally expected (Linn & Gronlund, 1995), studies employing internal consistency reliability found higher reliability, although this difference was statistically significant only for the Agreeableness domain.

Table 16.7 shows the comparisons of the different NEO versions (NEO-PI, NEO-PI-R, and NEO-FFI). The F ratio for each of the FFM domains was statistically significant at the $\alpha = .001$ level. It appears that NEO version is strongly related to the reliability of the scores, particularly for Openness ($\eta^2 = .58$) and Extraversion ($\eta^2 = .42$). For Neuroticism, Extraversion, and Openness, Tukey's HSD test ($\alpha = .05$) indicated that the NEO-FFI

Table 16.6   Mean Reliabilities as a Function of Type of Reliability Coefficient

Statistic	NEO Scale				
	N	E	O	A	C
Internal consistency (n = 47)					
M (SD)	.88 (.07)	83 (.08)	.79 (.13)	.76 (.08)	.84 (.84)
Test retest (n = 4)					
M (SD)	.82 (.05)	.81 (.15)	.78 (.06)	.58 (.11)	.76 (.18)
F(1,49)	2.56	.13	.04	5.65*	3.35
η^2	.05	.00	.00	.10	.06

NOTE: N = Neuroticism; E = Extraversion; O = Openness to Experience; A = Agreeableness; C = Conscientiousness.

*p < .05.

Table 16.7   Mean Reliability as a Function of NEO Version

Statistic	NEO Scale				
	N	E	O	A	C
NEO-PI (n = 21)					
M (SD)	.89 (.08)	.86 (.10)	.85 (.09)	.76 (.08)	.82 (.10)
NEO-PI-R (n = 10)					
M (SD)	.91 (.03)	.89 (.03)	.85 (.03)	.84 (.14)	.90 (.03)
NEO-FFI (n = 20)					
M (SD)	.83 (.06)	.75 (.07)	.65 (.12)	.67 (.08)	.80 (.06)
F(2,48)	9.01***	17.38***	33.69***	10.15***	12.29***
η^2	.27	.42	.58	.30	.33

NOTE: N = Neuroticism; E = Extraversion; O = Openness to Experience; A = Agreeableness; C = Conscientiousness.

***p < .001.

scores were significantly less reliable than either NEO-PI or NEO-PI-R scores, which did [245] not differ. For Agreeableness, each of the three versions differed significantly from the others. For Conscientiousness, scores on the NEO-PI-R were significantly more reliable than scores on either the NEO-FFI or the NEO-PI, which did not differ. Overall, therefore, in addition to sacrificing the ability to compute facet scale scores, users of the NEO-FFI are sacrificing some score reliability. At the extreme are the NEO-FFI Openness to Experience and Agreeableness scores, for which the average reliabilities across 20 samples are only .65 and .67, respectively.

Due to the fact that the NEO versions differ with respect to scale length (NEO-PI = 181 items; NEO-PI-R = 240 items; NEO-FFI = 60 items), an

Table 16.8   Mean Reliability as a Function of NEO Version, Corrected for Scale Length

Statistic	NEO Scale				
	N	E	O	A	C
NEO-PI (*n* = 21)					
M (SD)	.91 (.06)	.89 (.08)	.88 (.07)	.81 (.07)	.86 (.09)
NEO-PI-R (*n* = 10)					
M (SD)	.91 (.04)	.89 (.03)	.85 (.03)	.84 (.18)	.90 (.05)
NEO-FFI (*n* = 20)					
M (SD)	.95 (.02)	.92 (.03)	.88 (.08)	.89 (.07)	.94 (.02)
F(2,48)	11.35***	3.85*	.92	6.28**	23.16***
η^2	.32	.14	.04	.21	.49

NOTE: N = Neuroticism; E = Extraversion; O = Openness to Experience; A = Agreeableness; C = Conscientiousness; NEO-PI = NEO Personality Inventory; NEO-PI-R = NEO Personality Inventory-Revised; NEO- FFI = NEO Five-Factor Inventory.

*$p < .05$. **$p < .01$. ***$p < .001$.

[246] additional set of ANOVAs was conducted after correcting the reliability coefficients for differing numbers of items using the Spearman-Brown correction formula. The results of these analyses are shown in Table 16.8 and can be interpreted as answering the question, "Would the NEO versions differ with respect to score reliability if they were all the length of the NEO-PI-R?" The reliability of scores for each domain except Openness were significantly [247] different, but in most cases, it was the NEO-FFI that provided the highest score reliability.

For Neuroticism and Conscientiousness scores, the NEO-FFI had higher reliability than either the NEO-PI or the NEO-PI-R, which did not differ (by Tukey's HSD test, $\alpha = .05$), whereas for Extraversion and Agreeableness scores, the NEO-FFI had significantly higher reliability than the NEO-PI but not the NEO-PI-R. It is not surprising that the NEO-FFI tended to produce scores with the highest reliability given that the "best" items from the NEO-PI-R were selected for the NEO-FFI (Costa & McCrae, 1992a). If 180 more items could be manufactured with the same properties as the original 60 NEO-FFI items, scores on that hypothetical test typically would have higher reliability than scores from either the NEO-PI or the NEO-PI-R. Although the results in Table 16.8 are of theoretical interest, the fact is that the NEO-FFI only has 60 items, so the results in Table 16.7 are probably more substantively useful. Furthermore, the use of the Spearman-Brown correction formula assumes that the added items would have the identical intercorrelations and item reliabilities as the original 60 items, a somewhat unrealistic, and untestable, assumption. The most useful information gained by these additional analyses is that the differences observed in Table 16.7 for the uncorrected reliabilities are in fact due to the differing scale lengths.

Discussion

Situations Resulting in Inadequate Score Reliability

One of the most valuable results of reliability generalization studies is the identification of situations in which score reliability is low. Based on the present analyses, several situations (sample characteristics) can be identified. Although any cutoff for "adequate" score reliability is arbitrary, situations in which the average reliability was less than .75 will be noted here (Anastasi, 1988, p. 115; Kelley, 1927; Pedhazur & Schmelkin, 1991, p. 109) and can be interpreted as situations in which score reliability is at least potentially too low.

First, Agreeableness scores had low reliability when the referent of the NEO administration was the person completing the questionnaire (mean across 45 studies of .74). Similarly, Agreeableness scores had questionable reliability when the NEO was administered in English (mean across 41 studies of .73). Also, Agreeableness scores had low reliability when student samples were used (mean across 17 samples = .74). The Agreeableness score reliability was even lower when clinical samples were used (mean across 71 samples = .62). Openness scores had questionable reliability when the sample type was "other" (mean across 6 studies = .74). In terms of gender of subjects, male-only samples had questionable Agreeableness score reliability [248] (mean across 7 samples = .72). Test-retest reliabilities were very low for Agreeableness scores (mean across 4 samples = .58). Finally, both Openness scores (mean across 20 samples = .65) and Agreeableness scores (mean across 20 samples = .67) had low reliability when the NEO-FFI was used.

Agreeableness scores had low reliability across more situations than any other scale. This is perhaps not surprising because the NEO-PI-R manual (Costa & McCrae, 1992a) indicates that scores from the standardization sample on the Agreeableness domain were lower than for other domains for both the self-rating version of the NEO-PI-R and the NEO-FFI. However, somewhat contradictory is the fact that scores from the peer-rating version of Agreeableness from the NEO-PI-R standardization data had higher reliability than scores from any other domain, a result not found in this study. This apparent contradiction could be due to the fact that

Agreeableness ratings for one's self may depend on the type of mood one is in, whereas Agreeableness ratings of another person may be based on an average disposition, or general impression of that person, unconfounded with temporal instability.

This dimension of the FFM, at least as it is measured by the NEO scales, far more than the other four appears to be more ephemeral than enduring, a fact borne out by the low test-retest reliability averages in Table 16.6. Although scores on this dimension did have adequate internal consistency reliabilities (mean across 47 studies = .76), they were not temporally consistent (mean across 4 studies = .58). The scores are not meaningless in this context but must be considered more "state" than "trait."

This observation has implications for personality theory as well. There has been much debate (e.g., Costa & McCrae, 1992b; Eysenck, 1992; Zuckerman, 1992) regarding the number of personality dimensions that should be regarded as "basic." Temporal stability would, by most researchers' definitions, be a prerequisite for the label "basic trait" to be bestowed on a dispositional dimension. Costa and McCrae (1992b) have argued that Agreeableness is one of the basic personality dimensions and have therefore included it in their version of the FFM. Eysenck (1992), alternatively, argued that Agreeableness is one of the FFM domains that does not quite make the cut into the circle of basic personality dimensions (which is a rather exclusive club, by his definition, including only the Psychotocism, Extraversion, and Neuroticism dimensions of his P-E-N personality model). Although Agreeableness scores were, in this reliability generalization analysis, not completely lacking in reliability, their temporal stability leaves something to be desired. More research into whether Agreeableness scores are simply reflecting a respondent's mood or are defining a basic personality trait could help clarify this issue.

In short, there are many advantages to abandoning the idea of test reliability in favor of score reliability. In addition to being technically inaccurate, the concept of test reliability results in the omission of valuable information that [249] could be used to sharpen psychological research. It would be nice if reliability were a property of tests and a single study could determine exactly how reliable a test is. However, this is not the case, and to ignore this fact (either explicitly or implicitly—by not calculating and presenting score reliability information in substantive studies) is a mistake that could easily be avoided. Most articles present means and standard deviations for all measures employed in tabular format, and the addition of a single column for the reliability of the scores would greatly facilitate interpretation. In the case of a correlational study, reliabilities could easily be inserted along the diagonal of the correlation matrix, which usually contains 1s or dashes when reliabilities are not given. This would, in some cases, explain a failure to find the effects one was looking for (as Thompson, 1994, stated) and, perhaps as important, allow one to make the necessary statistical corrections.

Potential Limitations of the Present Study

Independence. This study has certain limitations that must be made explicit for the purposes of accurate interpretation of the results. In this study, statistical significance tests were conducted and reported in an attempt to highlight certain large effects. However, one of the assumptions required for these tests to be strictly accurate was more than trivially violated: The 51 samples included in this study did represent independent observations. As stated in the Procedure section, several articles provided more than one set of coefficients. This could have been remedied by combining certain coefficients or selecting only one set from each article, but the cost would have been to reduce an already small sample size. In any case, the statistical tests are of secondary importance to the effect size estimates.

Weighting averages. In some meta-analyses, samples are weighted by their size to compute the averages across homogenous samples. This was not done in the present study for two reasons. First, several of the samples were exceedingly large (highest $n = 3,856$), whereas many others were small (lowest $n = 21$). Had the score reliabilities been weighted by their sample sizes, the largest would have had 184 times as much influence as the smallest, making this a potentially problematic method. Second, there was not a statistically significant correlation between sample size and score reliability for any of the domains of the FFM, indicating that the differences between the weighted and unweighted solutions would be negligible. In fact, a parallel analysis was conducted using sample-size-weighted score reliabilities, and no differences were observed in terms of which sample characteristics were salient.

"Reliability file drawer" problem. In addition to potential statistical limitations, there may be a "file drawer" problem in the current study as with [250] other reliability generalization studies (e.g., Vacha-Haase, 1998). It may be the case that researchers who did present low score reliability estimates from their data may have had difficulty publishing their papers, resulting in their exclusion from this investigation. Similarly, researchers

who computed the reliability of scores in their studies and found them to be low may not have reported them, opting instead to include the reliabilities given in the tests' manuals, or none at all, due to a lack of understanding of the issues of score reliability versus test reliability discussed earlier. Concerns regarding a reliability file drawer problem are consistent with prior empirical studies of reporting practices demonstrating that authors of strikingly large percentages of articles (a) do not even mention reliability or (b) merely reference a previous reliability report for a different sample, perhaps without any direct comparisons involving the composition and variability in the prior study to these features of a given sample (Meier & Davis, 1990; Thompson & Snyder, 1998; Vacha-Haase, Ness, Nilsson, & Reetz, 1999; Willson, 1980).

Conclusion

Reliability estimates were given in only 15% (37/244) of empirical studies that employed the NEO personality scales examined in the present study. Given the importance of concepts of reliability in psychological research, this percentage is far too low. Forty-four percent of the 244 studies made *no mention* of reliability whatsoever. In the only other published reliability generalization study (Vacha-Haase, 1998), the percentages were similar but perhaps somewhat worse: 66% of studies employing the Bem Sex-Role Inventory (Bem, 1981) made no mention of reliability, and only 13% provided reliability estimates for the scores analyzed. From these two reliability generalizations, it appears that many researchers have an inadequate understanding of the concepts of reliability discussed in the present study. The primary reason for this is probably a lack of appropriate training in such issues in graduate programs. Virtually all graduate programs in psychology require certain statistical courses, but many do not require a course on measurement. Additionally, it may be the case that reviewers and editors at times discourage the inclusion of reliability data, in the interests of parsimony, also due to a misunderstanding of these issues.

The NEO personality scales produce scores with adequate reliability in most cases. The conditions under which the score reliability was inadequate were described above but should pose no serious threat to the use of the instrument in most circumstances. A major exception to this statement is that Agreeableness scores had low reliability in a variety of circumstances (including, most importantly, when temporal stability is required or when clinical samples are used). It is hoped that the present study will assist in allowing researchers to better understand score reliability. The sheer number

[251] of situations in which reliability was found to differ for samples with different characteristics provides empirical support for the importance of the notion that reliability is a property of scores, not tests. The manifestation of the shift away from concept of test reliability would be the reporting of reliability estimates in substantive studies, in addition to psychometric evaluations. This would have the outcome of more accurate effect size and other parameter estimates through, among other things, corrections for attenuation and restriction of range. Better reporting practices also would allow other researchers to conduct reliability generalization studies of other psychological measures to understand when they may provide reliable scores and when they may not.

References

*References marked with an asterisk indicate articles that presented reliability in a form acceptable for their inclusion in the present investigation.

*Adir, Y. (1995). The Israeli brain drain: A psychological perspective. *Journal of Social Behavior & Personality, 10,* 731-740.

Anastasi, A. (1988). *Psychological testing* (6th ed.). New York: Macmillan.

*Bagby, R. M., Joffe, R. T., Parker, I. D., Kalemba, V., & Harkness, K. L. (1995). Major depression and the five-factor model of personality. *Journal of Personality Disorders, 9,* 224-234.

*Ball, S. A., Tennen, H., Poling, J. C., Kranzler, H. R., & Rounsaville, B. J. (1997). Personality, temperament, and character dimensions and the DSM-IV personality disorders in substance abusers. *Journal of Abnormal Psychology, 106,* 545-553.

Bem, S. L. (1981). *Bem Sex-Role Inventory: Professional manual.* Palo Alto, CA: Consulting Psychologists Press.

*Bernard, L. C., Hutchison, S., Lavin, A., & Pennington, P. (1996). Ego-strength, hardiness, self-esteem, self-efficacy, optimism and maladjustment: Health-related personality constructs and the "Big Five" model of personality. *Assessment, 3,* 115-131.

*Blickle, G. (1996). Personality traits, learning strategies, and performance. *European Journal of Personality, 10,* 337-352.

*Bratko, D., & Marusic, I. (1997). Family study of the Big Five personality dimensions. *Personality & Individual Differences, 23,* 365-369.

*Church, A. T., Reyes, J.A.S., Katingbak, M. S., & Grirnrn, S. D. (1997). Filipino personality structure and the Big Five model: A lexical approach. *Journal of Personality, 65,* 477-528.

Costa, P. T., Jr., & McCrae, R. R. (1985). *The NEO Personality Inventory manual.* Odessa, FL: Psychological Assessment Resources.

*Costa, P. T., & McCrae, R. R. (1988). Personality in adulthood: A six-year longitudinal study of self-reports and spouse ratings on the NEO Personality Inventory. *Journal of Personality & Social Psychology, 54,* 853-863.

Costa, P. T., Jr., & McCrae, R. R. (1992a). *The Revised NEO Personality Inventory manual.* Odessa, FL: Psychological Assessment Resources.

Costa, P. T., & McCrae, R. R. (1992b). Four ways five factors are basic. *Personality and Individual Differences, 13,* 653-665.

*Costa, P. T., & McCrae, R. R. (1995). Primary traits of Eysenck's P-E-N system: Three- and five-factor solutions. *Journal of Personality & Social Psychology, 69*, 308-317.

*Costa, P. T., McCrae, R. R., & Dye, D. A. (1991). Facet scales for agreeableness and conscientiousness: A revision of the NEO Personality Inventory. *Personality & Individual Differences, 12*, 887-898.

Dawis, R. V. (1987). Scale construction. *Journal of Counseling Psychology, 34*, 481-489. [252]

Eysenck, H. J. (1992). Four ways five factors are not basic. *Personality and Individual Differences, 13*, 667-673.

*Fagan, P. J., Wise, T. N., Schmidt, C. W., Ponticas, Y., Marshall, R. D., & Costa, P. T. (1991). A comparison of five-factor personality dimensions in males with sexual dysfunction and males with paraphilia. Special Series: Clinical use of the five-factor model of personality. *Journal of Personality Assessment, 57*, 434-448.

*Foltz, C., Morse, J. Q., Calvo, N., & Barber, J. P. (1997). Self- and observer ratings on the NEO-FFI in couples: Initial evidence of the psychometric properties of an observer form. *Assessment 3, 4*, 287-295.

Ghiselli, E. E. (1964). *Theory of psychological measurement.* New York: McGraw-Hill.

*Gotham, H. J., & Sher, K. J. (1995). Do codependent traits involve more than basic dimensions of personality and psychopathology? *Journal of Studies on Alcohol, 57*, 34-39.

Gronlund, N. E., & Linn, R. L. (1990). *Measurement and evaluation in teaching* (6th ed.). New York: Macmillan.

*Heaven, P. C. (1996). Personality and self-reported delinquency: Analysis of the "Big Five" personality dimensions. *Personality & Individual Differences, 20*, 47-54.

*Holden, R. R. (1992). Associations between the Holden Psychological Screening Inventory and the Neo Five-Factor Inventory in a nonclinical sample. *Psychological Reports, 71*, 1039-1042.

*Holden, R. R., & Fekken, G. C. (1994). The NEO Five-Factor Inventory in a Canadian context: Psychometric properties for a sample of university women. *Personality & Individual Differences, 17*, 441-444.

*Hooker, K., Frazier, L. D., & Monahan, D. J. (1994). Personality and coping among caregivers of spouses with dementia. *Gerontologist, 34*, 386-392.

Joint Committee on Standards for Educational Evaluation. (1994). *The program evaluation standards: How to assess evaluations of educational programs* (2nd ed.). Thousand Oaks, CA: Sage.

*Katigbak, M. S., Church, A. T., & Akarnine, T. X. (1996). Cross-cultural generalizability of personality dimensions: Relating indigenous and imported dimensions in two cultures. *Journal of Personality & Social Psychology, 70*, 99-114.

Kelley, T. L. (1927). *Interpretation of educational measurements.* Yonkers-on-Hudson, NY: World Book.

*Kentros, M., Smith, T. E., Hull, J., McKee, M., Terkelsen, K., & Capalbo, C. (1997). Stability of personality traits in schizophrenia and schizoaffective disorder: A pilot project. *Journal of Nervous & Mental Disease, 185*, 549-555.

Linn, R. L. & Gronlund, N. E. (1995). *Measurement and assessment in teaching* (7th ed.). Englewood Cliffs, NJ: Prentice Hall.

*Luk, C. L., & Bond, M. H. (1993). Personality variation and values endorsement in Chinese university students. *Personality & Individual Differences, 14*, 429-437.

*Marshall, G. N., Wortman, C. B., Vickers, R. R., Kusulas, J. W., & Hervig, L. K. (1994). The five-factor model of personality as a framework for personality-health research. *Journal of Personality & Social Psychology, 67*, 278-286.

Meier, S. T., & Davis, S. R. (1990). Trends in reporting psychometric properties of scales used in counseling psychology research. *Journal of Counseling Psychology, 37*, 113-115.

*Mooradian, T. A., & Nezlek, J. B. (1996). Comparing the NEO-FFI and Saucier's Mini-Markers as measures of the Big Five. *Personality & Individual Differences, 21*, 213-215.

Nunnally, J. C. (1970). *Introduction to psychological measurement.* New York: McGraw-Hill.

*Ostendorf, F., & Angleituer, A. (1994). A comparison of different instruments proposed to measure the Big Five. Special issue: The Big Five model of personality in Europe. *European Review of Applied Psychology, 44*, 45-53. [253]

*Paulhus, D. L., &Bruce, M. N. (1992). The effect of acquaintanceship on the validity of personality impressions: A longitudinal study. *Journal of Personality & Social Psychology, 63*, 816-824.

Pedhazur, E. J., & Schmelkin, L. P. (1991). *Measurement, design, and analysis: An integrated approach.* Hillsdale, NJ: Lawrence Erlbaum.

*Piedmont, R. L. (1994). Validation of the NEO-PI-R observer form for college students: Toward a paradigm for studying personality development. *Assessment, 1*, 259-268.

*Piedmont, R. L., & Chae, J. H. (1997). Cross-cultural generalizability of the five-factor model of personality: Development and validation of the NEO-PI-R for Koreans. *Journal of Cross-Cultural Psychology, 28*, 131-155.

*Piedmont, R. L., McCrae, R. R., & Costa, P. T. (1992). An assessment of the Edward's Personal Preference Schedule from the perspective of the five-factor model. *Journal of Personality Assessment, 58*, 67-78.

*Pulver, A., Allik, J., Pulkkinen, L., & Hamalainen, M. (1995). A Big Five personality inventory in two non-Indo-European languages. *European Journal of Personality, 9*, 109-124.

*Riemann, R., Angleituer, A., & Strelau, J. (1997). Genetic and environmental influences on personality: A study of twins reared together using the self- and peer-report NEO FFI scales. *Journal of Personality, 65*, 449-475.

*Ruch, W., Angleituer, A., & Strelau, J. (1991). The Strelau Temperament Inventory-Revised (STI-R): Validity studies. *European Journal of Personality, 5*, 287-308.

*Schouwenburg, H. C., &Lay, C. H. (1995). Trait procrastination and the Big Five factors of personality. *Personality & Individual Differences, 18*, 481-490.

*Shaver, P. R., & Brennan, K. A. (1992). Attachment styles and the "Big Five "personality traits: Their connections with each other and with romantic relationship outcomes. *Personality & Social Psychology Bulletin, 18*, 536-545.

*Silva, F., Avia, D., Sanz, J., Martinez-Arias, R., Grana, J. L., & Sanchez-Bernardos, L. (1994). The five factor model: I. Contributions to the structure of the NEO-PI. *Personality & Individual Differences, 17*, 741-753.

*Strauss, M. E., & Pasupathi, M. (1994). Primary caregivers' descriptions of Alzheimer patients personality traits: Temporal stability and sensitivity to change. *Alzheimer Disease & Associated Disorders, 8*, 166-176.

Thompson, B. (1994). Guidelines for authors. *Educational and Psychological Measurement, 54*, 837-847.

Thompson, B., & Snyder, P. A. (1998). Statistical significance and reliability analyses in recent *JCD* research articles. *Journal of Counseling and Development, 76*, 436-441.

*Tokar, D. M., & Swanson, J. L. (1995). Evaluation of the correspondence between Holland's vocational personality typology and the five-factor model of personality. *Journal of Vocational Behavior, 46*, 89-108.

*Tokar, D. M., Vaux, A., & Swanson, J. L. (1995). Dimensions relating Holland's vocational personality typology and the five-factor model. *Journal of Career Assessment, 3*, 57-74.

*Trull, T. J., Useda, J. D., Costa, P. T., & McCrae, R. R. (1995). Comparison of the MMPI-2 Personality Psychopathology Five (PSY 5), the NEO-PI, and NEO-PI-R. *Psychological Assessment, 7*, 508-516.

Vacha-Haase, T. (1998). Reliability generalization: Exploring variance in measurement error affecting score reliability across studies. *Educational and Psychological Measurement, 58*, 6-20.

Vacha-Haase, T., Ness, C., Nilsson, J., & Reetz, D. (1999). Practices regarding reporting of reliability coefficients: A review of three journals. *Journal of Experimental Education, 67*, 335-341.

Webster, J. D. (1994). Predictors of reminiscence: A lifespan perspective. *Canadian Journal on Aging, 13*, 66-78. [254]

Wilkinson, L., & APA Task Force on Statistical Inference. (1999). Statistical methods in psychology journals: Guidelines and explanations. *American Psychologist, 54*, 594-604.

Willson, V. L. (1980). Research techniques in *AERJ* articles: 1969 to 1978. *Educational Researcher, 9*(6), 5-10.

Zuckerman, M. (1992). What is a basic factor and which factors are basic? Turtles all the way down. *Personality and Individual Differences, 13*, 675-681.

EXERCISE SET 4

As the previous four chapters made clear, RG is not a monolithic method. Some researchers examine score reliability, some the standard error of measurement (SEM), and some do both. To characterize typical score quality, some compute means, some weighted means, some medians. To characterize variability in score quality, some compute standard deviations of score quality characterizations (e.g., SD_α, SD_{SEM}), while others prefer graphical tools such as box-and-whisker plots. To characterize which measurement features predict or explain variability in score measurement quality, the whole range of methods within the general linear model (GLM) have been used (e.g., regression, canonical correlation analysis).

The best way to learn RG as a meta-analytic method is to do an actual RG study. Of course, a lot of effort is required to do so. The effort may be worthwhile if you are doing a dissertation or trying to publish a manuscript. But doing a real RG study may be unreasonably too much only as a way to learn RG.

The Table EX4.1 heuristic data were developed to facilitate exploration of RG analytic methods. Of course, a real RG study would involve many more than 12 studies as the basis for the meta-analysis.

RG Analysis of α

Input the Table EX4.1 data into SPSS. First, characterize typical alpha in various ways by executing a command such as:

```
frequencies variables = alpha/statistics = all .
```

Second, characterize the variability in the alpha coefficients. The standard deviation (SD) of the estimates is one way to formulate this characterization. You can also graphically summarize these dynamics by creating a box-and-whisker plot using the command:

```
examine variables = alpha/compare variable/
   plot = boxplot/statistics = none/nototal/
   missing = listwise .
```

Table EX4.1   Data for Heuristic "RG" Exercise

Study			SPSS Variable Name		
	"N"	"FORM"	"AGE"	"SD"	"ALPHA"
1	22	0	0	9.0	.15
2	49	1	0	15.9	.40
3	68	0	1	13.3	.71
4	33	1	0	16.5	.68
5	65	1	1	18.3	.90
6	54	1	0	16.6	.89
7	18	0	1	12.9	.88
8	305	1	0	11.1	.69
9	133	0	1	12.5	.66
10	98	1	1	12.7	.82
11	107	0	1	10.4	.74
12	59	1	0	13.7	.85

NOTE: In this heuristic example test form and sample age groups were "dummy coded." For form, "0" = short form; "1" = long form. For age, "0" = adolescents; "1" = adults.

Third, explore what measurement features explain or predict variability in α. One way to do this is to conduct a multiple regression analysis. For these data the regression can be conducted by invoking the command:

```
regression variables = all/dependent = alpha/
    enter n/enter form/enter age .
```

In making such predictions, to interpret your results ask two questions in a hierarchical, contingency-based approach:

1. Do I have anything? (i.e., Does my predictive model work reasonably well?); and

2. If "yes" (and *only* if "yes"), from where does my something originate? (i.e., Which measurement features work well in predicting variability in score reliabilities?)

To address the first question, consult the R^2 and other effect size indicators. Is the value sufficiently large that the predictive model seems to fit the meta-analytic data? If not, other predictors may be necessary.

If one moves to the second question (and *only* then), both standardized regression coefficients and structure coefficients should be consulted (Courville & Thompson, 2001). If a feature of the measurement protocol has both a near-zero β weight and a near-zero structure coefficient, this set of results indicates that this feature of measure does not predict variation in score reliabilities. This is important to know, because the result suggests that we may not have to worry about how we conduct the measurement as regards this protocol feature. On the other hand, variables with noteworthy (i.e., non-zero) coefficients do predict variation in score reliability. These analyses can be implemented in SPSS with syntax commands such as:

```
regression variables = all/dependent = alpha/
    enter age/enter n/enter form/
    save pred(PREDDV).
subtitle 'compute structure coefficients ****'.
execute.
correlations
    variables = n form age with PREDDV.
```

RG Analysis of SEM

If the reliability coefficients and score standard deviations have been entered into the data set, SPSS can be instructed to compute SEM_x via the command:

```
compute sem=sd* ((1 - alpha)**.5).
print formats sem (F9.5) .
```

The SEM is a "score-world" (i.e., unsquared) statistic, just as the mean and the standard deviation are "score-world" statistics. Because alpha is a squared-metric ("area-world") statistic, we compute the proportion of unreliable variance in the scores as $1 - r_{xx}$ and then take the square root (i.e., $.5$ or $1/2$) of $1 - r_{xx}$. This makes the SD and $(1 - r_{xx})^{.5}$ both in an unsquared metric, thereby yielding a result (i.e., the SEM) also in an unsquared metric.

As a heuristic exercise, conduct the RG analyses using the SEMs from the hypothetical 12 studies. Do the interpretations necessarily match those from analyses of the reliability estimates?

Reference

Courville, T., & Thompson, B. (2001). Use of structure coefficients in published multiple regression articles: β is not enough. *Educational and Psychological Measurement, 61,* 229-248.

EXERCISE SET 4

Index

About the Editor

Bruce Thompson is Professor and Distinguished Research Scholar, Department of Educational Psychology, Texas A&M University, and Adjunct Professor of Family and Community Medicine, Baylor College of Medicine (Houston). He is the editor of *Educational and Psychological Measurement* and of the series, *Advances in Social Science Methodology*, and past editor of two other journals. He is the author/editor of seven other books, and nine book chapters, 173 articles, 20 notes/editorials, and 11 book reviews. His contributions have been especially influential in moving the field as regards greater emphasis on effect size reporting and interpretation and promoting improved understanding of score reliability. He is a Fellow of the American Psychological Association and an elected member of the Executive Council of the American Educational Research Association.